Celebrating the Career of Terry L. Maple: A Festschrift

Edited by:

Michael P. Hoff, Ph.D.,

Mollie A. Bloomsmith, Ph.D.,

and Evan L. Zucker, Ph.D.

Red Leaf Press
Tequesta, FL 33469 USA

Printed by CreateSpace.com
United States of America

Front Cover: Shamba and her infant, Taz at Zoo Atlanta, 1989.
Photo credit: Michael P. Hoff.

Back Cover: A portrait of Terry Maple in Africa by Ellen Petty.

DEDICATION

This volume is dedicated to the memory of our deceased friends and colleagues who labored at our side and contributed so significantly to the success of our journey together: Guy Farnell, Carolyn Boyd Hatcher, Larry James, Erin McDole, Kathleen Melia, C. Dietrich Schaaf, and Jeff Swanagan.

CONTENTS

v

Part III: Professional Colleagues

Part IV: Family and Friends

Part V: Retirement Celebration

Part VI: Commentary and Addenda

ACKNOWLEDGMENTS

We thank Gail Eaton who skillfully organized the Festschrift celebration at the AZA conference in Atlanta in 2011; Gary Lee and his partners at CLR Design who sponsored the party. Dennis Kelly and the Zoo Atlanta Board of Directors for sponsoring a dinner soon after Terry's retirement with guest speakers Syd Butler (AZA), David Towne (Woodland Park Zoo), and Donald G. Lindburg (San Diego Zoo). Government proclamations were obtained and read by Tom LaRock. To celebrate his seventeen years at the helm of the zoo, Bob Petty sponsored an oil portrait of Dr. Maple, painted by his daughter-in-law Ellen, which was placed in the Ford Room in the Conservation ARC building. Kathy Hoff provided encouragement and expertise for the e-publication process, our first experience with digital publishing. Ruth Snyder is credited with the phrase, "knuckle-walk down memory lane" at the end of the Preface. Finally, Dr. Maple wants to thank Lessie Smithgall for her long friendship and significant financial support of Zoo Atlanta and his research program at the Georgia Institute of Technology.

x

FOREWORD

Terry Maple is a wonderful friend; a big, larger-than-life, lovable, compassionate, loyal, dedicated, and determined man who has made, and continues to make, this world a much better place. He mentored, developed, and inspired a large group of well-selected people who have made and will continue to make very meaningful contributions. Terry's vision, effectiveness, team building and mentoring, tenacity, academic discipline, and dedication in involving politicians, donors, board members, volunteers, students, and staff in creating today's Zoo Atlanta, while providing significant leadership in both academia and professional organizations will pay dividends for many years to come in both the animal and zoo worlds. He is truly a man who saw what needed to be done, did it, and left his indelible mark on zoos and animal welfare everywhere. We are grateful to him for all he has done and proud to count him as a friend. Terry changed many lives for the better.

In these pages, those who aspire to a profession in the animal world or in academia, will find the traits and skills necessary for a meaningful career. Those of us who know Terry will discover here, and marvel over, things we did not know. There may never be another Terry Maple, but this portrait and example will undoubtedly help spawn a new generation of people who contribute to increasing the scope of Terry's fields of interest in melding zoo and animal management, conservation, education, and academic research. Terry, a self-made-man, commented more than once to me that the knowledge attained in his studies of primate behavior is invaluable in dealing with corporate chieftains.

Not many of us can aspire to tributes from the likes of Ambassador Andrew Young, Stephanie Powell, Speaker Newt Gingrich, President Jimmy Carter and the other dignitaries who admired Terry. (Citing Jimmy Carter and Newt Gingrich in the same sentence demonstrates the reach Terry had across the political spectrum.) Equally important and impressive are the tributes by graduate students, employees, peers of all kinds, and friends and associates. Terry's living-life-to-its-fullest has indeed left indelible footprints in the sands of time. The world is a better place for his occupying a significant place in it. He is a big man, a gentle giant, with a large and enveloping heart.

Robert C. Petty
Atlanta, Georgia, September 1, 2014

PREFACE

In a 40 year career, Dr. Terry Maple has changed the world in important ways. He began his academic career at the University of California, Davis and then came to Georgia as an Assistant Professor at Emory University. Shortly after, he moved across Atlanta to Georgia Institute of Technology where he spent most of his career. But that academic and research career took a remarkable twist in 1984 when he took over the reins of the failing municipal zoo in Atlanta. Terry is best known for his visionary leadership in revitalizing Atlanta's zoo after one of the most publicized scandals in the history of American zoos.

An internationally recognized expert on the behavior, welfare, and conservation of great apes, Terry's ideas as a primatologist provided the ethological programming for Zoo Atlanta's innovative lowland gorilla exhibit, which, along with a ground-breaking orangutan exhibit, was instrumental in leading the turn-around of the zoo. The gorilla exhibit is acknowledged as one of the most important gorilla facilities in the world and it was the first designed for a population of gorillas distributed in four contiguous groups.

Over the years, millions of zoo visitors have learned to admire and respect primates by observing them in naturalistic enclosures at Zoo Atlanta. Terry's eighteen years as the Zoo Director and CEO re-branded Zoo Atlanta as a non-profit corporation, restored its credibility and the zoo became recognized as one of the world's most innovative. In 1987 and again in 2000, the zoo was honored by the Metropolitan Communities Foundation as Atlanta's "best-managed nonprofit corporation".

Honoring the quality of its design and reconstruction, the Association of Zoos and Aquariums (AZA) presented five awards to Zoo Atlanta for excellence in exhibit design. Zoo Atlanta's partnership with local television resulted in six Emmy Awards for local programming, and in 1991, the Georgia Wildlife Federation honored Zoo Atlanta as its "Conservation Organization of the Year." Based largely on the programs established by Terry from 1984-2002, Zoo Atlanta was recently honored with AZA's prestigious Edward H. Bean Award, for its fifty years of lowland gorilla conservation, exhibition, husbandry, propagation and research.

In Terry's letter of thanks for attending his 65th birthday party in Atlanta in September, 2011, he reminisced about the many friends and colleagues who were able to join him and his family in celebration of his birthday and career. That celebration was the impetus for this book. The three editors announced that we were organizing a *festschrift* to honor our mentor. We reminded our guests that festschrift contributions should be focused on Terry's career and the impact he has had on dozens of students, professional colleagues and friends over the years.

A *festschrift* is a publication that honors a respected academic. It can be composed of a variety of contributed papers and essays that in some way reflect on the honoree's contributions to his scholarly field. Thus, the contributions to Terry's *festschrift* are essays about personal experiences in graduate school or the business world that were impacted by Terry, a reflection of how each individual experiences with Terry shaped their academic or professional career, a contrast of the training received at the Center for Conservation & Behavior at Georgia Tech compared to previous or subsequent training, or a family story impacted by the experience of working with Terry, or it can be as psimple as a psong...

We encouraged contributors to tell their own stories about the influence that Terry Maple had on their professional and personal lives. We all had a story to tell and that was why we joined Terry in celebrating his life and career at the AZA national conference in Atlanta.

The story of the rebuilding of Zoo Atlanta is a remarkable one. But, it is just one of the stories of Terry's life and career. This book contains many warm and humorous stories, from the professional to the personal. They tell the story of Terry's influence on the lives of the people who worked with him and the animals that benefitted from our common cause. We thank Terry for having the opportunity to have shared in these many endeavors with him, and we are happy to honor his legacy with this volume. Join us on a "knuckle-walk down memory lane."

Michael P. Hoff
Mollie A. Bloomsmith
Evan L. Zucker

semi-mega-sans

To celebrate his career, Terry's good friend and long-time
design collaborator, Gary Hang Lee, created this portrait of Terry and
his alter-ego, demonstrating once and for all that Terry occupies the
same amount of space as a lowland gorilla.

Celebrating the Career of Terry L. Maple: A Festschrift

FESTSCHRIFT FOR TERRY MAPLE

PART I: STUDENTS

Hoff, Bloomsmith & Zucker, Eds.

1. LET'S GO TO THE ZOO (AND OTHER TALES OF THE TAILED AND TAILLESS)

Evan L. Zucker
Loyola University New Orleans

As I start writing this story, my contribution to the Festschrift honoring Terry Maple, it is February 21, 2012. It is Mardi Gras in New Orleans, where I live, but this year, I am not there. I am sitting at the table in the "Estacion de Investigacion Primatologica y Vida Silvestre" in Balancan, Tabasco, Mexico. Terry Maple has never been here, and it is likely that he has never seen a wild black howling monkey (*Alouatta pigra*) or any other species of howler in the wild, but that does not matter. My being here is due, at least in part, to the influences that Terry has had on me, my interests, my professional development, and my career.

When I was investigating graduate programs in Psychology, I had some ideas about what I wanted to do, but nothing definite. I knew I was interested in animal behavior, having taken a very good undergraduate course in Animal Behavior at the University of Maryland (with thanks extended to Dr. William Hodos). I had an interest in studying the effects of drugs on behavior, as I had had a very good undergraduate course in behavioral pharmacology (thanks to Dr. Lewis Gollub). I also had an interest in hormones and behavior (behavioral endocrinology), although I am not sure from where that interest came, and I knew I had an interest in primates, and like behavioral endocrinology, I am not sure from where that interest came. I also had some interests in Applied Behavioral Analysis, which developed from seeing what rats can learn via operant conditioning in an undergraduate lab class, taken in conjunction with a course about classical and operant learning (thanks to Dr. Roger McIntire). So, for graduate school, I applied to some programs in experimental psychology and some programs in Applied Behavioral Analysis, and the experimental psychology programs were at institutions that had some connection with primates. I did not necessarily plan to study primates, but if the opportunity presented itself, I wanted to be there and to be ready. Emory University accepted me, and as I wanted to live in the south, it was an easy decision (despite the cost!). I expected to be doing research with rats, which I thought were neat animals, and see where that took me.

I had been to Atlanta in early August of 1975 to find a place to live, and later that month, moved my meager collection of things to Atlanta. I walked into the Psychology Building on Emory's campus, went through the little entry way, looked right, looked left, and saw only one open door. It was at the end of the hall to my left, like a T-maze, and that's where Terry Maple was setting up shop, so to speak. He had arrived in Atlanta just a couple of weeks before I had, and he was unpacking some boxes of books. He was a brand new Assistant Professor; I did not know him, nor did I know his work. He certainly did not know me, as he was not involved in the graduate admissions process for that year. I walked down the hall to his office, we introduced ourselves, and the rest is history, as the saying goes. He told me about his work, he gave me reprints of his articles and chapters (which was quite a stack of paper), told me about wanting to do research at the Atlanta Zoo, where there were orangutans who actually moved, apparently a rare phenomenon for captive orangutans at that time. Then, from his mouth, came the words I will never forget and words that really changed my life. The words are the title of this article. Very simply, Terry said, "Let's go to the zoo."

Terry grabbed his camera and we were on our way, heading to the Atlanta Zoo in Terry's Mustang II with the "Ape Dr." personalized California license plates. If I remember correctly, and this was now almost 37 years ago, we actually saw some copulations or attempted copulations by the orangutans that day, and that started our study of sociosexual behaviors of these zoo-living orangutans. I returned to the zoo the next day or so, and data collection was underway. I knew essentially nothing about orangutans, nor the behavior of any other primate species, as I had expected that rats were in my immediate future, not apes. However, since that first day at the zoo, I do not remember ever thinking seriously about studying any other types of animals. Over the years, Terry and his students have, of course, become much more diversified in their choices of species to study, but I've stayed with primates. I certainly enjoy watching species other than primates, respect those other non-primate species, and respect those who study non-primate species, including many of my academic brothers and sisters. My interest in studying only primates probably kept me from pursuing (and/or getting) jobs in zoological parks early in my career, where a greater diversity of interest is required. While I believe in a comparative approach, the comparative approach I took kept me within one order, but over the years, I have studied a fairly wide variety of primate species, including New World monkeys, Old World monkeys, and apes. I have recently added Mexican black howling monkeys to that list.

When classes started at Emory that fall quarter, in mid-September of 1975, another new graduate student joined the team. He was Lindsey Brogdon, from South Carolina, and he took on the task of filming the orangutans at the zoo, films that became known as "fur flicks." Terry had gotten a new Super-8 movie camera, so we were quite "high-tech" then. Unfortunately for us, although maybe fortunate for Lindsey, whom Terry referred to as "The Giant," he enjoyed photography more than the science, and he soon left the program to pursue a career as a photo journalist.

At the zoo, we documented social play and other interactions between the adult male orangutan and his juvenile son, a topic that was of particular interest to Dr. Gary Mitchell, who had been Terry's major professor at the University of California at Davis, where Terry did his graduate work. This study was the first one we published (Zucker, Mitchell, & Maple, 1978 in *Primates*) about the Atlanta Zoo orangutans. We also collected data about sexual behavior and infant development, starting in 1975 and continuing for several years. As Terry became established at Emory, he attracted a cadre of undergraduate students who were interested in working on these zoo studies, and they contributed greatly to our success.

A little bit of an aside: I remember the day that the reprints of that "paternal play" article arrived - I was thrilled! The first person I showed one to was Ruth Snyder, who was a graduate student in the Developmental Psychology program. We were standing by the Coke machine in the basement of the Psychology Building, across from the room we called "home" - the Laboratory for the Study of Social Behavior. As I write this, I can tell you that she and I have been married 12.5 years now. It took us a little while to get our lives "in sync," but we finally did. She used to watch orangutans with me from time to time at the Atlanta Zoo, and when we visit zoos now, she still is willing to spend lots of time with me in front of orangutan exhibits, watching those wonderful apes.

I do not remember exactly when it happened, but there was an aggressive event among the Atlanta Zoo orangutans. When we started our observations at the Atlanta Zoo, the group consisted of an adult male (Lipis), two adult females (Sibu and Sungei), and the juvenile male Lunak (Lipis X Sibu). At the zoo, this group had had access to two adjoining indoor enclosures connected via a holding area. No one saw the aggression, but the end result was that Sibu was the victim, suffering the loss of part of one finger and a cut on her face that nearly detached her nose. Sibu and Lunak were removed from the group and returned to the Yerkes Primate Center, as it was from there that they were on loan to the zoo. Sibu healed, and she was returned to the zoo. However, Lipis and Sungei (and by this time, I recall, their infant female Hati) were limited to one enclosure, with Sibu put in the other, and a new male introduced to Sibu. This male was Bukit, and he had had limited social experience, as well as limited climbing and brachiating experience. This arrangement turned out to be quite fortuitous for us in our study of orangutan sexual behavior.

Barbara Mandrell sang about being country before country was cool. Ted Turner was described as being cable before cable was cool. Sibu and Bukit demonstrated proceptivity before proceptivity was cool.

Soon after these orangutans were introduced to each other, Sibu began showing increased general activity, including a lot of brachiation and play, including running and sliding along the floor and doing somersaults. This activity segued into her chasing the male, who would climb away from her, albeit awkward3

6

ly. More dramatically, while Bukit was brachiating slowly using the bars on the ceiling, Sibu would be below him, pulling his legs, and eventually getting him onto the floor and mounting him sexually. These changes in her behavior probably were from increased testosterone secretion, but back then, we did not have the means to assess testosterone fluctuations. I was observing these interactions (and collecting data), as was M. Beth Dennon, an undergraduate at Emory who was studying these orangutans as part of her honors thesis work. Over a 3-month period, there were clear "spikes" in female-initiated sexual behavior, approximately 30 days apart. Sibu conceived an infant during that third month, and these periods of proceptive behaviors ended. These data were published in *Behavioral Processes* (Maple, Dennon, & Zucker, 1979), and it is a study (and article) of which I am really proud to have been a part.

This article about orangutan proceptivity should have been published a little bit earlier, but in those days, manuscripts were typed (with typewriters) and mailed to the journal editor or editorial office. The editor of *Behavioral Processes* was in Canada, and the revised manuscript was lost in the mail. After not hearing from the editor for a while, Terry placed a call to find out what was happening with the manuscript, and it was then we learned that he had never received the revision. So another copy had to be sent, which slowed the publication of these data.

That article contained a graph (figure) showing the cyclic pattern of proceptive behaviors, and I still have the original figure that spans three pages of graph paper. When I talk about proceptivity in my Physiological Psychology classes, I unfurl that original graph to show students how we used to do graphs - hand-drawn, for the most part, with rub-on letters. There are traces of White-Out® on the original to cover mistakes in the drawing of the graph. Ah, the old days. I confess that I'm not sure that I could do a figure like that now that even with today's technology and computer applications.

While these orangutan observations were being done at the Atlanta Zoo, other graduate students came into the program and became part of Terry's lab. We were the Laboratory for the Study of Social Behavior (LSSB). In 2006, Terry organized a symposium for the Southeastern Psychological Association meeting that was held in Atlanta, a symposium that included four of his students talking about their work with endangered species. Terry asked me to give an overview of the history of the LSSB as an introduction, and in that presentation, I mentioned the graduate and undergraduate students who contributed to the success that we had at Emory, as well as mentioning the graduate students that Terry has mentored at Georgia Tech, although I did not know them nearly as well, and in fact, at the time, I did not know some of them at all. Since then, I have met a few more, as some attended Terry's retirement and birthday party this past September. These are my "long lost" academic brothers and sisters. I will mention the Emory graduate students here, and if anyone reading this wants a copy of that 2006 SEPA presentation, please contact me. In that presentation, I emphasized the presentations that we did at SEPA meetings in those early years.

Earlier, I mentioned Lindsay Brogdon as being another graduate student in my cohort who did some work with Terry at Emory. Another student that year was Thomas Goldsmith, who did some observations of the hybrid macaques at the Yerkes Field Station in Lawrenceville, GA. Tom really wanted to attend medical school, and when he was accepted, left the program at Emory, although I do not recall exactly when that was.

The next year, which would have been the 1976-1977 academic year, several more graduate students came into the program. Michael Hoff came to Emory from UC-Davis, where he had known Terry, although I do not remember the details of their prior connection. (See Hoff's *Travels with Terry* in this volume.) Mark Wilson came from Eastern Washington University, where he had earned a master's degree working with Bob Elton. Chuck Juno came from the University of Wisconsin, where he had done some work with Steve Suomi. Jane Reints also came into the program, but I do not recall from where she hailed, and I believe she stayed only a year.

Michael Hoff arrived in the summer of 1976, and immediately started observing the three infant gorillas that had been born at the Yerkes Field Station in March of that year. The study of these gorillas was a collaborative project involving Terry and Dr. Ronald Nadler, who was on the faculty of the Yerkes Regional Primate Research Center at Emory. A good number of articles about infant gorilla development came from this excellent longitudinal study. Mike has continued to observe gorilla development at Zoo Atlanta, and has spent more time around gorillas than most of the gorillas themselves.

Mark Wilson also got involved in observing gorillas, if I recall correctly, as well as doing some observations of orangutans. Mark focused on maternal behaviors, and did the primary analyses for the article about orangutan maternal behavior that was published in *Primates* (Maple, Wilson, Zucker, & Wilson, 1978). (Mark had written a satirical article about the behavior of pet rocks for the *Worm Runner's Digest*, in which he reported a correlation coefficient of r = .98 for something; one of the correlations calculated regarding maternal behavior also came to r = .98, and I remember being a little suspicious. But we went over the orangutan data, and it was, in fact, r = .98!). Mark also put together some comparative analyses of orangutan and gorilla paternal behavior that were presented at conferences, but not published. Mark wanted to do research that was more experimental and physiological, so he transferred to the University of Georgia, and worked with Dr. Irwin Bernstein. Mark continues to do behavioral endocrinology research at the Emory University School of Medicine and the Yerkes Primate Center.

Chuck Juno began working with nursery-reared chimpanzees at the Yerkes main facility, also with Ron Nadler, and I believe Jane Reints worked on the project at the outset, too. I know they did a study of reactions to strangers by nursery-reared and mother-reared chimpanzees. Chuck was at Emory a couple of years, and went on to earn his doctorate at the State University of New York at Stony Brook. I have very recently learned that Chuck is back in Wisconsin, in Green Bay, working as an Organizational Psychologist. We are back in touch with each other after about 20 years or so.

So in these first few years at Emory, Terry and his students had begun a number of studies of the three species of great apes. Bonobos, the fourth species, were not really in the picture then, although in that first year at Emory (1975-1976), Sue Savage also arrived in Atlanta, as did the first bonobos at Yerkes. Her studies of language capabilities of bonobos would start soon at Georgia State University and the Yerkes research center.

I've mentioned a few of my academic siblings here, and I definitely want to emphasize that academic family was very important to Terry - and still is. In his first year or two at Emory, he invited many of his academic siblings, as well as his academic father Gary Mitchell, to Atlanta and to various conferences. Meeting my academic grandfather Harry Harlow was truly a memorable experience, with that happening at a Western Psychological Association meeting in 1977 or 1978. The American Society of Primatologists was in its infancy in those first few years, and we all participated in the first meetings, April 1977 in Seattle and September 1978 at Emory in Atlanta. Those meetings were wonderful experiences for us all, both intellectually and socially, and it certainly shaped the direction that my life would take. Since the Society's inception, I have missed only one meeting (in 1984), and the friends and acquaintances made via ASP have been extremely rewarding in many ways. They are very much like family reunions. These days, the term "dysfunctional family" is heard so much more than "functional family" - we are very much a functional family.

Terry once described to me the atmosphere during his graduate school days as being somewhat competitive, with this competitiveness used as motivation. I remember him telling me that Gary Mitchell would throw out an idea to his graduate students, expecting one of his students to grab the topic or problem first and get started on the research, similar to "toss up" questions on old TV game shows. I think Terry liked that approach, as it did motivate graduate students to do more and more, but at Emory, I did not sense that Terry used that same motivational tool. All of us graduate students had our own projects, our own niches, and I did not sense any competitiveness among or between us. We all had plenty to do with our ongoing projects with our various (and respective) species.

Rather than encouraging competition, Terry tried to keep things fair amongst his graduate students and to distribute opportunities when they arose. This is the part of the story that brings me to how it is that I'm writing this in Balancan, Mexico. In the fall of 1976, the Yerkes Primate Center hosted a two-day meeting to commemorate the establishment of the original Yerkes Center in Orange Park, FL. Many distinguished scientists who had been associated with the research center attended and talked about their experiences and work there. Attending that meeting was Dr. Jay Kaplan, who was a new assistant professor in Anthropology at the University of Alabama in Birmingham and a "veteran" of doing rhesus macaque research on Cayo Santiago. I did not meet Jay at that meeting, but Terry did, and Terry learned of a field school that Jay would be conducting during that upcoming 1976-1977 winter break. Students were going to be spending a couple of weeks at Cayo Santiago (in Puerto Rico) and a couple of weeks at La Parguera (in southwestern Puerto Rico), then take a brief trip to St. Kitts to see vervet monkeys. Terry suggested that I participate, and I wanted to, but I could not afford the whole trip. The portion at Cayo Santiago was going to be the least expensive, so I inquired whether I could attend the first part of the field school there, and then stay on at Cayo Santiago to get more experience observing free-ranging rhesus monkeys. That plan turned out not to be feasible, but in the next year, Jay obtained some funding for a study of the free-ranging patas monkeys at La Parguera, and knowing I wanted to get field experience, and upon Terry's recommendation, I was hired as a research assistant.

I was able to spend a total of four months with the patas of La Parguera in 1977-1978. That work became my master's thesis project, and it resulted in numerous publications about patas monkey social behavior. I am grateful to Jay for this opportunity, but especially grateful to Terry for encouraging me to get field experience and for making the connections that turned opportunity into reality and productivity. It was this time in Puerto Rico that enabled me to meet those who worked at the Caribbean Primate Research Center (including Cayo Santiago) and become a small part of that very long and distinguished history (and family). That connection, made originally in 1977, persists, as I am currently collaborating with several researchers at the Sabana Seca facility of the Caribbean Primate Research Center in an analysis of possible matriline influences on reproductive and life history variables. That initial field experience, facilitated by Terry, prepared me for later work in Costa Rica with mantled howling monkeys, which in turn, connected me with researchers in Mexico with whom I am now collaborating, this time focusing on black howling monkeys here in Balancan.

By the way, I eventually did do some work with hormones and behavior, assessing fecal estradiol and testosterone concentrations in wild mantled howling monkeys in Costa Rica. My work in Mexico with black howling monkeys is in yet another direction, as I am performing urinalyses in the field as an index of overall monkey health, and will be assessing possible differences as a function of age and sex class, habitat type and quality, and group size, including adult female:immature ratios. This current study is quite different from observing orangutans at the zoo, but one thing just led to another, and another, and so it goes. That's science.

During the time that Terry was at Emory, all of his prior work had been with captive nonhuman primates. However, he always emphasized the need for field research and having data from wild and/or free-living animals with which to compare data from captive animals. As his first graduate student, I got the first chance to do field research, as I have described above. In the summer of 1978, through the Atlanta Zoological Society, I believe, Terry took a group to Kenya to see east African animals in the wild. Terry wanted to take an assistant, so this second opportunity to go to the field went to Terry's second graduate student Michael Hoff. Terry thought I might be disappointed (or angry?) not to have been asked to go, and explained that it was Mike's turn. From the outset, that was fine with me, and it had never been an issue, because as I have mentioned earlier, there was no feeling of competition between (or among) us. It was Mike's turn to go, and I'm certainly glad he had that opportunity. As Mike was studying gorillas, it made sense for him to go! I did get a Tusker Beer t-shirt as a souvenir (and a bottle of beer), and I think I still have that shirt stored away somewhere. The shirt had the Tusker elephant logo and the slogan, "Beer ni bora." Fortunately, it did not say, "My mentor and fellow graduate student went to Kenya and all I got was this t-shirt!"

Terry encouraged us all to DO and to GO, and as you will read, the instructions were in this order, not the reverse, as you typically hear. With respect to DO, a lot of the research we did in those "early days" was opportunistic, and frankly, might not be possible to do in quite the same way today, as prior institutional approval is now needed before data collection can begin. We had permission from the zoo director to do the observations at the Atlanta Zoo, but to my knowledge, we did not have to submit any formal proposals. The work we did was observational, and certainly ethical by any set of standards, then and now, but then, we could start collecting data without submitting protocols and waiting for Institutional Animal Care and Use Committee approval – those committees did not formally exist then. I recall there being only one study that we did that involved any kind of manipulation, and that involved pairing juvenile orangutans for short periods of time to observe their play interactions. The results of that study were published in *Developmental Psychobiology* (Zucker, Dennon, Puleo, & Maple, 1986), and it was, in my opinion, one of the better things we published, because it did involve some social manipulations. We found that the play behaviors of subadult orangutans contained many of the elements of the sexual behaviors of adults, with sex differences evident in these component behaviors of play. This study obviously did require prior approval of the administration and staff of the Yerkes main center and great ape wing. We also observed interspecies play behaviors between nursery-living chimpanzees and orangutans (described in a chapter in Smith's *Social Play in Primates* volume; Maple & Zucker, 1978), but my recollection is that these young apes were already being put together in the outdoor play area, so our study of them did not require any additional social manipulations.

With respect to GO, we attended a lot of conferences in a lot of places in those first few years, presenting a number of papers about great ape behavior, and I presented papers about patas monkeys after I had collected those data. We regularly went to regional and national meetings of the Animal Behavior Society, the Southeastern Psychological Association, the Western Psychological Association, and when ASP began, we, of course, were regular attendees and participants there, too. I recall one March going to three conferences in about a week's time. Several of us presented papers at the Southeastern Psychological Association in Atlanta, after which I went to the University of Georgia in Athens to present a paper at the American Society of Mammalogists meeting, and upon returning to Atlanta, driving with Terry to a regional Animal Behavior Society meeting at Purdue University in Lafayette, IN. Gary Mitchell and Joe Erwin had been in town for the Southeastern Psychological Association meeting, so we dropped them off in Nashville, TN, where Joe was living at the time. We played some pool, and then Terry and I went on to Indiana where he was going to give a talk about great ape metacommunication, if I recall correctly, in a symposium about primate communication.

Terry wanted us to do and to go, so we did and we went. In retrospect, I do not really know how we did all those things, how we managed to travel to all those conferences. Some trips are quite memorable, of course, like the drive to Seattle for the first ASP in 1977 and the trip to the Western Psychological Association meeting in San Diego in 1979, meeting up with a couple of former Emory undergraduates (Susan Wilson and Susan Clarke) who were then in graduate school at San Diego State University. There was an amazing

Mexican dinner at the Maple home in Chula Vista, CA, a confluence of Terry's academic and genetic families.

Something another graduate student said to me one Friday afternoon in Jagger's, a pub that was located across the street from Emory's campus, really exemplifies Terry's influence. This other student was in the clinical psychology program at Emory, and from across the table, looked directly at me and said, "How can you all be working so much and be having so much fun?" I do not remember what I said in response - I think maybe I was too surprised at the question to answer it, and shocked that other students were not enjoying their time in the program. Whatever I did say, I'm sure it was profound, especially after sharing a few pitchers of social glue, but what he said was right on target. We did a lot and we enjoyed the work that we did, individually and collectively.

Thinking back to the first day we met, the DO and GO attitude was evident even on that very first day, although I did not recognize it at the time. Terry could have easily suggested we schedule a time for the next week to go to the zoo to see what the possibilities were, but that was not the case. It was time to do; it was time to go. By the way, the data we started collecting that very first fall quarter were presented that subsequent February at a regional Animal Behavior Society meeting at the University of Virginia. We did, we went, and we did not waste any time.

Over the years, Terry has written a number of recommendations for me, and has shared many of those letters with me. I am truly appreciative of what he has said about me to others, but I have to say that I think he is a little prone to hyperbole, or at least, has exercised poetic license. But regardless of what he has said about me, when talking to me, Terry has always spoken highly of his other students and their accomplishments, and is always complimentary in what he says. He is obviously very proud of his academic descendants, and while I cannot speak for the others with certainty, I surely can say that I am proud to be one of his academic progeny and a member of this genealogy. And I really believe my academic relatives would say the same thing and be equally proud.

There are many, many more tales that I could recount from the Emory days and the years since we first met, and I will put some "key words" to some of these tales in an Appendix. This chapter is intended to be my personal tribute to Terry, to thank him formally for what he has done for me over all these years. These other tales are better suited for a biography of Terry Maple (or an informal social gathering). Some readers might recognize some of these terms or phrases and bring even other stories to mind.

There is a lot more to Terry and our relationship than what I have included here, of course, but the values imparted to me are really rather simple and straightforward:

1. Appreciate and respect your academic family.
2. Be fair and equitable with whom you work and/or instruct.
3. Be complimentary and respectful of others and of their work.

Thank you, Terry.

References

Maple, T., Wilson, M. E., Zucker, E. L., & Wilson, S. F. (1978). Notes on the development of a mother-reared orang-utan: The first six months. *Primates, 19*, 593-602.

Maple, T. L., & Zucker, E. L. (1978). Ethological studies of play behavior in captive great apes. In E. O. Smith (Ed.), *Social play in primates* (pp. 113-142). New York: Academic Press.

Maple, T. L., Zucker, E. L., & Dennon, M. B. (1979). Cyclic proceptivity in a captive female orang-utan (*Pongo pygmaeus abelii*). *Behavioral Processes, 4*, 53-59.

Zucker, E. L., Dennon, M. B., Puleo, S. G., & Maple, T. L. (1986). Play profiles of captive adult orang-utans: A developmental perspective. *Developmental Psychobiology, 19*, 315-326.

Zucker, E. L., Mitchell, G., & Maple, T. (1978). Adult male-offspring interactions within a captive group of orang-utans. *Primates, 19*, 379-384.

Appendix

Key Words to **Other Tales of the Tailed and Tailless**

PJ's and Speedies
Jagger's
Lullwater
Lada birth watch

Santa Gorilla
Captive graphs
Worm Runner's Digest
Journal of Irreproducible Results
"We still have half a keg left."
Zucker Inspection Test (ZIT)
"They'd better be here."
The Clam
Pavlov's All-Stars
"Nice threads."
"You're too big to eat here."
Chart House
Little Angels with Horns
Mrs. Sam's
Darwin Parties
Survival of the Fittest Punch
Alfred Russel Wallace Birthday Party
"What's it all about, Alfred?"
Motorpsychologists Club
UC-Atlanta
Psongs my Psychologist Taught Me
Tillie the Teller
"Put it to the Empirical Test"
"I…..forgot."
Quinn (the Eskimo)

2. TRAVELS WITH TERRY

Michael P. Hoff
Dalton State College

Meeting Terry

I was an undergraduate student at University of California, Davis, when I first met Terry in 1973. I was not a particularly focused student; I had chosen to attend UC Davis because it was relatively close to Squaw Valley and skiing, not because I had a particular academic interest in the university. I had gone to college with the assumption that I'd become a physician, the "appropriate" career pathway for members of my family, following the medical footsteps of my father and mother. I had no idea of whether I really wanted to be a physician but, pre-med did keep my parents off my back. My first quarter of college I had taken an Intro Psych class that I found very interesting. So, I continued to take psychology classes as electives and overload courses as I continued in the pre-med track.

In my second year, I was looking over the course offerings and came across a course entitled, "Aggression, Hostility and Violence." I signed up for it because, well, you just have to take a course called "Aggression, Hostility and Violence!" When I walked into the class for the first time, I realized that the instructor was somebody I had seen a number of times at The Antique Bazaar, a local pub; I had not met him before, but readily recognized him because he was, as we all know, memorable. It was Terry Maple.

The course that I took with Terry was based on a book that he and a faculty member from his undergraduate college had edited. I've just now pulled the book from my shelf and found the listing of assignments, exams and my grade from the class. The class was interesting, but it was not the course content that connected me to Terry. Instead, during the class, Terry noted that he was doing studies of interspecific sexual behavior between a male rhesus macaque (Romeo) and a female olive baboon (Julie); he said that sexual behaviors had been observed and they were hoping to produce a baby macboon. Terry asked if any undergraduates were interested in doing observations on the pair; I raised my hand because I really wanted to see a baby macboon! I never did see that macboon, but I did a number of observations on Romeo and Julie through their pairings. I didn't really know what I was doing, but Terry showed me how to fill out the data sheets appropriately and so I started my first primate observations.

I had always been a kid who liked to hang out at the zoo. In childhood, I would take the commuter train from my home up to San Francisco and spend the day at the zoo watching the animals and I had visited a number of zoos over the years. However, this was the first time that I had any sense that anybody watched animals for any reason other than pure pleasure. I continued to work with Terry on his primate studies, one involving pairing two infant female rhesus monkeys with two infant female savannah baboons. The pairs were raised separately for several months as interspecies pairs (baboon and macaque) and then all four individuals were put together; that is the point when I came into the project, observing and collecting data on interspecies and intraspecies behaviors and documenting the attachment behaviors among the individuals. I also did observations on a group of stump-tailed macaques at the Davis Primate Center. Then one day, Terry showed me what the future might look like when he asked if I wanted to go to the Sacramento Zoo...

To the Zoo with Terry

When we went to the Sacramento Zoo for the first time, we just walked around looking at animals. Terry talked with me about the work of Heini Hediger with zoo animals and Bob Sommer on environmental psychology. Bob had just published *Tight Spaces* (1974) and Terry talked with me about the hard architecture of the zoos of the day. We looked at the lions, the tigers and the bears, noting the concrete and glass enclosures, the lack of the ability of the various animals to escape the closeness of the zoo visitors and the complete lack of natural behaviors that the animals demonstrated. Of course, this visit and Terry's comments presaged the enormous change in the zoo world that Terry helped lead as animal exhibits were naturalized over the following decades. On that visit, however, I didn't see Terry's vision for the future. Rather, I saw his interest in doing research *in situ* - studying the animals of the zoo in the zoo environment.

We walked around for a while and then Terry set me free to figure out something to watch. I wandered around and found myself watching the people watching the animals. Then I noticed something that led to a publication several years later - some people seemed to be avoiding the reptile house at the zoo. I heard some individuals declare that, "I am not going to go in there with those snakes!" and then move away. I watched for a while and noticed that this was far from rare. Later on I talked with Terry about it and, interestingly, he had been considering reptile avoidance himself based on some conversations with his wife, Addie. As we talked about his ideas and what I had notice, he finally said, "Study it!" So, I did. I didn't know exactly what I was doing nor exactly how to do it. But, I'd meet with Terry and show him what I had and he would aim me in the right direction.

That project was interrupted by Terry and me both leaving UC Davis in 1975 - him finishing his post-doc and on his way to Emory University and me with my B.S. on my way home. Eventually, we resurrected that project at the Atlanta Zoo reptile house, replicating and expanding it and then publishing the results (Hoff & Maple, 1982) in the newly-formed *Zoo Biology* journal. One of the small outcomes of that study was Terry making sure that there were benches outside the reptile house at Zoo Atlanta when he took over as director in 1984; these were positioned for people who did not want to enter the reptile house. Another thing that I should have noticed from that study was the rather long time between the beginning (1974) and the publication (1982) of that study. That time lag, completely my fault, reflects my never-ending challenge - get the data published!

At the beginning of my senior year of college, I had an internship at NIH as a "normal volunteer" for their research programs. As part of that internship, we were able to work in one of many labs as research assistants. I chose to work in a cancer lab, largely spending my time cultivating, harvesting, isolating and purifying ascites tumors in mice. It was at NIH that I decided that I was interested in research as a career, although not biomedical research specifically, and I also decided I would not go to medical school. As I considered the possibilities, I recognized that animal behavior held a particular fascination for me and that I just might be able to follow that as a career.

I came back to Davis after that quarter and met with Terry, and spent some time talking with him about graduate school and the life of a college professor. He was, of course, very happy to talk with me, helping me define my interests and assuring me that there was a future in animal behavior research. As we were coming to the end of our time at UC Davis, him off to Emory and me graduating, Terry suggested that I might continue my primate studies over the summer by going to the Oakland Zoo where there was a large vertical cage housing gibbons and spider monkeys. He was interested in the patterns of interactive behaviors that these primates might show, reflecting the ongoing interest that he had in interspecific behaviors. I did go to the Oakland Zoo and conduct those studies, but we never did anything with the data.

That summer progressed and I considered my future as a college graduate working as a nurse technician (that's a nepotistic term for "orderly" if your father is a doctor...). I called Terry and talked with him about graduate school. Terry encouraged me to apply to Emory University, so I took the GRE and then in the fall applied to, and was accepted into, the doctoral program at Emory for the following fall (1976). With that arranged, I went back to work, saving money for graduate school. Then, in May of 1976, I got a phone call from Terry...

To Yerkes with Terry

Dr. Ronald Nadler was a research professor at Yerkes National Primate Research Center of Emory University. He had a particular interest in sociosexual behaviors in gorillas and, as those studies progressed three infant gorillas were born into a group of 4 adult females and a silverback male in March, 1976 at the Yerkes Field Station in

Lawrenceville, GA. Ron had a student working for him who left when the infants were a couple of months old. Shortly after, Terry called me and asked if I could come out to Atlanta to study those infants (RIGHT NOW!!!). I said I could, quit my job that day, told my parents I was going to Atlanta, went to the Stanford University bookstore to purchase a copy of *A Handbook of Living Primates* (Napier and Napier, 1967) to learn at least something about gorillas before I got there and then two days later hit the road to Atlanta.

When I got to Atlanta several days later, I drove directly to Terry's house in Stone Mountain. Unfortunately, I got there in the middle of the night; fortunately, the lights were on, I knocked on the door and Terry answered. I also met Addie at that time, a wonderful wife to Terry who has become a great friend of my wife, Kathy (see "*The Other Maple*," this volume). The next day, we went to the Yerkes Field Station.

On the way to the Field Station, I expressed some reservations. I had been listening to Terry for several years; he was full of ideas and possibilities and he wasn't blowing smoke - the things he thought were possible while he was in graduate school and I was an under-graduate were coming true. But, that didn't mean I was ready. I asked Terry how he came up with those ideas; how I would possibly ever have the breadth of knowledge that was necessary to earn a doctorate; and how could I possibly develop the research ideas that he had? He told me something I've always remembered - he told me that ideas come with knowledge and experience. That if we learn the literature about primates and then look at the gorilla literature, it will be clear that there are huge gaps in our knowledge about gorillas. The research ideas will simply fill those gaps and then extend the know-ledge. Of course, he was correct. And it was certainly comforting to hear.

After we came back from the Field Station, we went by the main Yerkes center and he introduced me to Ron Nadler. Ron, Terry, and I talked for a while about the possibility of my participating in Ron's research project and then Ron graciously offered to support me until graduate school started in September. Ron pointed out that histori-cally zoos had isolated pregnant female gorillas around the time of birth out of fear that males would kill the infants. Zoos would quickly remove infant gorillas from their mothers if the mothers were not immediately competent and raise them in nurseries.

As we talked, it reminded me of my visits to a major California zoo that had an infant nursery inside the front gate; I had seen those infant animals in diapers and cribs, being cared for by humans. It made for a great visitor experience, but not a great developmental outcome for the infants. Ron had hypothesized that group companionship around the time of birth was an important variable in developing competent mothering. So, when those three infants, Akbar, BomBom, and Machi, were born in the social group, they remained with their mothers and Rann, the silverback male. My job was to study them, documenting their development and the patterns of maternal and social behaviors in the adults.

I started those studies immediately and the first eighteen months of the data became the basis of my MA thesis - interestingly, my data collection for my masters was begun before I started graduate school and was completed before I actually had my MA proposal meeting. That gave rise to a question at my MA proposal meeting by Darryl Neill, a physiological psychologist on my committee, asking whether it would have been appropriate to propose the research for my masters before I actually did it. I really don't remember my exact answer, but it seemed to satisfy him since he signed off on my MA. Terry, Ron and I had numerous meetings over the years concerning research design, data collection, infant development and publication. It was a very fruitful relationship for all of us.

To Graduate School with Terry

After meeting Ron at Yerkes, Terry took me back to the psychology department at Emory where he introduced me to his first graduate student, Evan Zucker. I was immediately impressed with Evan as a truly nice person and also as my academic big brother, since he had a year of experience at Emory when I got there. Evan has a wonderful, wry sense of humor and I have enjoyed his company over the years. Many of our experiences together were at PJ Haley's Pub, about a mile from Emory. Terry had started the LSSB (Laboratory for the Study of Social Behavior) in the basement of the Psych department at Emory, of which Evan was the founding student. As I recall, we had a couple of desks in a small office and, later, a galago (Harry F. Galago) that we somehow acquired. Since everybody was very busy doing research (and, oh yeah, taking classes) we really weren't there very often. Instead, we would meet very regularly at PJ Haley's for a recap of the day over pitchers of beer. This proved to be a popular meeting and our LSSB meetings at PJ Haley's attracted a number of graduate students from other labs and programs in the psychology department at Emory.

When fall rolled around, I met the other new graduate students who came to Terry's lab. Two of them, Mark Wilson and Chuck Juno, joined the ape studies, Chuck studying young chimps and Mark studying both gorillas and orangs; measuring the paternal behaviors of Rann, the silverback male of the group of gorillas I was studying, as well as studying parental behavior in orangutans with Evan and Terry at the Atlanta Zoo. Mark later went on to University of Georgia to study with Irwin Bernstein and today is Division Chief of Developmental and Cognitive Neuroscience at the Yerkes National Primate Research Center of Emory University.

Terry has always had an overall plan of development for his graduate students. He has projects in mind and then has students do those projects. His first project at Emory was to study the orangutans at the Atlanta Zoo. When I got to Emory, that was Evan's project; I went out there and watched those balls of red fur and, as I remember, saw them actually move once or twice, but my infant gorilla studies at Yerkes really aimed me toward Willie B., the theoretical prolocutor of the primate house at the old Atlanta Zoo. His enclosure was a classic of the day - an indoor cage with concrete walls and floor, and a glass front. There was no place to escape from the visitors and his "enrichment" amounted to a tire on a swing and, later, a black and white television set.

Terry and I stood in front of Willie B.'s cage and Terry talked about the future of the infant gorillas at the Yerkes Field Station, being raised by their mothers in an outdoor enclosure with their father resident; this in contrast to Willie B. Terry had high hopes for those infants; hopes that have been fulfilled. The immature Willie B. came to the zoo in 1961 from West Africa and captivated Atlanta. He was named for the mayor of Atlanta, William B. Hartsfield. The Willie B. story eventually turned, of course, to the reconstruction of the zoo by Terry, Willie B. being socialized with female gorillas and then fathering five offspring many years later. More on that later...

Terry was my major professor in graduate school, of course, and served as my advisor for the classes I was taking. As we were determining my first quarter classes, he suggested that I do something different than did most students. At Emory, at the time, it was expected that new graduate students would take a statistics class in their first quarter. Terry suggested that there was good reason to wait and take that class the next year because the professor teaching it would be on sabbatical the next year and the class would be taught by that professor's senior graduate student. He didn't tell me exactly why it would be a good idea to wait, but I took his advice and did not take stats that first quarter, instead taking it the next year.

When I took it the following year, I benefitted from an advanced graduate student who did a great job in the class (and I also first studied with my eventual wife in that class). Later I heard that Terry had taken some significant flak from his chairperson since stats was considered to be a weed-out class for first year grad students and I had avoided that. I didn't know that at the time; I was simply taking the advice of my major professor. But, I have remembered that advice that Terry gave me through my tenure as a college professor and have regularly suggested to my advisees that they take one particular class instead of another. I don't ever tell students why, but wise students will take the suggestion of their advisor. I was lucky that I took Terry's suggestion about that stats class so many years ago. I understand that the Emory psychology faculty later formalized that requirement of taking statistics during the first semester of classes for new graduate students.

To Africa with Terry

Terry has always taken care of his graduate students. He arranges for support for them through their graduate school years and helps them find positions as they are finishing up. Terry helped Evan Zucker connect with Jay Kaplan from the University of Alabama, Birmingham to study patas monkeys on La Parguera on the coast of Puerto Rico during his second year of grad school. Evan's experiences are detailed in his contribution to this volume ("*Let's Go to The Zoo*"). In turn, when Terry decided to start an Emory in Africa program and take a group of students to Kenya, he invited me to go along as his assistant. I went to Kenya as Terry's assistant in two successive years (1978 and 1979), and then Terry had other graduate students go as assistants in the following years when he went to Georgia Tech.

When we first went to Kenya, we spent 6 weeks there with more than 30 students, most from Emory. We stayed at the University of Nairobi dormitories and went on many safaris to the major national parks of Kenya. We observed a wide range of animals on those trips and also visited several camps of researchers in Kenya. Terry knew many researchers and would call up and arrange to meet researchers whom he didn't know. We all benefitted from those meetings. The most memorable of those visits was to Cynthia Moss who started the Amboseli Elephant Research Project at Amboseli National Park in Kenya. Cynthia graciously met with us and overviewed her studies of elephants. She cautioned us to be very careful around the camp because of the elephants that were in the area. Several of us did manage to turn a corner and be faced with several elephants flapping their ears threateningly. Fortunately, they let us retreat back to the camp without a problem. Cynthia Moss started that research project back in 1972 and continues to study those elephants today - 42 years later.

The Emory in Africa program had course credit, so we had classes that met concerning animal behavior and research methodology. I taught some of those classes, but my primary job was to watch out for the students and to help cut deals with the locals so that we could actually do more travelling than we could otherwise afford. Because of the expense, Terry did not use a travel company to arrange our travels while in Kenya, rather he and I went to the Nairobi bus service and arranged to rent city buses to take us out on safari around the country. We did not have the most luxurious buses on safari, but those buses were surely the most cost efficient!

We learned a lot on those trips about field work and studying animals in the wild. One of our great experiences was in our second trip. Terry had met a Kikuyu graduate student from Kenya who was studying religion at Emory. Through this student, Terry arranged for the group to have a traditional Kikuyu feast for which the student's family "killed the goat" in honor of our group. His brothers were middle-management at Dole pineapple in Kenya (who knew that they grew pineapple in Kenya?) and his mother lived in the old family home.

Our group was invited to her home, and her family provided a feast of roast goat, goat head soup (I have a picture of that goat head) and associated foods. Before we got there, Terry suggested to the students that they respect the culture, enjoy the feast and don't ask too many questions. The value of that suggestion was demonstrated when one particularly curious young man asked what the wonderful stuffed meat was that we were enjoying. Through a translation we were told that it was stuffed goat uterus. When we heard that, Terry and I decided we needed to "man-up" and had seconds, demonstrating the appropriate visitor behavior to our students. Not many joined us in those seconds, however.

In the middle of my years of graduate school, Terry established a multi-year relationship with Kingdom's Three, a drive-through wild animal park south of Atlanta. Not only did he get access to the park to study the animals, he arranged for Kingdom's Three to supply a grant to help support his students, and he also served as a consultant to the park concerning animal issues. He got me a position as a research associate/ranger at the park through one year and we studied the various animals at the park. I studied gibbons, chimps, and lion-tailed macaques living on separate islands over that time.

We heard reports about monkeys raiding local farms at night, so we spent some nights there and found that macaques would swim off the island at night, leave the park and then come back, swimming back to the island. I don't remember if we had any sort of resolution to that problem for the park, but we were certainly impressed with the monkeys!

Several experiences from Kingdom's Three stand out. One day they were short-handed and asked me to control the gates between the lion area and African savannah area. When I got there, I was told to stay on the savannah side, of course, and was also handed a long pole with a Y-shaped end. I was told that there was an aggressive male ostrich which would slowly approach and then run the last couple of yards and kick (they kick forward and can be lethal with their kicks) and the way to stop him was to carefully aim the Y end of the long stick toward him and snag his neck as he approached. For some reason this did not bother me and I actually got quite good at snagging and stopping him as he ran toward me, at which time he'd run away and wait a while before approaching again. My other significant memory is taking turns caring for a lion cub which had been abandoned by his mother. Various people would take the lion cub home for the night and when it was my turn, I put him in my car and drove the interstate to Atlanta. I got many second looks from other drivers as they saw a lion cub wandering around the inside of my car!

Leaving Terry

Terry went to Georgia Tech in 1978 after Dick Davenport, a primatologist at Tech, tragically and suddenly took his own life. Not surprisingly, part of his negotiations with Tech related to his graduate students at Emory. We were offered admission to that program but chose to finish at Emory. That did not end our collaboration, but it did make it a bit more distant.

Sandy Pietrewicz was an assistant professor at Emory, and a good friend of Terry, who studied search images in blue jays. She offered to shelter me at Emory in the short term after Terry left. We did several studies of blue jays after capturing them from the wild. We also published a study on Mongolian gerbils, examining diurnal patterns of behavior as they colonized new areas. The next year, however, Kim Wallen joined the Emory faculty and agreed to be my doctoral advisor. I had assumed that Terry would serve on my dissertation committee, but the chair of the experimental psychology program at Emory denied me. I then met with the graduate school dean, John Palms, and told him I had been denied and asked him to override the chair; he did that and so Terry did serve on my committee. That, of course, did not endear me to the chair of the experimental psychology program. Oh well…

I finished all of my degree requirements in 1981 and joined the faculty of Dalton Junior College, a small teaching institution in Northwest Georgia. That same chair of the experimental program approached me after I accepted the position and sniffed that "Emory graduates don't go to junior colleges!" I disagreed and did go. However, I was not altogether sure of my choice, and so to give myself some flexibility, I did not turn in my completed dissertation until January of 1982, despite finishing it and getting all the signatures in September, 1981. I figured that if I was unhappy at Dalton, I could apply for other jobs as a 1982 graduate and use my Dalton time as teaching experience on my way to my "real job."

Terry was very interesting during the time I was looking for a job. I talked with him about my options as I was finishing up and, of course, he wrote me a very nice letter of recommendation. I was clearly doing something that Terry had not expected, but he was nothing but supportive. He did point out that a first job does not have to be a final job. But, I had taught psychology at the Atlanta

Federal Prison for Mercer University in my late years of graduate school and discovered something that I hadn't expected - while I liked doing research, I really loved teaching. So, I changed my career goals from a researcher who also teaches to a teacher who also does research. Dalton Junior College also came with a significant benefit. It was relatively close to the gorillas that I had been studying through graduate school. So, I accepted the position, became a teaching college professor and have been very happy in the years since.

Terry and I continued to associate for the next several years; we published a book on gorilla behavior (Maple & Hoff, 1982), we had daughters born a day apart and our wives became great friends. We published a few things that were left over from graduate school. And then the Atlanta Zoo was named one of the worst zoos in the United States and Atlanta Mayor Andy Young recruited Terry to take over and fix the zoo, Terry rebuilt the zoo and in the middle of that he called me…

Back to the Zoo with Terry

One of Terry's great goals of rebuilding the renamed Zoo Atlanta was to have a world-class gorilla exhibit. He negotiated with Yerkes a loan to Zoo Atlanta of the gorillas that weren't an active part of Yerkes' research programs. As part of the rebuilding of the zoo, Terry recruited Ford Motor Company as the first corporate sponsor of the new zoo. They provided a substantial contribution that allowed the building of the Ford African Rain Forest that encompasses 4 gorilla exhibit areas and 1 off-exhibit area, the Gorilla Interpretive Center and the gorilla holding area. Ford Motor Company has continued to be a major corporate sponsor of the zoo and in 2010, on the 25th anniversary of their initial sponsorship under the directorship of Terry, was given the opportunity to name the gorilla born to Taz (Taz was the 3rd Zoo Atlanta gorilla birth) and Kuchi. The company chose to name the infant gorilla Henry, after the founder of the Ford Motor Company, Henry Ford (Ford Motor Company, 2012).

The new gorilla exhibits were opened in 1988 with the gorillas on loan from Yerkes. Terry had a pretty good idea of what would happen about 8 months after putting a silverback male and several female gorillas together in an outdoor exhibit! He called me in the spring before that was going to happen and asked me if I wanted to come back to the zoo to study the infants that he was sure were to be born. I wrote a proposal in the spring of 1988 for a Dalton College Foundation Award (we were no longer a junior college) that would allow me 6 months released from teaching for an independent study at the zoo. I put the start date of my study at 8 months past the date that the gorillas were scheduled to be released in the new Ford African Rain Forest exhibits. Fortunately, we were both correct in our timing and my independent study began the same month that the first two gorillas, Kekla and Mia moja, were born at the zoo (March 1989), followed several months later by Taz (see front cover of this volume). Today Taz is the silverback gorilla who is leading the major social group at the zoo and has sired 6 surviving infants to date.

Of course, the Willie B. story is core to Zoo Atlanta. On May 13, 1988, Willie B. was released outdoors for the first time since he was captured in infancy. Willie took a tentative step outside, looked around, stood on his hind legs, and then grabbed some leaves from an oak tree and ate them. The Zoo Atlanta website (Turnaround, 2012) has an iconic picture of Willie B. engaged in this behavior. Willie B. was introduced to females slowly over several months. Terry, of course, was intimately involved in the decisions and processes involved with Willie B.'s rehabilitation. There were numerous meetings and discussions about the best way to proceed. A consistent aspect of these decisions is that they were all data-based and scientifically driven.

While there were no data at the time on isolate gorilla rehabilitation, there was such literature on monkeys. Terry considered those findings as the plans to rehabilitate Willie B. were developed. Needless to say, those plans were successful; Willie was introduced to two females at the beginning and then, over time, several more. When Willie B. fathered his first offspring on Feb 8, 1994, Atlanta erupted in celebration. Over the next 6 weeks, 60,000 potential names were submitted for the infant and 104,000 people voted on the name (Atlanta Zoo's, 2012). And the name was Kudzu, later changed to Kudzoo. Over the following years, Willie B. sired a total of 5 offspring. Willie lived a long life after being released outside. Many thousands of zoo visitors watched Willie as he sat in front of the Gorilla Interpretive Center and watched them back.

In January of 2000, Willie got ill with pneumonia that led to congestive heart failure. Willie died on Feb 2, 2000 at about 1:40 pm.

I happened to be doing observations that day and my last observation on Willie B. was at 1:10 pm. His whole group was indoors because of his illness, so I sat just several feet from him and his group. Willie didn't move during that observation; I observed another gorilla, and then another, and then looked back at Willie B. and he wasn't breathing. I called the veterinarian staff and the primate curator, Charles Horton. They came and attempted to resuscitate Willie to no avail. The whole city, including all of the Zoo Atlanta staff, mourned the passing of Willie. Terry and Ambassador Andrew Young eulogized Willie B. to a crowd of 5000 people (see *"Remarks at Willie B.'s Memorial,"* this volume). I've talked with Terry a number of times about the passing of Willie B. and both of us find great comfort in knowing that his passing was painless as he just stopped breathing.

My studies of the gorillas at Zoo Atlanta have continued since those first infants were born in 1989. There have been 19 surviving infants born at the zoo over those years. Since I do developmental work, that work will continue as long as the animals continue to develop. Terry retired from Zoo Atlanta in 2002 and then went on to be named President and CEO of the Palm Beach Zoo until retiring in 2011. And then we all met in Atlanta for Terry's 65th birthday and to plan this Festschrift for Terry Maple.

What I've learned from Terry

Terry has been a major influence in my life. My wife has noted several times that I've known Terry longer than I've known her (By the way, I had also known Willie B. longer than I knew my wife when he died!). My academic pathway, my career, and my professional style have the footprints of Terry all over them. Over the years, I've learned many things from Terry.

I've learned to be nice to others, particularly to students and subordinates. I've learned to share credit for work done. I've learned to be careful as I give advice to students because it might mean much more to them than it does to me. I've learned to take chances in life because those chances might not come around again. I've learned to have expansive horizons because that will lead you beyond your expectations. I've learned to study things beyond my academic training and focus. And I've learned that marital and academic families are forever.

Thank you, Terry, for what you've taught me.

References

A Zoo Growing Up and the Arrival of Willie B (2012). Retrieved 2/16/2012 from: http://www.zooatlanta.org/home/history/advent_of_willie_b.

Atlanta Zoo's Gorilla of Yet-Undetermined Gender Given the Name "Kudzu." (2012). Retrieved 2/16/2012 from: http://news.google.com/newspapers?nid=2026&dat=19940323&id=17wjAAAAIBAJ&sjid=rtAFAAAAIBAJ&pg=3522,2402671.

Ford Motor Company Names Infant Gorilla (2012). Retrieved 2/16/2012 from:http://www.zooatlanta.org/home/article_content/ford_names_gorilla.

Hoff, M.P., & Maple, T.L. Sex and age differences in the avoidance of reptile exhibits by zoo visitors. *Zoo Biology, 1*:263-269, 1982.

Maple, T.L & Hoff, M.P. (1982). *Gorilla Behavior*. New York. Van Nostrand Reinhold Co.

Napier, J.R. & Napier, P.H. (1967). *A Handbook of Living Primates*. New York: Academic Press.

Sommer, R. (1974). *Tight Spaces*. Englewood Cliffs: Prentice Hall.

Turnaround - From Worst to World Class. (2012). Retrieved 2/16/2012 from: http://www.zooatlanta.org/home/history/from_worst_to_world_class.

3. BEHAVIOR MATTERS

Mollie Bloomsmith
Yerkes National Primate Research Center

Terry has more ideas than anyone I've ever known. Some of his
ideas are insightful, some are ground-breaking, and many are wacky.
It was some of these ideas about caring for captive primates that
made me decide to apply to study with him at Georgia Tech when I
was considering graduate school. I'd met Terry once, while I was
playing a softball game at U.C. Davis. My intramural team, the
"Psyclones" (with players from the Psychology and Genetics departments), was playing a game and I was playing first base. I made an
uncharacteristic leap to catch a throw that was going well over my
head. Good thing I caught the ball because it turned out Terry was
standing a ways off of the first base line behind me and might well
have been hit in the head if I had missed the ball. I might have spared
him a serious headache. Terry was an academic relative of mine,
since I was an undergraduate student of Terry's academic father,
Gary Mitchell. So I guess Terry was my academic older brother, soon
to become my academic father. You know how convoluted these
primatology families can be.

I decided to study with Terry for my graduate school years
because I liked the idea of applying what I knew about the science of
animal behavior to improving the lives of captive animals. By that
time I had already spent a few hundred hours as an undergraduate

collecting behavioral data on monkeys at the then, California Regional Primate Research Center in Davis, and I was hooked on the idea of continuing my study of primates. The notion of getting to study great apes, with Terry Maple at the Yerkes Regional Primate Research Center in Atlanta, was very appealing. Once I met Terry and experienced how fun he was to talk with, I was sure that Georgia Tech was the right place for me. It was a good decision. Terry worked from a positive reinforcement approach when he dealt with his graduate students. He pointed out the positive, was encouraging and excited about his students' ideas, he loved to talk about our new research projects and our research findings. Terry seemed to truly enjoy the accomplishments and successes of his students and colleagues, and we all thrived in that positive environment.

Terry made many opportunities available to his students. He sent some graduate students to Kenya, Brazil, or China, but me, he sent to Bastrop, Texas. In the summer. Little did I know when I first went to that wonderful chimpanzee facility at the M.D. Anderson Cancer Center, Science Park in 1983, that I was taking the first step toward what would, three years later, become my first "real" career job. That first summer I got a good tan while collecting behavioral data on chimp groups from the roof-top observation platforms, observing large, multimale/multifemale groups of chimps. I completed a simple evaluation of a feeding enrichment device that summer, and later published it with Terry, Ken Riddle and Pat Alford (two vets from the Bastrop chimp facility) as co-authors. I remember Terry calling to check up on how I was doing and I answered from the rooftop phone. I was in the midst of more than 125 chimpanzees who started pant hooting (it must have been meal time) while I was on my call, but I could still hear the excitement in Terry's voice as I shared my preliminary findings with him. His enthusiasm was (and still is) infectious, and as a young grad student I felt that my work was important partly because he seemed to think it was.

I did get my trip to Africa in 1986 with Terry and an eclectic group of a local television show host and crew, a zoo architect, zoo supporters, and zoo scientists - I went along as a "scribe." Terry had recently taken over as the director of Zoo Atlanta, and as part of the work to develop the concept for the naturalistic gorilla enclosures at Zoo Atlanta, we took a trip to see gorillas in the wild. It was the trip of a lifetime for me. The animal parks in Kenya were incredible, but hiking into the mountains of Rwanda to spend a few hours amongst mountain gorillas was better than I ever could have ever expected, and I had expected a lot. I remember swimming in a pool at the beautiful Mount Kenya Safari Club with Terry, and us agreeing that it doesn't get much better than that.

Terry doesn't see firm boundaries to what he can or should do, and because of that, his career is a little difficult to pigeon-hole. He is best known for his work in revolutionizing zoos, and many of the contributions to this volume focus on that, but Terry has also had an important role in making improvements in primate laboratories, which is where much of my own career has been spent. When a new issue arises, the first thing Terry recommends is to "go to the literature" to read about it. He followed his own rule when he participated in an NIH Ad Hoc Task Force on the National Chimpanzee Breeding Program in the late 1970s. As a part of the deliberations of the group, Terry wrote a technical report titled, "Chimpanzee Reproduction, Rearing and Rehabilitation in Captivity" which was presented to the group in 1980. It is a 94-page literature review of what was known about behavioral issues related to the normal and abnormal behavior of chimpanzees, and an assessment of the likelihood of the success of rehabilitation efforts, should they be taken. The behavior and social organization of wild chimpanzees is reviewed, and critical comparisons are made between the wild and captive situations on topics like infant development, parental behavior, and environmental requirements for maintaining these apes. The review also covered management approaches such as "behavioral engineering" (now more often called animal training), minimizing aggression, using enrichment to reduce abnormal behaviors, and the conduct of introductions of unfamiliar chimpanzees with one another. In the report Terry states, "… so little research has been conducted on applied problems. Activity in this important area may result in the development of an 'applied comparative psychology'. Experimentation is clearly called for, the results of which will be useful indeed" (p. 85-86). He recommended, among other things, that "In-house research or visiting research programs should be developed for the purpose of assessing behavior problems and testing therapeutic procedures." Looking back at this technical report recently, it is shocking to see how many of Terry's insights, suggestions and predictions have been acted upon. My own research program on chimpanzee well-being over the last 30 years has grown from many of the themes Terry detailed in this report.

Immediately following my trip to Africa, I packed my 1969 Toyota and moved to Bastrop, Texas, where I worked for the next 11 years. By this time, regulations on animal welfare were beginning to change. In 1986 the formal process had begun to amend the Animal Welfare Act to include the concept of promoting the psychological well-being of non-human primates (this amendment was finalized in 1991). Dr. Michale Keeling was the Chair of the Science Park at M.D. Anderson in Bastrop. As a vet, Mike saw the need for working with people with a behavioral science background to ensure that the field of "enrichment", as we then called it, was based on more than subjective opinion. Terry and Mike were fast friends, and Terry consulted on the design and operation of the Bastrop chimpanzee facility for many years. Mike and Terry shared a visionary outlook for where things should go for laboratory chimpanzees, and together created a behavioral scientist position that would focus on doing research to improve the care and well-being of the chimps, just as described in Terry's technical report mentioned above. I took this position before completing my Ph.D., and I believe the position was the first in the country in a laboratory primate facility. Now similar positions for Ph.D. behavioral scientists are commonplace in large primate laboratory facilities.

During my years at the Bastrop facility I learned so much about chimpanzees and rhesus monkeys, working with veterinarians, writing grant proposals, publishing research, and managing people. It was a tremendous work experience, and along the way I got married, bought a house, and gave birth to a couple of Texans. After a decade of life in Texas, my husband Craig and I were ready for a change, and I mentioned this to Terry during a visit to Atlanta. I was so surprised when he made yet another wonderful opportunity available to me, and offered me a job working for him at Zoo Atlanta. From 1997 to 2003 I worked as the Director of Research at Zoo Atlanta, during part of Terry's tenure as the Zoo Director. Even though my career focus had been as a primatologist, my years at Zoo Atlanta taught me that I could do more. I found that most of the animals on site - whether it be Giant Pandas, elephants, flamingos, or Aldabra tortoises - could benefit from having behavioral scientists around. While I was accustomed to thinking about all of the things we didn't yet know about chimpanzees and needed to discover, in comparison many of these other creatures were still a huge mystery. At the zoo it was fun to be a part of a facility where behavior mattered so much, to so many. With a large number of Georgia Tech grad students and with several Ph.D. behavioral scientists on staff, we studied everything. At one point I made a list of behavioral research projects underway and those being planned, and there were more than 100 on the list. We even studied ourselves with a project focusing on the role of science in the zoo. Having this huge scope of research was just fine with Terry, although at times it was overwhelming to me.

During my years at the zoo, as I helped Terry to supervise a large number of his grad students as they conducted research at the zoo, I again observed his mentoring style, but this time from the other side of the fence. I saw that Terry believed that his students were capable of doing anything and he did his best to make sure they had a myriad of opportunities. He thinks grad students are perfectly capable of designing studies, publishing papers, speaking at conferences, reviewing articles for journals, writing book chapters, editing books, serving on AZA committees, teaching, traveling to Africa, Asia or South America to study animals, leading students on international trips, taking on leadership roles in professional organizations-and much more. Terry expects that they can do these things, and his students tend to rise to that high expectation and perform brilliantly. I think this experience has been especially empowering for many of his young, female graduate students, some of whom came into the program not yet fully confident in their own abilities, but left the program with a long list of accomplishments, with demonstrated competence, and with the confidence to match.

In 2002, things were changing at Zoo Atlanta. There were funding reductions and we lost some of the research positions that had been in place for some time. When I was contacted by the Yerkes National Primate Research Center about beginning work there, and although I hated to leave the zoo, I felt that Yerkes was my best option. Now, 11 years later, the behavioral management program at Yerkes has grown to 15 people. We are conducting behavioral research and implementing a day-to-day program to promote the welfare of the Yerkes primates. Yerkes is a great example of the major shift in how laboratory primates are cared for—the psychological side of the equation is now seen as an important thing to attend to, and psychologists and other primatologists are integral to the daily operations of the facility.

It has been 34 years since my initial foray into a primate laboratory, when I first started observing monkeys at the California Primate Center. In my opinion, primate laboratories have made remarkable changes and improvements during this period of time with regard to the psychological well-being of their primates. Improvement has taken place in the research evaluating animal welfare, in facilities, in the daily care of the animals, in opportunities to learn about these topics, and in the people providing the care. The research documenting which potential improvements are effective and which are not, has grown exponentially. There are now many hundreds of peer-reviewed articles published that evaluate a wide variety of approaches to improving the welfare of many species of laboratory primates, and the scientists publishing this work are leading the way toward meaningful change. There are books and newsletter-type publications widely available to those working with laboratory primates. There are entire conferences devoted to environmental enrichment and there are many workshops teaching about improving laboratory primate welfare. There are commercial companies that provide enrichment supplies and equipment. Alongside jobs in animal care and veterinary care, there are now positions that specialize in animal behavior, environmental enrich-ment, training of primates using positive techniques, socialization methods, and behavioral management. These types of jobs are ubiquitous in primate labs, although 30 years ago, virtually none of them existed. Animal facilities now include more innovative housing that provides better social opportunities and more complex and interesting environments to laboratory primates. Primate facilities have environmental enrichment programs with the budgets and re-sources needed to carry-out the daily tasks of increasing environ-mental stimulation in species-appropriate ways. Behavior of the primates is routinely assessed to identify problems, and treatments are implemented. Many laboratory primates are now being trained to cooperate with husbandry, veterinary and research procedures using positive reinforcement training techniques, eliciting the animals' cooperation rather than relying on coercive methods. Some labora-tory primates are now retired to sanctuaries following their time in biomedical research.

Many of these changes are already considered the routine way of caring for primates - the "new normal" - and other improvements are still under development. The primate laboratory community is not yet finished making improvements or learning what needs to be done to further enhance animal welfare, but the progress has been real. I don't think it is an exaggeration to call this a revolutionary change in caring for laboratory primates. It has been very rewarding for me to play a small part in this transformation. I know that Terry had an early and influential role in starting this revolution in improving the welfare of laboratory primates. Terry has articulated the need for primatologists working in many settings, and he has essentially defined the various roles that primatologists can and should play in these differing capacities. Many primatologists are now employed studying animal welfare in zoos, laboratories, and sanctuaries, in part due to Terry's vision for the need for this work.

One of the most important things I learned from Terry is to be proud of our study of behavior, and to know that psychologists have something special to contribute to the lives of captive animals. Psychologists can bring our unique skills and knowledge to the table when we work with professionals of many stripes - veterinarians, architects, field biologists, immunologists, virologists, politicians - and we need to feel that our expertise is as valuable and as relevant as is the expertise of others. Those with behavioral training deserve to have a strong voice in how captive animals are housed and cared for. Behavior matters, and the scientific study of behavior should be the foundation of how we move forward in improving animal welfare.

Terry emphasizes the value of our shared academic family and his desire for all of us in the family to keep in touch and to help one another achieve our goals, and he points out that it is a lot more fun to do what we do with our friends. The culture of Terry's lab has always been about sharing - developing projects together, coauthoring papers, consulting together, traveling together, having a beer or some barbeque, and keeping those academic family ties strong. Few of my colleagues from other academic lineages feel the type of bond and shared history with their own academic relatives that I feel. It is truly one of the joys of my work life and I thank Terry for nurturing this sense among all of us in his academic family.

I have also been lucky enough to know and love Terry's biological family. His wife, Addie, has put up with Terry by frequently employing her own superb wit, and she has supported Terry's strange career throughout. Their daughters, Molly, Emily and Sally, are all truly unique, bright and talented young women, whom I had the pleasure of occasionally babysitting during their early years. It has been a load of fun to watch them grow up and find their niches in this world. Terry and Addie have been great role models as parents (if you haven't read Terry's article on "Natural Parenting", look it up sometime), and they have been encouraging to my own sons whom they have watched grow up. I am so grateful for my personal relationships with all of the Maples.

I hope that I can play my part in continuing Terry's legacy of hard work, influencing change, improving the lives of captive animals, and having a ton of fun along the way.

4. MENTORING MY INNER APE

Ken Gold

When I was Terry's student he went to Switzerland with his brother, a filmmaker, to interview Dr. Heini Hediger (the visionary thinker and developer of the concept now known as "zoo biology"). During the filming Terry interviewed Hediger in front of the Rhino exhibit at the African House at the Zurich Zoo, which he designed in 1965. This visionary building was designed with varied topography, plants, skylights, natural materials, and most-importantly moated exhibits, not barred enclosures, and walls that varied from the traditional 90 degree angles.

Terry and Dr. Hediger also walked thru the grounds of the Zurich Zoo, where Hediger was director from 1954-1973. Hediger was celebrating his 80th birthday the year Terry interviewed him, but still very sharp. Terry asked Hediger about some of the concepts of zoo biology, and elicited detailed descriptions from Hediger about concepts of animal psychology and how this was incorporated into revolutionary thinking about zoo animal behavior, and the development of appropriate zoo animal management and exhibit design.

After Terry returned from Switzerland I was eager to see the footage, and after much cajoling, Terry passed to me a few unedited VHS tapes of the interviews, which he told me he planned to edit into a TV special. The footage was spectacular, and captured on film a true revolutionary thinker who had the vision and opportunity to change the captive animal world, describing a small portion of his life's work to an insightful interviewer. Unfortunately, Dr. Hediger died within a couple of years of the filming, and other things became a priority for Terry and delayed the final editing for two decades. I am pleased to say the final product was worth the wait. It was debuted at the annual meeting of the World Association of Zoos and Aquariums in Orlando in 2013. One of Terry's former students, Jackie Ogden, played an important role in the final edit, proving once again that academic families stick together forever.

As a student of Terry's during the time he restructured Zoo Atlanta (ZA) into one of the premier zoos in the world, Terry was a busy man. In addition to being a zoo director he was a full professor at Georgia Institute of Technology, an editor of the American Journal of Primatology, and the founding editor of Zoo Biology journal. His students were lucky to get brief moments of his time at the zoo, and he was a bit more accessible at Georgia Tech, where he truly mentored his students.

Upon completion of the defense of a Ph.D. dissertation, the last step prior to graduation, Terry had a long standing tradition of cracking open a bottle of Dom Perignon to drink with the successful student. I was due to graduate with a Ph.D. in Psychology, with a minor in Architecture, as one of my main interests and passions was appropriate design of spaces for captive exotic animals. When Terry asked me when I would be available to continue this tradition, I deferred, and told him what I really wanted instead was to walk around Zoo Atlanta, alone, just he and I for an hour, so I could ask him questions about what he thought was successful, what could be improved on, and his general thoughts behind the resurrection of Zoo Atlanta.

What I got was more than I had hoped. Terry enjoyed the time so much, as he was mostly office bound, that we spent over two hours walking around the zoo grounds. Walking around that day at ZA with Terry was for me, probably what it was like for Terry to walk around with Heini Hediger, discussing his legacy. Terry said our walk that day at ZA was very insightful for him, and he needed to do it more often with his students. I am not sure if he did, as I left Atlanta soon afterwards, but I hope it started a new tradition. Terry also insisted on sharing the bottle of Dom Perignon, so I got two memorable graduation gifts from Terry. I still have the cork from that bottle.

5. BRIDGES BUILT AND CROSSED

Kyle Burks
Denver Zoo

More than twenty years ago, if I had been asked to describe the role that Dr. Terry Maple would play in my career, my response would have been narrow, short-sighted, and, for the most part, wrong. As a fledgling graduate student, my myopic view would have been focused on the role he would play in shepherding me through the academic hurdles that one must face in graduate school while on the journey toward a career of research and scholarship. Dr. Maple certainly did those things, and I could justifiably laud that journey between advisor and student as a crucial component in my professional career. But, of greater import than the academic journey we shared were the bridges that Dr. Maple built for me, bridges he built with me and the journeys taken to cross those bridges. As I reflect on his impact on my career, those bridges are the things that I have carried forward with me far more than the foundation of scholarship that has been always at the core of our relationship. Dr. Maple has a unique and somewhat frightening ability to recognize and create opportunities to span gaps between what at times might appear to be diametrically opposed places and positions. This ability, and its practice, has provided the most valuable lessons I have learned from someone rich with lessons to share.

Through twists of fate that have been chronicled in detail elsewhere comes the first instance of gap recognition and bridge construction that would impact my career. The formal practices of science have a long and robust history in zoos and aquariums. However, no one truly and successfully bridged the gap to connect the university, and more importantly, its students, directly with the zoo or the aquarium until Dr. Maple began his tenure leading Zoo Atlanta. It is one thing to have established relationships between the institution of a zoo and the institution of a university; it is quite another to firmly plant one foot in each and ensure a seamless connection between them. Ironically, it was this blending of the two institutions that allowed me to recognize that a life in academia was one to which I am not uniquely suited. However, without Dr. Maple's ability to recognize and demonstrate the power of connection between the university and the zoo, I would not have been able to cross that bridge in my own development as a professional. Nor would I have carried the critical foundation of solid scientific inquiry and practice with me into a career as a leader in zoos. And now, twenty years later, if one were to take a broad view of the connections, formal and informal, that exist between universities and zoos in our society, many of those connections can be traced back to Dr. Maple through his scholarship, his students, their students and the value of the bridge he constructed that so many have crossed.

While the bridge connecting university and zoo is one that many will cross, Dr. Maple has also been critical in building a singularly unique bridge designed for one specific animal to cross. This bridge allowed Ivan the gorilla to cross from a solitary life into a social one more appropriate for his species, and this bridge perhaps has had the most significant impact on my career. In the early 1990s, one would have been hard pressed to find someone with the desire, much less the ability, to bridge the gap between the polarized parties that were involved in deciding the Ivan's future. Not only did Dr. Maple help bridge that gap for Ivan, but the example that was set—one that demonstrated that the animal welfare community can work successfully with the zoo and aquarium community toward a common goal—is one that will continue as a legacy for any who desire to work toward improving the welfare of any animal in a captive setting. This bridge not only set the foundation for my own academic pursuits studying the dynamics of social group formation in captive species, but also helped me recognize the need for strong, sincere and enduring relationships between all of the individuals and parties who desire to improve animal welfare.

I have described but two bridges, and each alone could stand in their own right as a noble legacy for any professional or academic. But, these are just two of many that Dr. Maple has constructed and helped others to cross. There have been bridges between Atlanta and China, across which pandas and the science of their management have freely crossed. There have been bridges between conservation and politics, across which the ideas and agreements necessary to protect all species have successfully crossed. There have been bridges between the public and their zoos, across which the support that each needs from the other has freely flowed to the benefit of all.

And the list could, does and will continue as Dr. Maple continues his legacy of building bridges and shepherding animals, people and ideas from the places where they are to the places that they should be. It has been my distinct pleasure to have crossed but a few of those bridges and it is my distinct honor to have been included in the journey.

6. SHAPING ZOO BIOLOGISTS

Beth Stevens
Lori Perkins
Jackie Ogden
Rebecca Snyder
Megan Ross
Megan Wilson
Kristen Lukas

The late 80's and early 90's was a special time to be at Zoo Atlanta - it was a period that ushered in many of today's AZA and conservation leaders. We were lucky enough to be there at that time and to get our start under the mentorship and counsel of Terry. One thing we all have in common is that Terry gave us opportunities and experiences that ignited our passions and shaped our careers. He believed in us and he gave us tremendous freedom to explore the field and make a difference.

∞ ∞ ∞ Beth Stevens ∞ ∞ ∞

I first met Terry in 1980 when I was an undergraduate at Duke University. I saw an ad in our school newspaper for a class called "African Animal Behavior" offered by Georgia Tech in Kenya - Terry Maple was the professor. The trip to Kenya was life-changing. Terry introduced us to many scientists and conservation programs in Kenya - it was exhilarating. And, luckily, when a Masaai chief tried to make a trade with Terry - 12 donkeys for me - Terry declined! I returned from Kenya one day before my senior year at Duke. I changed my entire course plan for the year - I no longer wanted to go to vet school, I wanted to go to graduate school to study animal behavior.

When I finished graduate school, thanks to Terry's influence, I decided to pursue a curatorial internship at the National Zoo. At the end of that internship, Terry offered me a position as research biologist at Zoo Atlanta - and so began that special period for me at Zoo Atlanta.

Terry's inspirational vision for the scientific management of zoos gave me the opportunity to learn how to work with curators, keepers, educators, scientists and lots of students. He gave us the freedom to pursue all kinds of research studies and educational program development. He urged us to attend conferences, share our research and publish our scientific results. He supported us as we got involved with all kinds of AZA committees and conservation groups. We hosted the "Ethics on the Ark" meeting and published the book that is now available in hard copy and electronically on the Kindle. We were part of the first distance learning programming in the state of Georgia. We developed a Young Scientists program for middle schools. There were so many firsts - everything we did was forging new territory. I owe so much of my career to Terry. His leadership, mentorship and inspiration gave me the confidence, courage and conviction to carry on his legacy to use science to help make the planet a better place.

∞ ∞ ∞ Lori Perkins ∞ ∞ ∞

I first heard Terry Maple's voice on the radio, in 1982 or 1983. I was at work at a mindless and soul-sapping post-undergraduate job outside of Boston, and when the radio program host said he was about to play an interview with Terry, I perked up - this was the guy to whom I'd recently sent my grad school application! Of course I'd heard of him - my undergrad advisor, Melinda Novak, had spoken often of his work with apes, but how exciting - he was on the radio, too! I knew I wanted to go to graduate school in Atlanta, because of the opportunity to work with apes at Yerkes, but I hadn't decided between the three major universities there. I can't say that the radio broadcast convinced me, but Terry's interview about the ape mother-infant bond fascinated me, and the memory is still vivid, 30 years later.

I came to Georgia Tech in 1983 with the idea of doing basic research. Terry assigned me to work with Mollie Bloomstrand (later Bloomsmith), collecting data on elderly chimpanzees at Yerkes, to help me learn about apes (since I'd worked only with rats and rhesus monkeys until then). He also encouraged me to spend time at the zoo, where he studied the solitary male gorilla Willie B. I knew nothing about gorillas, but I started spending more and more time at the zoo, happily playing hide-and-seek with Willie, and watching those puzzling orangutans out of the corner of my eye when it was my turn to hide.

In 1984, Mayor Andrew Young and his commissioner of Parks, Recreation and Cultural Affairs, Carolyn Boyd Hatcher, asked for Terry's help in turning the zoo around, and by that point I was spending many hours a day at the zoo and had befriended many of the keepers. One of the major issues at the zoo was the state of its animal records, and, with an eye to providing his student with gainful part-time employment, Terry proposed that I redevelop the records-keeping system. I remember my abject terror when I had to meet with Mayor Young and Commissioner Hatcher for informal job interviews, and I remember how they both had such clear faith in Terry's ability to make the zoo into the world-class institution it has become.

I found my career in working at the zoo. Those odd orangutans, unwilling (or too dignified?) to play hide-and-seek with me, became my passion, and my species of research focus. Thanks to Terry's encouragement and guidance, I was able not only to study them scientifically, but to become deeply involved in their captive management and their conservation in the wild. And because of the many doors Terry opened for me, I had the opportunity to become involved in the zoo's redevelopment as well as in larger national and international zoo organizations, from AZA to ISIS to CBSG. I've become lifelong friends with the generations of graduate students who came after me, and have marveled at how so many of them have gone on to become leaders in zoo management and science. What an amazing legacy Terry has created! I'm so proud to be a part of that, and to have been fortunate enough to have been a part of his team throughout most of his own zoo career.

∞ ∞ ∞ Jackie Ogden ∞ ∞ ∞

Late on a Friday evening some 26 years ago, I was sitting in my studio apartment in Seattle when Terry called me. I had never met him, but had recently contacted him regarding possible graduate school opportunities. My goal was eventually to land in zoo/conservation administration, but I had been discouraged from admitting anything other than a purely academic focus. So imagine my surprise, when this deep voice introduced himself, and asked if I had ever contemplated an eventual career in conservation-related administration. After I overcame the intimidation of talking to this larger-than-life character, suffice it to say I found myself moving to Atlanta. This move resulted in some amazing opportunities. First, I was able to study the introduction of Willie B. - Zoo Atlanta's famous gorilla - to not only his first outdoor exhibit, but to female gorillas (including video documentation of his first "close encounters"). This socialization was important not only for Willie B. as an individual, but also provided an opportunity to examine the broader psychological implications of such socializations to gorillas in managed settings. Terry gave me the opportunity to be not simply a graduate student doing research at a zoo, but really to be a part of the overall team. It was - and is - a tremendous team, and working with them provided me many opportunities to learn and to grow, including friendships that I cherish. He generously supported me to attend many conferences - through which I not only learned to over-come my fear of public speaking, but had incredible opportunities for networking and building professional friendships. And he facilitated my eventual pre- and post-doc positions at the San Diego Zoo, where my interest in working with both people and animals - continued to grow. I have learned a great deal from Terry, and value my friendship with him and with his family. And I will be forever indebted to him for the opportunities he has provided me.

∞ ∞ ∞ Rebecca Snyder ∞ ∞ ∞

I first found Terry Maple through his books, *Gorilla Behavior* and *Orangutan Behavior*. Even my primate deprived undergraduate alma mater, Iowa State University, had those books in its library. I applied to Georgia Tech because of those books, and also applied to several other universities with faculty conducting research on mammalian behavior. I had some vague idea about wanting to use research to improve captive breeding for endangered species. I was overjoyed when I received my acceptance letter to Georgia Tech and stunned when Terry personally invited me to visit the school and Zoo Atlanta. As soon as I met Terry, who was warm, funny, and immediately paternal, and saw the zoo I knew Terry's unique program at Georgia Tech was the right choice. No other program had the powerful university and zoo connection that allowed Terry's students to access to a wide array of species to study. And my interest in the captive breeding of endangered species fit perfectly.

Most of Terry's students chose to take advantage of Zoo Atlanta's exceptional primate collection for their research projects. But I was drawn to the less social species, particularly carnivores. One the reasons Terry is an extraordinary mentor is because he always encourages his students to follow their passions. He was supportive of my desire to study solitary species and taught me how to apply what he had learned in the areas of primate sexual, mother-infant, and developmental behavior to carnivore research. I got started studying tiger reproductive behavior for my master's thesis and was living my dream to conduct research on captive breeding of endangered species!

Terry also taught me that it's okay to have fun with your research. His orangutan mating videos or "fur-flicks" were notorious among the psychology graduate students; even the IO students who took Terry's comparative class remembered those videos fondly. Soon I had my own collection of tiger fur flicks which were quite a hit at grad student parties!

For my dissertation I dared to dream the impossible, because with Terry as your mentor, the impossible became possible. I still vividly remember telling Terry in Zoo Atlanta's Holder Board Room that I wanted to go to China to study captive giant panda reproductive behavior. Most advisors would have had some hesitation about this course of study. Not Terry. He was so enthusiastic that it was as if he had simply been waiting for a student to suggest such a seemingly outlandish idea - and maybe he had. With Terry's unfaltering support, I was in China in less than a year collecting data on giant pandas! This study eventually grew into a whole program of giant panda behavioral research, involving many of Terry's students, both in China and at Zoo Atlanta, with the arrival of the pandas in 1999.

Looking back, I am still amazed by the incredible opportunities Terry provided to me and all of his students. The dreams he enabled all of us to fulfill are like Terry himself - larger than life.

∞ ∞ ∞ Megan Ross ∞ ∞ ∞

As the Vice President of Animal Care at Lincoln Park Zoo in Chicago, I get asked how I got to where I am today in my career by students and other interested parties. Unfortunately, mine is not the typical response, and virtually impossible to replicate. So I thought I would share with you my step-by-step process of getting into graduate school and starting my career working in zoos:

(1) **Follow up on your hobby.** While working for a software company, I asked a family friend if she knew anyone who banded birds in the Atlanta area. I had banded birds during undergrad, and thought I would take it up again as a hobby. She recommended that I ask her friend who might happen to know some birders in the area. She put me in touch with Terry Maple and we arranged a meeting.

(2) **Insult the work of your potential mentor by showing disinterest.** When I met Terry, he asked me about my interests and experiences. He then asked me why I had not applied to be his graduate student. I was very quick to inform him that I did not like, nor was I interested in, non-human primates. I preferred birds, which to me was the obvious reason as to why I would not want to be his graduate student.

(3) **Let them laugh at you (and be a good sport about it).** Terry laughed at my response of not liking non-human primates. I was pretty sure that I had offended him in that moment, but he was quick to put me at ease. He reminded me that there were more animals at the zoo than just primates, which in hindsight is pretty obvious.

(4) **Then mention that you don't know much about the person's field of work.** In this case that was zoos. Lucky for me, Terry likes a challenge and he carefully laid out his points for all of the amazing work that zoos do with welfare, conservation, research and population management. He made a pretty convincing argument.

(5) **Last, and most importantly, make sure that your meeting is with Terry Maple.** I am fairly certain that my ingenious "plan" to get into graduate school might never have worked if the person I was talking to was NOT Terry Maple. This is a man who can convince you to quit your well-paying job, go to graduate school with him as your mentor, and start to do research at a zoo over the course of an hour when you only went in to see if he knew someone who might be able to help you band birds.

I am so indebted to Terry for getting me to where I am today. Without that meeting on that fateful spring Tuesday afternoon, I have no doubt that I would not be where I am today.

∞ ∞ ∞ Megan Wilson ∞ ∞ ∞

"Where else did you apply?" he asked.

"Nowhere," I replied.

"What will you do if you don't get into the program?"

"Keep applying until I do."

That's pretty much how my first conversation with Terry went. If I sounded confident that I should be working with him at Georgia Tech and Zoo Atlanta, I wasn't. But I knew that I wanted to study animal behavior and I knew that Terry was at the top in his field. A short time after that conversation, I somehow managed to finagle my way into a graduate program with Terry as my advisor, and I've never been the same since.

I had a master's degree when I began working with Terry, but nothing really prepared me for the opportunities that my relationship with him would offer. I was fortunate to have some experience doing research at a different zoo on seals and sea lions - I loved marine mammals. Despite the fact that I was committed to a graduate career in Atlanta with Terry, I was still a bit skeptical that I would find something to love as much marine mammals. What I didn't realize, though, was that being one of Terry's students wasn't going to be the typical advisor/advisee relationship. Terry got me involved in giant pandas right away and I was fortunate enough to spend some time studying them in China. Terry's passion for elephants was contagious and I soon became involved in several research projects on elephant welfare and management. I was given the opportunity to travel both locally and abroad and had the privilege of making trips to Austria and Africa as a graduate student. I was blown away by Terry's ability to find me opportunities for growth.

Today, looking back at my time as a graduate student, I'm still blown away by what I experienced working with Terry. His advice and support have shaped my career in so many ways and I'm grateful for my opportunity to work with such an incredible mentor.

∞ ∞ ∞ Kristen Lukas ∞ ∞ ∞

In my senior year at Bowling Green State University, I was sitting on the couch in my apartment with my then-boyfriend (now-husband) Corey Taylor when a National Geographic show on gorillas came on. Other than a childhood fascination with Curious George's antics, and a lifelong admiration of Jane Goodall's chimpanzee studies, my knowledge of ape behavior was very limited so we nestled close and settled in for the duration of the program. I remember leaning forward, my eyes getting wider and wider, while I became completely transfixed with the story of Dian Fossey and her work with the mountain gorillas. I became enamored with the gorillas and just *knew* I had to do something to help them.

Fortunately I was just starting an animal behavior class and my professor used his connections to set me up as an intern at the Toledo Zoo. Glenous Favata agreed to take me on as a volunteer keeper but, sadly, after only hours of cleaning the gorilla exhibit my teary eyes, constricting lungs, and runny nose revealed a severe allergy to hay that would prohibit me from working behind-the-scenes. I felt crushed. Glenous knew I desperately wanted to work with gorillas so she suggested I conduct a behavioral study of the introduction of their new male, Kwashi, to three females.

Although my BGSU professor specialized in the flight behavior of homing pigeons, he taught me the basics of ethograms and behavioral research methods so I could apply them to zoo research. Most importantly, he pointed me to the library where I found Maple and Hoff's (1982) book, *Gorilla Behavior*. I spent hours reading and re-reading that book and called it my "bible," constantly referring to it during the three months of my gorilla behavior study. When I was ready to apply to graduate school, I boldly wrote to Terry Maple and told him about my research and my desire to be his student. I applied and was accepted at both Georgia Tech and University of Georgia so

I planned a trip to Atlanta.

I arranged a flight to Atlanta in the spring of 1993 and couldn't believe how sunny and warm Atlanta was compared to the dull and cloudy Cleveland I just left behind. The rental car company didn't have any economy cars so I had to drive a blue convertible to my appointment at Zoo Atlanta. Atlanta felt like paradise to me, so bright and promising, and I was so excited when I arrived at the Zoo and walked in to find that bear of a man, Terry Maple, behind his desk. I was completely star struck! Could this really be him? The best part was that he was so warm and kind to me - it was the first of many meetings where he made me feel like the most promising young scientist in the world who could do absolutely anything I desired. He offered me a tuition waiver and stipend on the spot and I felt I had won the lottery. Incidentally, the next day I had to exchange the convertible for a compact car and drive to the University of Georgia in the rain for a defeating interview with Irwin Bernstein; but it really was Terry, not the convertible, that influenced my decision to go into the program at Georgia Tech and Zoo Atlanta!

It is a decision I have never regretted. The next six years were positively wonderful. I spent hours upon hours on the roof of gorilla holding observing four dynamic groups of gorillas housed in outstanding exhibits. Terry not only taught me the nuts and bolts of gorilla behavior and exhibit design but showed me how to dream big and push myself to do better and better. He maintained a clear and inspiring vision for the role of science in zoos and the importance of animal welfare that still guides my work daily. When it was time for me to leave the Zoo Atlanta nest, he advocated for me and helped me gain the opportunity to interview for my first job as a scientific primate curator at Lincoln Park Zoo and again when I moved back home to Cleveland. As Curator of Conservation and Science at Cleveland Metroparks Zoo I launched a graduate program in Animal Behavior in partnership with Case Western Reserve University that models almost exactly what Terry established at Georgia Tech; it is one of the few zoo-university programs in the country where students can earn graduate degrees in biology while conducting zoo-based research.

Beyond the vision, leadership, and inspiration he has shown over the years, Terry has been like a father to all of his students. He created an environment at Zoo Atlanta that emphasized family, whether it was providing a place where my working-mother role models, Beth Stevens and Mollie Bloomsmith, could enjoy work-family balance or advocating a primate style of mothering that many of us implemented in raising our own children. He introduced me to many new friends and colleagues including Tara Stoinski and Megan Ross, who are still like sisters to me, and Chris Kuhar, who is not only like a brother to me but is now Executive Director at Cleveland Metroparks Zoo. It is a joy to come to work every day knowing a member of Terry's extended family is, like Terry, ensuring that science, conservation, education, and welfare are at the top of the zoo's priority list and that his employees can maintain a healthy work-family balance.

I am deeply grateful to Terry for accepting me into to his program that sunny day in Atlanta. He continues to provide inspiration and leadership to all members of his zoo family who strive to realize his vision for zoos.

∞ ∞ ∞ ∞ ∞ ∞

All of us met at Zoo Atlanta because of Terry. Today, thanks to our start at Zoo Atlanta during this special period in the 80's/90's, not only are we among many who are carrying on Terry's legacy in the zoo and conservation field, we have also developed friendships that will last a lifetime. Thanks Terry!

7. IN PURSUIT OF THE WILD

Gwen Murdock

It is an honor to be invited to share in this celebration of our mentor, professor, friend and colleague, Terry Maple and the celebration of his retirement from a productive and impressive career, just as it was a privilege to share in the celebration of his 65th birthday in Atlanta in 2011.

At the birthday celebration, I was happy to see and catch up with graduate school friends. I was impressed with the trajectory each person's life has taken since Georgia Tech (and Emory). We have demonstrated the value of the discipline of psychology in that none of us followed the same pathway, yet we are all working in and contributing to our field and to our communities. We all have an interesting story to tell. I was happy to hear about some and look forward to reading about more. What follows, is the story of my time at Georgia Tech and the ways that I satisfied my real passion, which is to learn how animals live by being with them in their natural environment. Along the way, I have had wonderfully good fortune to meet people who inspired me to stay on my quest, including, of course, Terry.

Unlike most students in our program at Georgia Tech, I had no background in psychology. When I first came to Georgia Tech (in 1980), I had only taken a zoo animal behavior class taught by the invincible David Chizsar at the Denver Zoo, where I worked while completing my Master's in Biology. My first year at Georgia Tech involved taking undergraduate psychology courses, starting with introductory psychology. It turned out that it was an ideal set up, because there was pressure to do well, but nothing like the pressure of "Marr papers." Terry was instrumental in getting a job for Linda Conradsen and me working for engineers testing the influence of microwaves on rats' mating behavior (Seaman, Murdock & Conradsen, 1981). We learned how to ovariectomize female rats and watched and recorded their behaviors. It would be one of my few experiences doing laboratory experiments with any kind of animal, but one I share with students when talking about proceptive female mating behavior.

I was attracted to Georgia Tech and to Terry's interest in zoo animal behavior because I loved working with primates during my 5 years as a zookeeper at the Denver Zoo. When I first came to Georgia Tech, I was intent on working at Yerkes Primate Research Center. I had conducted primate projects, one of which was my MA thesis, on the woolly monkeys under my care (Murdock, 1977; 1978; 1981; Quiatt, Everett, Luerssen & Murdock, 1981). I was looking forward to a career studying primates' social behavior. I always enjoyed reading and thinking about the varieties of social organization among the taxa. I also loved the intimate one-on-one interactions I had with my zoo charges and knew that I would desperately miss them. I hoped that continuing to do research would substitute for that personal contact.

Then, Terry invited me to visit his research site at St. Catherine's Island Wildlife Survival Center for the break between fall and winter quarters. Other students in the program had warned me that staying on the island was a primitive, remote experience. I still wanted to go, because more than anything, being in remote exotic places was something I thought I would like. I asked Terry if I should bring my tent and sleeping bag. Terry very casually said, "They have accommodations for the researchers."

I was completely shocked by my experience! True, to get to the island, one had to travel by boat at very specific, pre-arranged times. True, there was no way to get in touch with the outside world, except for going back to the mainland. True, most of the accommodations were not air conditioned, in spite of summer daytime temperatures around 100° F. True, there was no access to television or any other media source, except local radio. But it was hardly primitive, not in my mind. As other students who also made this trek will attest, we slept in nicely furnished cabins, ate meals in a common cabin that had a fully functioning and air conditioned kitchen. During the summer months, the swimming pool was always available, if one didn't want to visit the nearby unspoiled, empty beach. If one wanted a shorter respite from the grueling, arduous task of data collection, one could always take bread to the alligator hole and feed baby alligators. The wildlife on and around the island was as interesting as the captive exotic species.

The meals we ate on the island were far superior to what any graduate student had a right to expect. While Terry and we students were always frugal in what we ate, when we were there alone, it was still more than interesting and filling. (I remember roasting my first turkey in St. Catherine's kitchen.) If one of our visits coincided with the archeologists' visits, we were in for real treats of which we never would have indulged ourselves - fresh strawberries and artichokes, in winter, come to mind.

Conversations in the communal kitchen with other researchers were one of the highlights of the end of a day's worth of data collection. Besides conversations with Terry and other psychology students, there were biologists studying woodpeckers and ticks, geologists studying beach erosion, archeologists digging up pre-Columbian settlements, and interns working for the New York Zoological Society. If these people's visit happened to coincide with our own, it was a special bonus.

Hippotraginae

But more importantly, when I discovered that bovid species showed the same variety of social organizations as primate species, I was intrigued. My zoo experiences hand-rearing a variety baby primates and ungulates suggested to me that while primates are proactively social and suffer severely when socially isolated, bovids are also social, but not so proactively. I was curious about what might characterize the differences. One generalization I discovered in a quick search of the literature intrigued me more: whether primate or bovid, the taxa that live in social organizations of monogamous pairs tend to occur in tropical rain forest environments, the taxa that live in single male and multi-female social groups typically occur in grassland environments, and the taxa that live in multi-male and multi-female social groups tend to occur in desert environments.

St. Catherine's Island happened to have four species (addax, gemsbok, Arabian oryx, and sable antelope) that belong to the Hippotraginae subfamily, the horse antelopes. This was very lucky, for me and for our research. It was a perfect opportunity to do truly *comparative* psychology. Terry took advantage of the situation and with him and many Georgia Tech students (Lynn Howe, Bill Stine, Linda Conradsen, and Scott Ellington), we published papers on many aspects of antelope behavior, particularly the sable antelope (Howell, Stine, Murdock, & Maple1981; Maple et al., 1982; Maple, Murdock, & Lukas, 1981; Murdock, Stine, & Maple, 1982; Murdock, Stine, & Maple, 1983, Stine, et al., 1982).

Terry, as most readers of this volume know, was a great mentor in finding opportunities for students. He challenged me to come up with a way to determine which of the Hippotraginae species was "more social" for a symposium that he invited me to participate in at the WPA Convention in Los Angeles. This challenge ended up being the basis of my dissertation.

I devised a way of measuring behavioral synchrony, reasoning that herd animals, while easily detected as a herd by predators, could hide within the herd only if their behavior was synchronized with other members of the herd. My initial pilot data was nearly a failure, because I tried to measure the behavior of all the individuals in the sable antelope herd, every minute. This nearly drove me crazy, because just as soon as I finished noting which individuals were lying, standing, grazing, moving, or engaging in other behaviors, it was time to record another instantaneous sample. Luckily, with the benefit of time series analysis, I determined that instantaneous scan samples taken every 10 minutes were statistically independent of each other, even though the samples were taken of the same individuals. In the end, my results showed that the sable antelope were synchronized a mean of 84% of the time, whereas the addax and Arabian oryx were synchronized significantly less. The utility of this measure was validated by the fact many herd species, including the Hippotraginae, separate themselves from the herd to give birth or if an individual is ill or injured. If one can synchronize one's behavior with the herd, then one can hide within the herd. But, if one cannot, because of being in labor or being ill, then it is better to avoid the easily detectible herd and hide alone. Consistent with this idea is the fact that sable antelope live in savanna-grassland type habitat with greater numbers and taxa of predators than the desert habitat of the other three species. So, even though the Hippotraginae on St. Catherine's Island had no predators, they synchronized their behavior as if there was still a possibility. My observations suggested that these species' behavior in captivity was consistent with what would have been predicted of their behavior in the wild.

Near the end of my time at Georgia Tech, in addition to looking for potential academic and zoo jobs, I was also trying to figure out what the next research project should be. Given how money for research was drying up under the Reagan administration in the mid-1980s, I felt very pessimistic about being able to do field research on African antelope, even though I dearly wanted to. Then, I started thinking that the American plains bison was as worthy of people's adoration as African species, and that the logistics for doing research on bison might be more feasible on a limited budget. My family's cattle ranch in western South Dakota meant that I had regular contact with the bison at Custer State Park and Wind Cave National Park. From reading the literature on bison social behavior, it was apparent that most people who studied bison limited their observations to the summer months, when the weather in the west was favorable. Also, it was apparent that the summer months are dominated by bison calving and rutting activities. While those are certainly interesting, I took to heart Jeanne Altmann's observation that people should also observe animals, when the animals don't seem to be doing anything. For 10 months out of the year, bison herds consist of cows and immature bulls. Only during the rut, do bulls join the herd and compete with each other for access to the cows. Observing bison behavior year round seemed like a logical way to make a contribution.

Bison

Luckily, in 1985, a teaching job was available for me at Missouri Southern State University (MSSU). I was hired to teach physiological psychology, sensation & perception, and experimental psychology. I was assigned to fill in my 12 hour load each semester with courses in developmental psychology, applied statistics and general psychology. Initially, I taught animal behavior as a "special topics" course, before integrating it into the regular required curriculum.

Equally lucky was the fact that a bison herd had just been established at Prairie State Park in Liberal, Missouri, 40 miles away. After the first semester, my schedule was arranged so that I could teach almost all my classes three days per week. For the next 10 years, I collected instantaneous scan samples and focal animal samples on the bison herd, as the herd grew from 12 individuals to 58 (Murdock & Larson, 1986). The nice thing about this set up was that I was able to identify individual bison as they matured. I also consulted with park staff about how to cull the herd and ways to educate the public about bison behavior (Larson & Murdock, 1988; Murdock, 1996). Collecting data and teaching a 4-4 load, meant that I rarely had time to do much in the way of data processing and analysis. Nevertheless, this was the nicest combination of the intellectual stimulation of teaching and research, as well as the physical challenges of conducting research in the field.

Among the physical challenges was dealing with nearly 100 degrees of difference between winter and summer field conditions. In the winter, bison typically would stay on the highest hill, taking the full force of the winter wind. Almost invariably, I would give up fighting the cold after a couple of hours. Then when walking back to my car, I felt like I had "wimped out" until I realized that taking notes, while standing still, generated less body heat than walking through a ravine or behind a hill away from the wind. After two winters of experimentation, I figured out what to wear to stay warm enough - a surplus artic-wear Air-Force jacket and insulated snow-mobilers' pants.

In summer, bison do not seek the shade of the few trees in the ravines or cool themselves by standing in water. Instead, they soak up the summer sun's force. Protecting myself from the sun, while also staying cool was a summer challenge. Long durable trousers are necessary to walk through black-berry brambles. I remember one day, in particular, feeling like my brain was frying from the sun. I later learned that the temperature that day was 108° F.

Then, in 1992, the herd tested positive for brucellosis. I was heartbroken. Bison are in the worst possible situation in two ways. First, bison are classified as livestock, not wildlife. This creates the problems reported around the animals who escape from Yellowstone National Park. Second, bison originally contracted brucellosis from cattle imported by Europeans in the 1600s. Bison carry brucellosis, but suffer the consequences (miscarriage) for, at most, one year, unlike cattle who suffer for several years. Because cattle producers view brucellosis as a threat to their livelihood, most states have laws similar to Missouri, where the herd had to be destroyed. Prairie State Park staff obtained a special permit to ship the bison cows to Texas A&M University for a research study on brucellosis in bison. However, the fully adult bulls were killed and their horns and hides were used for museum exhibits, including the visitor center at the Park. Now, I surreptitiously stroke the hide of "AA," and the horns of "BZ," which make up the specimen standing in the visitor center. Because BZ's horns were spectacularly wide and long (more than any bison bull, I have seen in Oklahoma, Nebraska, South Dakota, Wyoming, or Montana), they were used as the form for multiple museum exhibits, not just in the U.S. but also in Germany.

Fortunately, the loss of the herd did not end my research. The next spring, Prairie State Park started a new bison herd, and this allowed me to replicate my study with a whole new set of individuals (Murdock, 1994).

Among the things I discovered were that as the herd got larger, it segregated into two groups: 1) mature cows (5+ years old) and their calves; and 2) younger cows, their calves and immature bulls. Unlike what I expected to find, the only cows that associated with each other, more than chance would have predicted, were cows and their now mature first born heifers, whose mothers had been barren the following year. It seems that body size and activity level determined associations among individuals (Murdock, 1995). This led me to wonder, how do calves develop independence? Do cows initiate independence or do calves? When do cows stop protecting their offspring from predators?

Bison and Wolves

Fortunately, Erich Klinghammer had the perfect set up for answering these questions at his Wolf Park facility in Battleground, IN. From April to November, the public could visit Wolf Park in the evenings on Thursday, Friday and Saturday, view the wolves and hear an interpretive talk about their behavior. Then on Sunday afternoons, the resident bison herd was lured into a pasture bound by a wolf proof fence and up to four wolves were introduced to the pasture.

The focus of the interpretive talk was how wolves interact with bison. This was a perfect natural experiment of how the calves and mothers interacted as the calves matured in the face of "potential" predation. For the most part, the wolves and bison teased each other, after which the wolves gave up and started hunting rodents in other parts of the pasture. The Wolf Park staff chased and enticed the wolves, like untrained dogs, to return them to the pack's territory.

In 1995-1996, Erich allowed me to conduct bison observations on Saturdays, and again on Sundays before, during and after they interacted with the wolves. A series of natural events revealed the answer to my main question, "When do adults stop trying to protect calves from wolves?" A yearling heifer was suffering from pink eye and her eye was swollen shut. Erich was concerned that she would be especially vulnerable to the attention of the wolves since she was blinded on that side. She was put into an adjacent pasture out of the wolves' reach, but not out of their sight. The wolf-bison demonstration that day consisted of the wolves ignoring all the other bison and instead seeking to get through the fence to the one-eyed heifer. The other bison ignored the wolves and instead just enjoyed the apples that were used to keep them near the area where they could easily be seen by visitors.

About 6 months later, one of the cows, Ruby, appeared to be seriously ill. I observed her yearling bull, B1, standing next to her as she lay isolated from the herd. A short time later, he approached the herd, and then almost immediately returned to her side. The cow moved very slowly, yet attempted to keep up with the herd as they moved and grazed around a 40 acre pasture. This pattern of B1 leaving and returning to his mother repeated itself all morning. When it was time to lure the herd into the wolf-proofed pasture, the yearling followed the herd, but then immediately turned and ran to the gate that separated him from his mother. Erich directed the staff to let the yearling into the pasture with his mother, because he feared that if B1 stayed at the gate, away from the herd, the wolves would harass him. As soon as he was locked into the other pasture, he tried to return to the herd, rather than to his mother. The calf spent the entire Wolf-Bison demonstration running back and forth along the fence, trying to join the herd.

As soon as the wolves were released into the pasture, they ran to the gate where the calf was running. Then, the entire herd, led by a "leader cow," Dagmar, ran to the gate and harassed the wolves, who were harassing B1 on the other side.

In the first instance, the yearling heifer was being harassed by the wolves while it was on the other side of the fence, but the rest of the herd ignored her and the wolves. In the second instance, the rest of the herd harassed the wolves who were harassing the yearling bull. One difference between these two instances was the fact that there were younger calves in the herd when the heifer was being harassed, but the yearling bull, B1, was in the youngest cohort. One might conclude that the youngest cohort elicits protection from other adults. Of course, these observations were confounded by the fact that the heifer was ill with pink eye, whereas B1 was perfectly healthy (Murdock, 2002).

The experience at Wolf Park was tremendously enhanced by the fact that while I was conducting my observations, I was camping next to the wolf enclosure. It was an absolute thrill to go to sleep and wake up each morning to the sound of wolves howling behind a nearby 8 foot high chain link fence.

Tanzania

When Missouri Southern instituted its International Mission, one of its intentions was to internationalize the curriculum by encouraging faculty to travel. I organized a sabbatical in Tanzania, studying antelope at Mikumi National Park. It was my first experience away from the North American continent and a wonderful experience, though with a number of significant logistical challenges. I spent August 1997 to December 1997, staying in the research facilities organized by Sam Wasser and Guy Norton. (Their research involved studying a baboon troop for over 20 years and employing local rangers and international research associates to collect data year round.) I stayed in a little metal "banda" without access to electricity. Some evenings, I would enjoy the company of the other researchers in the main research house, which had electricity. This situation was nearly like the St. Catherine Island's experience. Sometimes in the night, African buffalo, elephants and zebras grazed on the grass adjacent to my banda. If I spent the evening in the main house, then I would use a flash light to check for lions, before returning to my banda. One evening, as I stepped outside the house, there was a group of zebras 50 feet away. As I shined my light towards them, their eyes gleamed, then they started to move away. It was absolutely magical to see seven or eight shiny tapetums rotating in space as I heard their hooves hit the ground. In the middle of another night, I awoke to hear the low growly rumble of a mother elephant talking to her calf. I looked out the window and came eye to eye with her, as she pulled up the long grass growing next to the banda's wall.

One of the rangers, Charles Kidong'o, worked with me on the days he wasn't employed by the baboon researchers. He had worked at the park for 20 years and was very familiar with its landscape and wildlife. On the days we worked together, we would go searching for sable antelope in the miombo woodland in the foothills of the Uluguru Mountains. Most of the park rangers, the park warden, and even the park ecologist had never seen the sable antelope who resided in the park. With Charles' help, we were able to track down a herd of 13 individuals and determine the locations of three bulls. On mornings we worked together, we very, very slowly, and stealthily drove along a road constructed to maintain the power line that crossed the park. When we came to selected hilltops, we would sit on the top, looking across the landscape searching for sable antelope. On 30 of the 40 days, we saw them.

I always thought that St. Catherine's Island sable antelope never knew that they were not under predatory threat, but were still remarkably well habituated to vehicles and human activity. Watching truly wild Mikumi sable antelope was significantly more challenging. Charles was masterful in spotting sable horns emerging above tall grass. But, the slightest sound would make the sable run. When they ran, they ran so amazingly smoothly (not like the loping wildebeest & hartebeest). Their front legs stretched out in front of their chests and their back legs out behind their tails, so that the underside of their bodies seemed to be completely flat, from front hooves, chest, belly, to hind hooves. While the sable antelope on St. Catherine's Island were confined to a 2.7 hectare pen, they still seemed to stay in a cohesive group. The herd that I came to know in Mikumi split up, on occasion. Charles and I found some individuals 3 kilometers from the others. A few days later, we saw that the two groups had reunited (Murdock, 1999). The Mikumi sable antelope showed no signs of habituating to our presence, requiring that we try to avoid their detection. At the same time, I had reservations about the impact that I might have if I were to habituate them to my vehicle or to us.

People who lived adjacent to the park, if they could avoid detection by rangers, would hunt for bush meat in the park. I worried about contributing to the demise of the sable herd.

On days when Charles was not available, I drove to spots where I could observe wildebeest in the Mkata Plain. On these trips, I drove past the "hippo pool," which always had hippos under a surface covered in duck weed, but also occasionally a crocodile sunning itself and often lions lounging on the side. It was always a thrill. While driving to the wildebeest observation site, I discovered a family of jackals living in a culvert under the road. The adult pair immediately ran away when the car approached, but the juveniles stayed close by and let me photograph them.

On some evenings, I enjoyed the warm beer and the company of the park's professional staff at the little bar for park employees. Occasionally a bureaucrat in the park system would visit the park. Invariably the discussion would turn to the threats to Mikumi's future. The park staff had a very pessimistic view of the park's potential because a rail road, a major highway (albeit two lane), a power line, and a gas line all crossed the park. The staff would bemoan the fact that the park was not pristine. I kept thinking about all the "intrusions" in Yellowstone National Park and my bison research site, Prairie State Park. I would reassure the staff as best I could that Mikumi was still worth preserving, in spite of these intrusions. I was struck by the parallel circumstances between the origins of Tanzania's Mikumi National Park and Missouri's Prairie State Park. Prairie State Park was on a landscape that was too rocky for farming, so the tall grass prairie was never plowed and consequently available to be preserved. Mikumi National Park was on a landscape where the tsetse flies were too dense for people to raise cattle, so it, too, was preserved. Land that cannot be used by humans as an agricultural resource can be used by humans as a natural history resource.

Living in Mikumi, completely surrounded by wildlife, was an idyllic experience. Working in Tanzania was also a very intense social experience negotiating new cultural norms in an extremely inter-dependent society.

Back to Teaching, but Traveling Whenever Possible

Even though I started graduate school with a clear vision of myself conducting research rather than teaching, it has provided me with considerable satisfaction. While many students attending more selective institutions than MSSU have intellectually enriched upbringings, generally MSSU students have not and some grew up under distressingly brutal circumstances. Many are very bright and hard working. Their sacrifices for education are truly impressive. Among the students in my first animal behavior seminar were Sandra Guzman, who won an NSF Minority Graduate Fellowship to pay for her graduate education, and Cindy Cogbill, who became a naturalist at Prairie State Park. One of the highlights of my teaching career has been seeing students take on challenges far beyond the immediate community. I was honored by students who recommended me and by faculty who selected me to be Outstanding Professor in 1992.

Over the years, my former and current colleagues had developed a strong psychology program that was unusually research focused (Cathey & Murdock, 2008). All undergraduates completed a minimum of three research projects, from start to finish, in their undergraduate careers, including a senior thesis project. It was common for half a dozen students to travel to regional undergraduate psychology conventions to present their research. Many of our students had projects published in the *Journal of Psychological Inquiry*, of which I was a founding associate editor. I am very proud of the accomplishments of our students. About half the graduates from our program eventually earn masters degrees, a significant number have also earned Ph.D.'s (Sandra Guzman, Chad Phipps, and Wade Stipp in human factors; Deborah Cherry, Greg Kohler and Blake Webster in clinical psychology; and Clay Rutledge in social psychology to name a few with whom I have stayed in contact).

Missouri Southern's president, Julio Leon, developed a multi-faceted focus for the campus on international studies, sending faculty and students on international trips, developing an international major, and bringing scholars and artists to campus to share their international expertise (Gray, Murdock & Stebbins, 2002). It was a way of developing the community into something a little bit more cosmopolitan than it was naturally inclined to be. I think it had a wonderful impact. Part of Missouri Southern's International program involved focusing on one geographic region each semester. When I returned, the president designated the semester of 1998 as the "African" semester. There were many ways that I was able to share my experiences in Tanzania with MSSU faculty and students.

MSSU also made it possible for me to attend the Ethological Conference in India in 1999, where I traveled for 3 weeks, two weeks in South India and one week in Kashmir. Then, I lead student groups to Cuba for 10 days in 2003 and to India for 6 weeks in 2005. Both were satisfying experiences for me and our students. The trip to Cuba involved leading four journalism students and three other faculty members in anticipation of the Cuban Semester in the fall.

It was a privilege to visit Cuba in 2003, when Fidel Castro was still in power. It meant that the culture was relatively undiluted by influences from the United States. That trip, involved lots of intense social interaction, but few wildlife experiences. The journalism students explored many facets of Cuban culture, tourist sites, factories, schools and historic sites. Experiencing Cuban art in multiple venues, and music and dance through live performances was a special treat. Cuban governmental support of the arts was impressive. It made me wish the U.S. and local governments did a better job of supporting the arts as a way of distracting people from the struggles of everyday living.

On the first trip to India, I spent a week in Bangalore, participating in a truly international conference. I met researchers from across the U.S., Europe and Israel. It was lots of fun not only attending the sessions but also exploring the city with the group of new found friends and fellow researchers. When I returned to India six years later, the students and I traveled over most of the country, from Mumbai, Kerala, Chenai, Hyderabad, to Agra and Jaipur. We managed to ride elephants into the fort at Jaipur and see gaur in Bandipur National Park, thar in Eravikulam National Park, and nilgai in Bharatpur Bird Sanctuary. We spent 4 weeks on the campus of the University of Hyderabad, where the students conducted research projects. The psychology students conducted research on the division of household labor, mental health institutions in India, and adolescent experiences.

In the meantime, in 2001, our very hard working and dedicated psychology department head, Betsy Griffin, accepted a job in Academic Affairs. It was a position well suited for her, but that left an opening for our department. My colleague, Brian Babbitt and I, decided that one of us should take over as department head, but neither one of us really wanted the job. Brian won our debate, and I became department head.

I enjoyed the opportunity to develop the department in new ways and facilitate further development of faculty teaching. I also delighted in using my honed Tanzanian and Indian negotiation skills on behalf of the department. I feel I made some significant contributions as department head, for example, designing an animal lab for the soon to be built Health Sciences Building, facilitating the hiring of strong faculty colleagues, and being the buffer between administration and faculty. I was proud that our department met the challenge of developing an assessment of our program that met our standards for validity, but while not intruding on academic freedom (Huffman, Adamopoulos, Murdock, Cole, & McDermid, 2011). We also developed a human research ethics protocol that provided appropriate oversight of students' projects, but was nimble enough that students were able to start their projects without unnecessary delays. Our assessment and our human research ethics protocol became models that the rest of campus followed. In spite of these achievements and satisfactions, the department head was the person on whom "the buck" finally rested for many issues, which was stressful.

Bishkek, Kyrgyzstan

In 2008, I was awarded a Fulbright Award to teach psychology at American University of Central Asia (AUCA), in Bishkek, Kyrgyz Republic. I also officially retired from MSSU. At AUCA, I was assigned to teach physiological psychology, developmental psychology and to team-teach cognitive psychology, and psychological testing. Even though it was long ago, it was a relief to have in my repertoire the broad psychology background that I acquired at Georgia Tech.

I loved teaching at AUCA, because of the warm welcome from departmental and university colleagues. While the teaching style was completely in step with my experiences in the U.S., it was interesting to observe the dismissal of the "student as customer" model that prevails in the U.S. Instead, faculty members were accorded considerable respect consistent with Kyrgyz tradition. My departmental colleagues represented the tremendous diversity that is found in Kyrgyzstan as a result of the social engineering of the Soviet system. I taught with colleagues who were ethnically Korean,

Chinese, German, Jewish, Ukrainian and Russian. Kyrgyz psychology still adheres to many facets of the Psychodynamic system, where discussion of ego defenses was commonly bandied about the office. I found all these differences very stimulating and feel very fortunate to have had this opportunity. Since returning to the U.S. I have continued to collaborate with my Kyrgyz colleagues on presentations at the Midwestern Psychological Association meeting in Chicago (Molchanova, Galako, Zubareva, Mukambetov & Murdock, 2010; Murdock & Kim, 2010).

While in Kyrgyzstan, I had many privileged experiences, one of which was visiting a snow leopard rehabilitation center and visiting the field site of C.J. Hazell, who was studying wolf behavior and trying to devise ways to help farmers avoid losing their livestock to wolves.

Pittsburg State University

While living in Bishkek, I started searching for my next academic job. Unfortunately, my search started after the 2008 stock market and academic job market decline. I wanted to move further west, but there were only six tenure track jobs west of the Mississippi River that were a good fit for my interests and experience. Luckily, one of those was at Pittsburg State University (PSU), 10 miles west. Now, I teach courses in conditioning & learning, physiological psychology, research methods, and history & systems. The conditioning & learning courses (one graduate, one undergraduate) and the history & systems courses were brand new preparations for me. It was fun and continues to be stimulating to pursue this new phase of my academic life. In many ways, I felt like I was starting over. While I was familiar with the campus and knew many colleagues in the psychology department and elsewhere, I was surprised by the differences between PSU and MSSU. The administrative infrastructure at PSU is much more supportive of faculty focusing on teaching and research. PSU is a much more traditional campus with a Greek System and very successful athletic program that is wildly championed by the whole community, whereas MSSU is a commuter campus with much less extra-curricular involvement. I feel very fortunate to have solid relationships with my colleagues at both institutions.

Because PSU is the only university with a nonhuman primate mascot, it captured Terry's attention in the early '80s. Anytime I cross campus, I see that I am surrounded by gorillas. Some of them are statues, but most of them are living Pittstate Gorillas. One of the mottos of PSU is "Once a gorilla, always a gorilla." I am happy to be in the troop.

References

Cathey, C. & Murdock, G.K. (2008). A successful departmental model: Missouri Southern State University. In R. Miller, R. Rycek, E. Balcetis, S. Barney, B. Beins, S. Burns, R. Smith, & M. Ware (Eds.) *Developing, Promoting, and Sustaining the Undergraduate Research Experience in Psychology* (pp 82-85). Washington D.C.: APA Division 2: Society for the Teaching of Psychology, an ebook available at http://teachpsych.org/resources/e-books/e-books.php

Gray, K.S., Murdock, G.K. & Stebbins, C.D. (May/June 2002) Assessing study abroad's effect on an international mission. *Change, 34* (3), 44-51.

Howell, L.L., Stine, W.W., Murdock, G.K., & Maple, T. (1981 June). Proximity in a Free-ranging Herd of Captive Sable Antelope (I): A Longitudinal Study of Social Change. Presented to Animal Behavior Society Meeting, Knoxville, Tennessee, June 1981.

Huffman, L., Adamopoulos, A., Murdock, G., Cole, A., & McDermid, R. (2011). Strategies to motivate students for program assessment. *Educational Assessment, 16,* 90-103. doi: 10.1080/10627197.2011.582771

Larson, L. & Murdock, G.K. (1988) Small bison herd utilization and impact on tall grass prairie. *Proceedings of the Eleventh North American Prairie Conference* pp. 243-245.

Maple, T.L., Lukas, J., Murdock, G.K., Bunkfeldt, L., Bigg, K., Conradsen, L., Ellington, S., & Christenson, T. (1982) Notes on the birth of two sable antelopes (*Hippotragus niger*). *International Zoo Yearbook*, 22, 218-221.

Maple, T.L., Murdock, G.K., & Lukas, J. (1981) Birth weights of african antelopes on St. Catherine's Island. *Zoologische Garten, 5,* 288-390.

Molchanova, E., Galako, T., Zubareva, M., Mukambetov, A., & Murdock, G. (2010 April) Clinical classification systems in

Kyrgyzstan: Why are mental health specialists not happy with ICD-10? Presented at the annual meeting of Midwestern Psychological Association, Chicago, IL.

Murdock, G. & Kim, E. (2010 April) Supplementing Psychology Classes with *Forty Studies that Changed Psychology* (Hock, 2009). Presented in the CUPP Creative Department or Program session at the annual meeting of Midwestern Psychological Association, Chicago, IL.

Murdock, G.K. (2002 July) Relationships Between Bison Responses to Wolf Harassment and Bison Herd Composition. Presented to the Animal Behavior Society Meeting, Bloomington, IN.

Murdock, G.K. (1999) Sable antelope (*Hippotragus niger*) behaviour in Mikumi National Park, Tanzania. *Advances in Ethology 34: Supplements to Ethology, 160*, p. 263 (abstract).

Murdock, G.K. (1996 February). Effects of Management Practices on the Social Behavior of Bison on Tallgrass Prairie in Missouri. Presented to the Missouri Forests, Fish and Wildlife Conference, Osage Beach, MO.

Murdock, G.K. (1995 July). Analysis of Cow Social Relationships in a Small Bison Herd. Presented to the Animal Behavior Society Meeting, Lincoln, NE.

Murdock, G.K. (1994 April). A Comparison of Social Behavior in Two Small Bison Herds on Tallgrass Prairie. Presented to Midwest Animal Behavior Conference, Carbondale, IL.

Murdock, G.K. (1981) Observation of sexual behavior of woolly monkeys at the Denver Zoo and the Los Angeles Zoo. *American Journal of Primatology, 1*, 352-353 (abstract).

Murdock, G.K. (1978) Maintenance and breeding of white-faced saki (*Pithecia pithecia*) at the Denver Zoo. *International Zoo Yearbook, 18*, 115-117.

Murdock, G.K. (1977) Observation on the behavior of three species of Pongidae at the Denver Zoo: Curiosity and object manipulation. *Journal of the Colorado-Wyoming Academy of Sciences, 9*(1), 2 (abstract).

Murdock, G.K., & Larson, L. (1986) Behavioral study of a small bison herd at prairie state park. *Proceedings of the Tenth North American Prairie Conference* No. 07.03.

Murdock, G.K., Stine, W.W., & Maple, T.L. (1983) Observations of maternal-infant interactions in a captive herd of sable antelope

(*Hippotragus niger*). *Zoo Biology*, *2*, 215-224.

Murdock, G.K., Stine, W.W., & Maple, T.L. (1982 April) Mother-Infant Behaviors in a Captive Sable Antelope Herd. Presented to Western Psychological Association Meeting, Sacramento, CA.

Quiatt, D., Everett, J., Luerssen, S., & Murdock, G. (1981) Problems in representing behavioral space-time. *Proceedings of the VIIIth International Primatological Congress, Primate Behavior and Socio-biology*, Chiarelli and Corruccini (Eds.), Berlin:Springer- Verlag, 121-129.

Seaman, R.L., Murdock, G.K., & Conradsen, L. (1981 August). Pulsed micro-waves may affect rat mating behavior. Presented to Bioelectromagnetics Society Meeting, Baltimore, MA.

Stine, W.W., Howe, L.L., Murdock, G.K., Newland, C.M., Conradsen, L., & Maple, T.L. (1982) The control of progress-sion order in a captive herd of sable antelope (*Hippotragus niger*). *Zoo Biology*, *1*, 89-110.

8. ENABLING APE WELFARE

Andrea Clay

I was a zookeeper at Zoo Atlanta for eight years. Before that, I was a research technician at the Language Research Center for three years. At both jobs, most of what I did was animal care. That is, I cleaned cages, and shifted animals, and fed animals, and handed out medications, and gave out enrichment, and monitored the behavior and physical well-being of the animals in my care. I loved my job, and I loved the apes that I worked with. I started with bonobos and, sometimes, chimpanzees; moved on to gorillas and, sometimes, orangutans. Occasionally, I worked with different types of monkeys and once or twice with a sloth. I actually loved every part of my job, including chopping up produce and cleaning cages. But of course, there was never any question that the best part of my job was the opportunity I had to get to know individual apes and learn about the different ape species first hand.

After eleven years, however, I started to chafe. I knew a lot, by then, about the animals I worked with. I had a lot of opinions about how best to work with them, too. I had less patience with people who prevented me from doing what I thought best or who did things that I thought were ineffective or even possibly harmful for the animals. I was hungry for more than following someone else's instructions. Throughout the time that I was at the zoo as a keeper, I had seen graduate students in our zoo director's Ph.D. program come into gorilla holding to collect information, design studies, implement research, and gather data. I had seen for myself that people holding Ph.D.'s often had more influence over the animal management programs at Zoo Atlanta than did the people actually managing the animals on a daily basis. I started to imagine myself pursuing a Ph.D. and finally having more control over the things that, as a keeper, I could not control. Ultimately, I left Zoo Atlanta and applied to the graduate program at Georgia Tech. My zoo director boss became my graduate school advisor.

Graduate school was not what I thought it would be. It wasn't just a tool to get me into a better position when I returned to my keeper career: it was a learning experience that not only shaped my understanding of my past career but also completely revolutionized my goals for the future. And this happened not once, but many times over the seven years that I studied at Georgia Tech. By the time I was finishing my Ph.D. data collection, I was sure that I wanted to be a middle school teacher inspiring kids to really learn about science - this was a long way from the Ph.D. ex-zookeeper Curator of Primates job that I was sure I wanted when I started classes at Georgia Tech. It was, however, a natural result of having learned how incredible and useful and crucial an understanding of science is to really learning anything at all about the world that we live in. I wanted more people to have that understanding.

As it turned out, though I did teach part-time in a middle school science classroom for 2 years, I did not become a career teacher. As I was finding it hard to land a full-time teaching job pre-certification, a position opened up at the Yerkes National Primate Research Center in Atlanta. I worked as a graduate student at Yerkes for a number of years in Mollie Bloomsmith's behavioral management department and also collected all of my masters and Ph.D. data at the center. I knew and liked the people in the behavioral management department, and the job that had opened up was with the chimpanzees, which meant working with great apes again, and that was likely incentive enough for me to apply for the job. However, there was something much more.

Probably the most important thing that I learned in Dr. Maple's lab was that science is not just important for better captive animal management - it is indispensable. It is science that allows someone with a gut feeling about an animal in their care to explore that 'gut' feeling and study it and assess it and either find or not find evidence with which to convince someone else that one's pure intuition is, in fact, likely to be right on the mark. It is science that allowed a zookeeper with some strong opinions to start testing and assessing the correctness of those opinions and share the results, whether they supported opinions or made them suspect. I knew that science was also indispensable for Dr. Bloomsmith, and that working for her I would be required to be, ethically, a scientist. I knew that I would be required to apply the many things that I learned at Georgia Tech to my job at Yerkes, every day. I knew that if I did, I would get support from my boss, from my supervisor, and from my coworkers when I pushed for changes in animal management. It seemed like the perfect fit for me, and so far, it has been.

By the time that I really got started at Tech, Dr. Maple had moved to Florida. I didn't interact with him as much as many of his other past graduate students interacted with him. But I am grateful to him for having established the laboratory at Tech where I was able to experience a unique post-graduate education, one that perfectly mirrored my desire to learn more about captive primate management. I am also grateful that Dr. Maple had folks like Dr. Jack Marr and Dr. Mollie Bloomsmith working with our lab and holding us all to high standards, all the time. I am immensely grateful for the opportunity to work with Dr. Bloomsmith as she is now my boss and, though she certainly can be demanding, she is also someone that I know will always be open to new ideas and opinions - IF they are supported by science.

I never would have thought, when I first got face-to-face with a great ape, that I would be working with apes 17 years down the line. But here I am! And in my current position, I have the benefit of not just over fifteen years working directly with primates on a daily basis, but also have the benefit of excellent training to be a scientist, training I received in Dr. Maple's lab at Georgia Tech. I will always be grateful that I was accepted into the program at Tech and that I was given the opportunity to complete my Ph.D. and concurrently conduct research at the zoo and at Yerkes. I will always be grateful for the rigor of Dr. Marr's behavioral science classes, for Dr. Bloomsmith's high expectations where productivity was concerned, and for Dr. Maple's confidence in his students and his program. I may have come through at the tail end of his time at Georgia Tech, but the experience I had reflected the uniqueness and the importance of the program that he directed for many years.

So, thank you Dr. Maple and Happy Festschrift!

9. FROM ATLANTA TO AFRICA AND BACK AGAIN: THE CONTINUING INFLUENCE OF TERRY MAPLE

James L. Weed
Centers for Disease Control and Prevention
National Center for Emerging Zoonotic and Infectious Diseases
Atlanta, GA

The year was 1979. I was finishing my undergraduate degree requirements in biology at the University of Georgia. During my senior year I had enrolled in several advanced biology courses such as evolutionary, developmental, and cell biology. However, the course that sparked my greatest interest that year was animal behavior. What struck me right away was the fact that the instructors for the class were not even faculty in the biological sciences program. They were psychologists and had to travel across campus to teach their course in the biology building. I was hooked and unfortunately having focused almost all my coursework in the biological sciences, I wasn't sure what the next step would be. Most biology majors went right on to graduate school to continue their studies in biology. Some of my classmates enrolled in our veterinary school. I, however, had no clue what I was going to do or where I would be going. Then the most fortuitous thing happened. I often scanned the biology bulletin board which was situated between the large classrooms at one end of the biology building and the faculty offices at the other. Someone had been kind enough to put up a flyer advertising a summer course in African Animal Behavior to be held in Africa and taught by a Georgia Tech professor. At that time I had no clue who Terry Maple was or whether there would be any room left in the course to enroll for that summer. I don't recall whether I called Terry right away or sent a letter asking about available space. This all took place long before the internet was a popular medium and before cell phones were readily available to students. Needless to say, Dr. Maple indicated that there would be room in the program that summer.

I returned home that spring and began preparations for a trip to Africa. Terry typically hosted a pre-trip meeting with students to address logistics and answer questions. I was living in upstate New York at the time and couldn't make those meetings. Terry provided sufficient details to get me going. I booked my flight to New York City. My first face-to-face meeting with Terry would be in the Pan American terminal at JFK airport. I arrived early on the day of departure and literally wandered around for several hours before realizing there was another half to the Pan American concourse. I finally found my way to the gate. My first meeting with Terry left me a little concerned. Several students as well as Michael Hoff and Terry were sitting around a table engaging in all that pre-flight banter. Terry was very good at providing a description of how to spot him in a strange airport. I was to look for the guy who looked like a lowland gorilla. Once I made my way to the scheduled departure gate, it wasn't hard to determine which of the folks seated in the lounge was Terry. The first thing I spotted besides him was the liquor bottle in the center of the table. This Africa trip was my first overseas flight. I wasn't sure what exactly I had gotten myself into. As sometimes happens, our departure was delayed by 4 hours. Needless to say there wasn't any liquor left in the bottle by the time we all boarded the plane.

We finally departed New York and headed for Africa. We hopscotched our way across Africa on that flight. First stop was Monrovia, Liberia. We were allowed to look out of the windows on that stop. We picked up the Swaziland Prime Minister in Monrovia then it was on to Abidjan, Cote D'Ivoire; Lagos, Nigeria; and finally to Nairobi, Kenya. Before landing some of us got to see the sunrise from 30,000 feet above Africa. I will never forget that sight. Since we had been delayed in NYC as well as along the way, arrival in Nairobi was at 4 am. Fortunately for us, our local hosts were at the airport to provide us with a ride to the Nairobi University dormitories. Since the day was just beginning, we stayed up and explored Nairobi. For some it was just another international city. For me it was the city where all those jungle safaris began. Terry and Michael went off to rent vehicles for our first safari.

During that trip to Africa Terry introduced us to several scientists as well as other individuals who lived in Kenya. Some of those tales are described elsewhere in this volume and need not be repeated here. Needless to say the students were exposed to a great many things that must be experienced first-hand rather than through television or movies. One of the most salient aspects of that trip was the realization that it was possible to conduct field research in Africa, that primates were everywhere, from the Arboretum in downtown Nairobi in the Kenyan interior all the way to Diani Beach on the Indian Ocean coast. Terry, as others have noted, was always thinking about potential research projects, even going so far to describe a Pachydermobile – a research vehicle disguised as an elephant which could make it possible to get up close and personal with wild elephants. Finding colobus monkeys living within walking distance of Diani beach presented some interesting research possibilities. Since colobus monkeys are folivores, what mechanism was in place to help them adjust to a diet which potentially had a higher salt content than that typically eaten by other colobines living much further inland? I'm still interested in this question.

All too soon that trip was over. I returned to Rochester, NY to tend to family business and review my future options. During the Africa trip, Terry had shared some thoughts about potential work with colleagues of his. He saw that I had an interest in zoo design as well as primate behavior. He suggested I contact Joe Erwin to see if he might have any thoughts about possible work opportunities. Joe was just one of several individuals whom I contacted. As is often the case jobs were few and far between at that time. I stayed in touch with Terry and ultimately found myself fortunate enough to be in a position to go back to Africa for a second time. I would volunteer to be his assistant on this trip. The return trip to Africa with Terry and the other students was just as enjoyable as the first. Needless to say, one should always be careful about volunteering to do anything. In my case that meant finding alternative housing for one night in New York City; assisting students with missing passports; chasing down lost luggage in Amsterdam; removing a tick from the program director's leg; fixing a broken throttle cable in our van while stuck on the Mara; and pointing out to Terry that having two vans full of students completely surrounded by an elephant herd in the middle of Amboseli National Park was probably not the safest thing to do. We all came back safely from that trip and the colobus monkeys were still living right behind the huts at Diani Beach.

I was hooked on the possibility of studying primate behavior after that. I put in some time as a research assistant at Cornell University and as a behavioral technician working on Morgan Island off the coast of South Carolina. Terry has several suggestions for other field opportunities. Somewhere I still have a letter from Dian Fossey indicating that the position I had inquired about working at Karisoki would not be available that year. While I was disappointed at not getting out into the field to conduct research with primates or at finding a job as a primate research technician, I did find my way into the graduate program in the Psychology Department at the University of Georgia. I was back taking classes with those two faculty members who first exposed me to the idea of studying animal behavior. During those graduate school days I kept in touch with Michael and Kathy Hoff, both still living in Atlanta and attending Emory University. They were kind enough to suggest some research opportunities at Zoo Atlanta and I would stay at their apartment while performing some observations on several primates at the zoo including work with Willie B.

My research continued first at the Yerkes Regional Primate Center, working with rhesus monkeys, and then in the animal behavior laboratory at the University of Georgia working with other laboratory animals including monkeys. Time came to graduate and I found myself contacting Joe Erwin again. This time, Joe was in need of someone to assist with the management of an environmental enrichment program for non-human primates. The position was working in an NIH supported infectious disease laboratory in Rockville, Maryland. I gained a great deal of experience working with primates in that laboratory. Work there led me to take a post-doctoral position with the National Institute on Drug Abuse. We were working with monkeys as part of the National Institute on Aging project on calorie restriction. Folks at NIH had seen me around during the post-doctoral days.

When my stint with NIDA and NIA was over, I was fortunate enough to apply for and receive an offer to start up a program to provide environmental enrichment for laboratory housed animals within the Veterinary Resources Program at NIH. I stayed there for approximately sixteen years. When I first told Terry of my new position as manager of an environmental enrichment program at NIH he said "We have a mole at NIH." Maybe not a mole but at least I had remembered all the lessons taught by Terry and several of his colleagues about providing the best environments for non-human primates housed in laboratories. I was pushing the established status quo by recommending enhanced and possibly more stimulating naturalistic types of housing systems not only for the non-human primates but for all laboratory animals housed at NIH and elsewhere. We had come a long way since the first meetings to discuss providing environmental enrichment for laboratory animals.

Terry was the first individual who pointed me toward the literature of Alfred Russel Wallace. He is also the only individual whom I know who regularly celebrated Darwin's birthday with a party. One of Wallace's more interesting papers was republished in a two volume set titled "Studies Scientific and Social" (Wallace, 1900). I was fortunate enough to find a copy of this set in a used book store in Washington, DC. In this volume, Wallace republished some of his collected works including his paper on primates "Monkeys: Their affinities and distribution", that originally appeared in *Contemporary Review*, December, 1881. In this paper Wallace provides great detail regarding potential ways to house great apes in captivity. As Terry is a prime example of yet another individual who champions the cause of great apes as well as other primates housed in zoos and laboratories I think it appropriate to end with a quote from Wallace.

> These great apes, like many of the smaller monkeys, are very liable to lung-disease in this country, and soon die from confinement. This is no doubt due to the want of pure air and exercise, and it is unfortunate that none of the Zoological Societies of Europe have made suitable arrangements for giving them these essentials of health. All that would be necessary would be a rather large and lofty conservatory, containing two or three moderate-sized trees, and opening out of this a larger enclosure containing a

few clumps of loftier trees. This enclosure might be surrounded by a deep and wide trench sloping inwards, from the outer margin of the bottom of which would rise a wall or fence of a sufficient height, and perfectly smooth inside, so as to be unclimbable by these apes. Even if it were twelve feet high such a fence would offer no obstruction to the view, as the earth excavated would form a bank on the outside, reaching nearly as high as the top of the wall. Fruit trees, such as apples, crabs, damsons, cherries, chestnuts, &c., would be suitable as furnishing both food and exercise; and on mild sunny days throughout the year the orangs or chimpanzees would spend most of their time out of doors, only coming into the conservatory in very cold or wet weather. There seems no reason why, under these more favourable conditions they should not live to a fair old age. Each species should be kept separate, and the experiment should begin with two or three young animals, whose association would be another factor tending to health. The opportunities for observation of the whole life-habits of these singular animals would be of greatest interest, and the experiment would probably pay its cost as a public exhibition...; but even in England I feel sure that, with an arrangement such as I have suggested, these most remarkable and interesting creatures might be kept alive for many years, and might even breed in captivity. (Alfred Russel Wallace, 1900)

Those of us who have been fortunate enough to work with Terry know of his passion and commitment for working with non-human primates but especially the great apes. While I was never an official student of his, I'd like to think that his influence on my life and career can be seen in the work I continue to do to this day. The comparative approach to addressing research questions is never far from my mind. I know that Terry had more than a passing influence on my career. As he once said, my meeting him changed my entire life as well as my ultimate career path. Nothing could be more true and I thank him for it.

References

Wallace, A.R. (1900). Monkeys: Their affinities and distribution. In A.R. Wallace, *Studies Scientific and Social, Volume 1*. London: Macmillan & Co, Ltd.

10. THAT WAS ME IN THE GORILLA SUIT

Ted Finlay

That was me in the gorilla suit at Terry's AZA party. How did the VP of Research at a major advertising firm end up in a gorilla suit roasting one of the premier primatologists of all time?

I ended up in the gorilla suit because I was fortunate enough to have Terry Maple as my mentor when I began graduate school at Georgia Tech in 1982. I'm not sure how I ended up at Terry's doorstep, but I do remember a phone call to him 6 months earlier expressing my interest in animal behavior and zoos. I remember him saying "Come on down." So I did. Apparently neither he nor the folks at Georgia Tech remembered that because my appearance that fall seemed to take them all by surprise. But Terry, being Terry, took care of it all in stride and I became part of his band of researchers along with Mollie Bloomsmith and the next year Lori Perkins.

Within the year, *Parade* magazine named the Atlanta Zoo as one of the 10 worst zoos in the country. The city debated closing the doors, unable to find anyone willing to risk their career on the atrocity in Grant Park. Terry Maple rose to that challenge and took his graduate students along for the ride. Over the next five years the zoo became our research site, our dissertation material, and our employer. We studied behavior, naturalistic design, environmental enrichment, and a myriad of other topics.

My area of study migrated to how the physical design of zoos influences people's perception of the animals themselves. I learned that we could change the physical facilities of the Atlanta Zoo from bathroom tile cages to open air naturalistic enclosures. The animals responded positively and quickly to their new habitats. The people didn't.

Reality had changed but perceptions had not. The people of Atlanta had a perception of what the Atlanta Zoo (now Zoo Atlanta) was like. This attitude would not change easily. But why? What did people think about the zoo? What did they think about the animals in the zoo? As a researcher, my first instinct was to measure and quantify the situation. And as a graduate student in psychology I had recently taken a course in social psychology in which we spent a great deal of time learning about attitudes. So, with the help of a local market research firm we set about Zoo Atlanta's first customer satisfaction survey.

The seeds were sown for a life of measuring people and later consumers' attitudes and behaviors, rather than animal behavior. With his simultaneous fatherly approval and reservations, Terry blessed my move to market research and the business world. I will always be grateful.

Terry taught me many things and I want to thank him for that. He taught me that the best tasting beer in the world is a Tusker, when liberally consumed after a long, hot day in the Masai Mara.
He taught me, if you're not the first author on a paper, then be the last (serial position effect).

He taught me the proper words to the Georgia Tech fight song. *Ramblin' baboon from Cameroon and a hell of an omnivore…* Terry taught me good science. Good experimental design. Good observational methods. I have tried to rigorously apply those in the world of consumer research.

As I write this, I feel like I have come back to my roots a bit in the animal world. Besides my personal zoo of critters, I am now the head of global market research for Merial, the leading companion animal pharmaceutical company in the world. Once again I'm surrounded by animal researchers, veterinarians, and other scientists.

Thank you bwana, friend and mentor.

Addendum
About that gorilla performance at Terry's party. The video is on YouTube.

11. A DIK-DIK TO LOVE

(a Terry Maple-inspired psong)

John Fowler

(psung to the tune of Robert Palmer's ***Addicted to Love****:*
http://www.youtube.com/watch?v=XcATvu5f9vE)

With tiny hooves, and matching horns
It is for love, that you were born
Your tail shakes, your legs twitch
There's a seduction, that makes me itch

Your tuft of hair, your eyes like beads
Your twiggy legs, they spark my needs
Scent mark I will, surrounding twigs
To claim for mine, the one I digs

WHOA, you like to think that you're not sturdy
enough...OH YEAH!
It's closer to truth to say you're made for the stuff
You might as well face it, you're a dik-dik to love

You make me rut, I strut my stuff
You walk away, like that's enough

It blows my horns, when you're in season
Forget all that, I need no reason

Here in the bush, I know you're there
You like to act, like you don't care
You tic at flies, you nibble grass
I flip my lip, when you shake that...tail

WHOA, you like to think that you're not tough
enough...OH YEAH!
It's closer to truth to say you're made for the stuff
You might as well face it, you're a dik-dik to love
Might as well face it, you're a dik-dik to love (5 x)

Just look my way, take what you need
Stop in your tracks, I want to breed
Give me a nod, don't make me brag
I have been told, I'm quite the stag

WHOA, you like to think that you're too dainty for
love...OH YEAH?
It's closer to truth to say you're made for the stuff
You know you're gonna have to face it, you're a dik-dik to love
You're gonna have to face it, you're a dik-dik to love (5 x)

12. HAPPY HAPPY BIRTHDAY TERRY: THE ONTOGENY OF A PSONG

Evan L. Zucker
Loyola University New Orleans

Terry Maple published a set of "brutally rewritten" songs in a 1976 issue of the *Worm Runner's Digest*, a humor and satire journal. The *Worm Runner's Digest*, started in 1959, published both science and satire until 1966, when it became two different publications bound into a single issue; the truly scientific side was called *The Journal of Biological Psychology*, with the satirical side retaining the original title. Included in this set of psongs ("Psongs my Psychologist Taught Me") were such destined-to-be-classics (at least for some constituencies) as, "Baboon (You Saw Me Standing Alone)," "The Hamadryas Love Song (You Always Herd the Ones You Love)," "Chim-Chimpanzee," and "Give Your Regards to Ardrey." I am not sure where or when "Happy, Happy Birthday, Darwin" debuted, but it was circa 1977. This song was originally penned and performed by the Tune Weavers in 1957, and Ronnie Milsap recorded a version in the 1980's with slightly different lyrics from the original. The original Tune Weavers' lyrics are provided below. Terry revised his initial version of this psong in 1979, making minor changes, and that version is also included here.

As Terry's birthday/retirement party was being planned, I was asked by Gail Eaton (of the Palm Beach Zoo), and I believe at

Terry's suggestion, to rewrite his brutally rewritten "Happy, Happy Birthday, Darwin" to honor Terry on his birthday. My task was to write the lyrics to "Happy, Happy Birthday, Terry." My version is included here. It was completed under pressure, much like the 1980 "What's It All About, Alfred?" – a psong to commemorate the birthday of Alfred Russel Wallace. I had requested that Terry write a psong for a Wallace Party I was hosting – and it was finished with minutes to spare. I truly believe Terry waited those 31 years to put me under the same pressure – but I managed to get it done with about a week to spare, maybe a little less!

The lyrics to my brutally rewritten psong were distributed with the program at Terry's retirement party (9/13/2011), and the psong was performed by a gaggle of Terry's students (and their significant others) who were present. It was monumental! And likely never to be repeated.

Original Version by the Tune Weavers
(Music and lyrics by Sylvia & Lopez, 1957)

Happy, happy, birthday baby
Although you're with somebody new
Thought I'd drop a line to say
That I wish this happy day
Would find me beside you.

Happy, happy, birthday baby
No, I can't call you my baby
Seems like years ago we met
On a day I can't forget.
'Cause that's when we fell in love

Do you remember the names we had for each other
You were my pretty, I was your baby
How could we say goodbye?

Hope I didn't spoil your birthday
I know I'm acting kinda crazy

So I'll close this note to you
With good luck and wishes too.
Happy, happy birthday baby

Do you remember the names we had for each other
You were my pretty, I was your baby
How could we say goodbye?

Hope I didn't spoil your birthday
I know I'm acting kinda crazy
So, I'll close this note to you
With good luck and wishes too.
Happy, happy, birthday baby...

Rewritten for Charles Darwin's Birthday
(Words by Maple, 1979)

Happy, happy birthday, Darwin.
Though your theory's not so new,
Thought I'd write the psong to psay,
That I hope this modern day,
Reveals the ape inside you.

Happy, happy birthday, Darwin.
Can you see us masticating?
Seems like years since you got wet,
On that ship we can't forget,
'Cause that's when you found your finches.

Where's your rejoinder,
For names we for our
Forefathers;
Australopithecus, Homo erectus,
Why did they say good-bye?

Hope we all survive your birthday,
As our species' radiating,
So we'll end this psong to you,

With "good luck" to Wallace, too;
Happy, happy birthday, Darwin.

Rewritten for Terry Maple's Birthday and Retirement Party
(Words by Zucker, 2011)

Happy, happy, birthday Terry
Although you're at another zoo
Thought we'd gather here to party
That we wish this happy day
Will let us honor you.

Happy, happy, birthday Terry
Yes, our academic daddy
Many years ago we met
On days we can't forget.
'Cause that's when the lab was born

Do you remember the names you had for each other?
He was Romeo, she was his Julie
How did those days go by?

Hope this is a happy birthday
Surviving years of acting crazy
So we'll psing this psong to you
With data, love, and wishes, too.
Happy, happy birthday Terry

Do you remember the Fur Flicks and P. J.'s Speedies?
Ape Doctor Mustang, too big for Antoine's
How did those days go by?

Hope this is a happy birthday
Surviving years of acting crazy
So we'll psing this psong to you
With data, love, and wishes, too.

13. THE LAST GENERATION

Suma Mallavarapu
Estelle Sandhaus
Bonnie Perdue
Ursula Anderson
Stephanie Allard
Angela Kelling
Diann Gaalema
Allison Martin

Although many others would likely argue the same, we consider ourselves to be the luckiest generation of Terry Maple's students. We are the last subset of Terry's students, and like many of those who came before us, we formed a family of our own during graduate school. We feel lucky in so many ways that Terry has touched and forever changed our lives:

❖ *Lucky that we had the honor of working with Terry just before his well-deserved retirement.*

❖ *Lucky that Terry always treated his academic family like a true family, and we were all adopted into that family.*

❖ *Lucky to have the academic brothers and sisters around the world to help guide our paths.*

❖ *Lucky that Terry so willingly opened doors for us to travel down new and unchartered waters.*

Anyone who has met Terry knows that his energy and spirit fill whatever room he enters - so much so that his enthusiasm and vision often push open the doors as well! But what makes Terry stand out from others is that he holds those doors open for those around him to walk through as well. For most of us, we are early in our careers, and the full paths that we will travel have yet to be determined. Yet, we will always be united by the common thread that Terry has opened doors for us and provided opportunities so rare and special that they will forever alter the paths of our lives. Here we reflect on how Terry shaped our course up to this point, but only time will tell where we go from here...

∞ ∞ ∞ Suma Mallavarapu ∞ ∞ ∞

I first met Terry in December 2001 when he invited me to visit him and his research lab at Zoo Atlanta/Georgia Tech., right after I graduated from college. While working on an undergraduate honors thesis on play behavior in captive juvenile gorillas, I had read several of his publications on gorilla behavior. These were of great help to me, and were instrumental in fostering an interest in great ape behavior. Meeting him in person strengthened my resolve to gain experience studying primate behavior in a zoo setting. I was grateful for the opportunity to work in his lab from 2002-2009, during which time I gained invaluable experience conducting research on primate social behavior, welfare, and comparative cognition. Terry always encouraged and inspired me, and gave me confidence in myself by believing in me. I will always have a deep appreciation for the doors he has opened for me. By creating a unique research lab at Zoo Atlanta, he was instrumental in helping me create and maintain a research program, as well as a rich network of contacts, both of which continue to move my career forward. As an assistant professor at Kennesaw State University, I have been fortunate to be able to continue to conduct primate research at the zoo. More importantly, I have been able to involve undergraduate students in zoo research and will continue to do so, while here at KSU. I will always be grateful to Terry for opening doors not just for me, but for other young scholars who are following in his footsteps.

∞ ∞ ∞ Estelle Sandhaus ∞ ∞ ∞

When I was growing up in southern California, the plight of the critically endangered California condor was well-known; the topic came up from time to time at our family dinners. I had no idea that one day I would be studying the nesting behavior of the reintroduced progeny of that remnant population. Terry Maple led me down this path.

I vividly remember the day that Terry walked through the door of the San Diego Zoo's giant panda building with his friend and colleague, Don Lindburg. Under Don's leadership, a team of researchers and volunteers was carefully studying the behavior and development of Hua Mei, who would become the first American-born cub to survive into adulthood. As an undergraduate at the University of California at San Diego, I was given the exceptional opportunity to volunteer on the project. The day that Terry was visiting, Hua Mei had engaged in object play for the first time. I enthusiastically shared this news with Terry and Don, not realizing that when Terry walked through that door, a door had just been opened for me. After graduation I joined Terry at Georgia Tech and Zoo Atlanta to pursue my graduate studies.

During my studies at Georgia Tech I had the opportunity to study a number of animal species not only at Zoo Atlanta, but also giant pandas at the Chengdu Research Base of Giant Panda Breeding and the Chengdu Zoo in Chengdu, China, in 2001 and 2005. Benefitting from the solid partnership built by Terry and my academic siblings before me, I enjoyed exciting intellectual collaboration and warm friendship with our Chinese colleagues. I also feel fortunate to have had the opportunity to live in China during a decade of rapid change. The Chengdu of 2005 looked very different from the Chengdu of 2001, and I feel privileged to have experienced firsthand something that will no doubt be an important study in urbanization for years to come.

As the Director of Conservation and Research at the Santa Barbara Zoo, I am proud to continue Terry's tradition of the empirical zoo and to share the excitement of science and conservation with students at all levels of study.

∞ ∞ ∞ Bonnie Perdue ∞ ∞ ∞

It was the fall of 2009. I was feeling a little light-headed from having been "encouraged" to take another shot of what must be one of the strongest liquors on the planet - baijiu. It is often translated into "rice wine," but in my estimation neither resembles rice nor wine in any way. In my haze, I began to reflect on how on earth it came to be that I was at a dinner table in China drinking liquor with some of the leaders of the Chengdu Research Base for Giant Panda Breeding. In reality, the answer was actually pretty simple - Terry Maple.

Through Terry's work at Zoo Atlanta and the continued work of his students, I had the amazing opportunity to travel to China to study giant pandas as part of my dissertation work. Fortunately, several of Terry's other students had travelled this path before me and I was not venturing into unchartered territory alone - but being guided by the experiences of those in my academic family. Of course, this didn't completely diminish the nervous excitement I felt at traveling alone to live in another country, nor the amazement I felt at having the opportunity to actually live in China and be fully immersed in the culture while collecting data for my dissertation. It was truly an experience that I will never ever forget, and one that would not have been possible if Terry Maple had not opened that door and encouraged me to go through it.

I will be starting a position as a professor in the fall of 2013. I hope to continue the tradition that Terry began and work to inspire in future generations the passion for animals, zoos and science that he has instilled in me.

∞ ∞ ∞ Ursula Anderson ∞ ∞ ∞

I have not written an essay since 1999. My essay writing days were over soon after I spent the summer of 1999 interning at TECHlab at Zoo Atlanta. It took one summer working alongside Terry's other graduate students - I apologize for the entry errors with the boxes of lemur data and for letting the visitors distract me such that I skipped scans during flamingo observations - for me to become fixated on the science of zoo biology. I remember my first day at the zoo. I, the rising college senior, met with Mollie on the second floor of the administration building and soon after met with Terry in the big office on the ground floor. As a seasoned researcher, I now know that it is odd for a zoo director to meet with interns -

odd for every other one, but not for Terry. He is devoted to zoo research, even as Emeritus Director. After that summer internship, there was never any other choice. I became a graduate student at Georgia Tech. I secured a desk near the door in the trailer next to Orang Holding, got a badge that proclaimed me to be a Research Associate at Zoo Atlanta, and proceeded to spend the next decade of my life with Terry Maple at Zoo Atlanta and Georgia Tech.

Now I am a lowly postdoctoral fellow, working in the realm of cognitive development with the other nonverbal ape - the human infant. From this vantage point, I can fully appreciate the Terry Maple mentoring style: freedom to explore, freedom to fail, but most importantly, freedom to excel. The zoo-university academic model that Terry innovated doesn't exist anywhere at the level that Terry was able to create. It is, though, the academic legacy that Terry has left me and that I hope to continue one day.

∞ ∞ ∞ Stephanie Allard ∞ ∞ ∞

I have hit many milestones in my life and some really stand out. I went to Africa (that's one I hope to repeat multiple times), I got my first real zoo job, and I received my Ph.D. (once is definitely enough). All three were made possible in great part thanks to Terry Maple. I first met him in 1999 as I prepared to travel to Africa for the Georgia Tech/Zoo Atlanta field course in animal behavior. That trip changed my life and set me on the course upon which I still travel. In the years since, I have had many conversations with Terry that, at the time, seemed like typical theoretical discussions between a mentor and student. Looking back, I see that what appeared like pie in the sky ideas were actually goals that he continues to achieve. Terry has pushed me to take chances by not letting me doubt myself and by always making sure I knew I had his support, no matter what. I have walked through many doors that he has pointed out, unlocked, and opened and each time I feel fortunate that I am part of Terry's academic family and that by sharing his vision with us, he has made it possible for us to see the world as it could be and how we could contribute.

∞ ∞ ∞ Angela Kelling ∞ ∞ ∞

I still remember the beautiful Atlanta spring day I decided I wanted to be an animal behaviorist. I started Georgia Tech intending to be a chemical engineer, but decided I did not want to work in a lab day in and day out. I considered transferring to University of Georgia to become a veterinarian, but I knew dissections and euthanasia would be difficult for me. My path was actually made possible by my suite mate signing up for Terry's undergraduate comparative class. On the day I got my UGA acceptance letter, I knew I wanted to stay at Georgia Tech and I began down a path only Terry Maple could have paved. The opportunities his Ph.D. program opened up are unparalleled. Where else could you examine the color vision of giant pandas and the salivary cortisol of African elephants? I am eternally grateful for these and many other experiences throughout my graduate career. Additionally, I was able to get many teaching experiences, including the opportunity to teach Comparative Psychology, the very course that changed my career goals.

∞ ∞ ∞ Diann Gaalema ∞ ∞ ∞

As was common with many of Terry's last crop of students, I was moving in while he was moving out. I was a little surprised that after my first year at Georgia Tech Terry moved to Florida. However, it was not a case of out-of-sight, out-of-mind. Even if Terry wasn't physically near he was invaluable to me in other ways. First of all he handed mentoring duties over to Jack Marr, which likely changed the course of the rest of my career, putting me on the path of behavior analysis. But really the best thing Terry gave me was access to his connections. I was able to work on problems I loved, in populations I never would have had access to on my own, because of him. When I was starting out Terry knew I enjoyed working with reptiles and so got me set up with the reptile curator at Zoo Atlanta. I was then able to use those initial connections to work on a wide range of research problems. This included from the seemingly mundane, but surprisingly difficult, task of training giant tortoises to stand still to be weighed to studying how flexible certain lizards are in their learning abilities. When I wanted to expand my studies on learning in monitor lizards it was once again Terry who was able to get me access to other populations, in other zoos, so that I could have a reasonable sample size. Even when I went on to study other animals at other institutions it was those connections that Terry had initiated that allowed me to perform studies I would not thought feasible. Even now, when my research looks quite a bit different than it did then, it is those lessons

I learned from Terry about nurturing connections that serve me time and again.

∞ ∞ ∞ Allison Martin ∞ ∞ ∞

I will be the last of Terry's Ph.D. students at Georgia Tech. As such, I am the latest in a long line of graduate lab instructors for a very unique laboratory created by Terry Maple and Jack Marr. Our unique experimental analysis of behavior laboratory takes place at Zoo Atlanta and is a shining example of many of the things that Terry has championed throughout his career, including encouraging collaboration between institutions, engaging students in learning, conducting science in the zoo, and promoting programs to enhance animal welfare. Instead of training pigeons or rats in a laboratory, Georgia Tech's undergraduate psychology students come to the zoo each week and apply the classical and operant conditioning techniques that they learn about in lecture to train the animals in Zoo Atlanta's contact yard. The goats and sheep get individual training and enrichment that they might not otherwise receive, and the undergraduates get the very unique experience of training a goat or sheep. The training all takes place in full view of the public, so the laboratory also serves to educate the public about positive reinforcement training. Some of the behaviors taught to the animals - such as allowing a harness to be placed on the head or raising a hoof for inspection - have direct benefits to the keepers at the zoo and the general husbandry of the animals. Sometimes the behaviors are a bit more creative though. People visiting the zoo during this time may encounter a goat bowling, untying a knot, navigating an obstacle course, or even doing the electric slide. We hold a "Goat Show" at the end of each semester where the students give a training demonstration of their work throughout the semester and compete for the coveted "Golden Goat Award." The lab is a lot of fun, and students often rate this lab as the best they have ever taken at Georgia Tech. Perhaps even more importantly, the students also learn how to apply these behavioral principles to their own lives. Through the laboratory, students have used these principles to stop smoking, salvage a relationship, or improve their grades. I cannot count the number of students who have told me that this laboratory changed their life, and that is all because of what Terry started.

On a more personal note, I have developed disabling medical

problems during my graduate career. My medical problems have slowed my progress through the Ph.D. program at Georgia Tech, and this has meant that Terry has had to be a long-distance advisor as he transitions into retirement. Although not always physically present, Terry has made sure that I have had local mentors to help to guide me through the program. My health problems have made even the simplest tasks seem insurmountable at times, but Terry has met each set back with encouragement and compassion...never with criticism. As with all of his graduate students, Terry has continued to champion my strengths, allowing me to explore the research area that interests me (in, my case, behavior analysis) and giving me the tools to do so. Always the optimist, Terry has never focused on what I cannot do...always on my potential. When I get my Ph.D., I'll look back on all of the hard work and determination that went into that degree. I'll also reflect on an advisor who saw my potential, encouraged me to pursue my academic interests, and insisted that I never give up. Thank you, Terry.

14. WELLNESS IN THE WEST: HOW TERRY COLLECTED ONE MORE CAUSE ALONG THE WAY

Valerie Segura

I must begin by prefacing with a bit of honesty. Non-academic writing is not my strongest suit, but writing a piece for Terry Maple's Festschrift is one of the few times in my life that I will get to express how utterly grateful I am for having met and worked with him.

I have the great fortune of knowing the exact day and moment that I met Terry Maple. For me, that day was May 2, 2013, 12:00pm, in the Psychology Building, Room 118, at the University of the Pacific in Stockton, CA. By that time, I had been anticipating that day for about two weeks. I'll back up and explain in a bit more detail.

I had received an e-mail informing me that a Pacific Alum was going to be coming to visit the campus for a talk about his work in zoos. Although I knew this must be a very special person coming to our campus, I had no way of knowing that I was stumbling upon the tip of the iceberg that is Terry Maple's reputation for "working in zoos." A few days prior to Terry's talk, I received an e-mail that we may have to cancel if more RSVPs did not arrive. I was determined to not let that happen, so I asked my fellow graduate students to write an e-mail (or otherwise comment) to express interest in securing the talk. Thankfully, the students' interests were heard and Terry Maple arrived on that day in May.

Terry's talk was a huge success. He captivated the interest of every person in that room, and we were all blown away at the fact that Terry had done so much for animal welfare and the promotion of the empirical zoo in his career. The audience heard about Atlanta Zoo becoming Zoo Atlanta, the amazing story of Willie B., the history and development of the science of animal welfare, and the work of his students and colleagues.

In that talk, Terry recognized the very notable mentors in his life that helped, in some capacity, shape the trajectory of his career. He cited Robert Sommer, renowned environmental psychologist, as someone that reinforced his curiosity and encouraged him to pursue the "big stuff," no matter how daunting the task. Terry spoke the following words that day, and they resonated with me. "Every time I talk about this stuff, I just need to tell you how I was lifted by people I admired or people I knew, in this case it was Robert Sommer... who encouraged me to pursue this effort and my dreams."

Terry had no way of knowing, but I desperately needed to hear his talk that day. Up until that point, I was making plans to abandon my work applying the Science of Behavior with the mental health population, and instead move towards becoming a dog trainer specializing in the science-based behavior analytic approach to problem-behavior treatment. Each subject Terry mentioned evoked a series of questions that I wanted to follow up on. Taken from my notes on that day, "Does Dr. Maple think it would be possible for a behavior analyst to practice in zoos, is there any room for me?" I had no way of knowing at the time, but Terry changed the trajectory of my career on that very day in May.

I knew I had crossed paths with a remarkable person. I decided that regardless of the outcome, I'd like to learn more about his work and stay in touch. So I did. I emailed Terry a few days after the talk, and again after I attended a conference, and once again to see if there were opportunities to work together in some capacity. On a humorous note, I tried very hard to curb my enthusiasm in those initial emails to Terry for fear of being annoying! Needless to say, it was incredibly difficult. However, Terry was encouraging in his responses and his optimism was reinforcing enough to keep me writing. In July of 2013, I was able to see Terry in action for the first time when I was invited to sit in on some of his meetings. It was confirmed; he was (and still is) a "mover and shaker." We had a serious conversation about the field of behavior analysis and the possibility of reviving and growing its influence in zoos. We agreed on many subjects and points and when I left that meeting, I was filled with great optimism for the future. Little did I know, Terry had already decided to take on yet another cause, and this particular one aligned perfectly with my career and academic aspirations. With that, our collaborative efforts to work together to promote and further the influence of behavior analysis in zoos, was born.

Since then, Terry has been the most important mentor in my academic and professional career, without question. In August of 2013, Terry helped me secure a position at the San Francisco Zoo as a Hal Markowitz Research Fellow, and advocated for my project placement. This allowed me to demonstrate my ability to develop and maintain a behavior-based observational study. Terry and I collaborated on my very first manuscript, a paper addressing the need to re-connect the Science of Behavior (i.e., behavior analysis) with zoos and aquariums (Maple & Segura, *in press*). Since meeting Dr. Maple, I have met fascinating people, all of whom contributed (and continue to contribute) in significant ways to a scientific under-standing of non-human animal behavior and the science of animal welfare and wellness. I have also come to know and build relation-ships with like-minded people within my field of behavior analysis who share our vision of working to promote the animal welfare movement in zoos and aquariums.

I am positive that Newton's famous quote, "If I have seen further it is by standing on the shoulders of giants," has been used by former students, colleagues, and friends to reference Terry Maple. In this *Festschrift,* it will once again be used by me. I have yet not "seen further" in any sense of the word, but I have been bolstered and supported by Terry Maple in a way that makes me feel very optimistic about the many years of hard work I have ahead of me. I am very grateful to have met Terry Maple, a person that I consider to be a "giant" in his field, and one of the single most impactful people I have ever had the honor of meeting. I will continue the great work of promoting the Science of Behavior in the animal welfare and wellness movement, and that is directly due to the mentorship and the benefit of Terry Maple's leadership that I have received.

Thank you, Terry, for the honor of letting me contribute to your festschrift.

References

Maple, T.L. and Segura. V. (2014). Advancing behavior analysis in zoos and aquariums. *The Behavior Analyst*. Advance online publication. doi: 10.1007/s40614-014-0018-x

15. TERRY'S TURTLE TUTORIAL

Larry Wood

I first met Terry Maple when I was the curator of a small sea turtle rehabilitation facility near West Palm Beach Florida. He was fairly new to the area, and had recently taken on the lead role at the Palm Beach Zoo. During his first visit to our center, I could sense his keen interest in sea turtles, and by the end of the visit, he was happily handling a young green turtle, flippers flapping and water flying, all the while with a huge grin on his face. As with so many of his students and colleagues, the day I met Terry Maple, all said and done, was a really good day.

Our next meeting was under considerably different circumstances. My 20+ year service at the sea turtle facility had come to an abrupt and unexpected end, which not only weighed heavily on me personally, but also threatened to cut-short my hawksbill turtle research that had just begun to become so productive. In somewhat of a panic and not knowing where to turn, I recalled his visit to our facility and his interest in sea turtles. I decided to send him an e-mail informing him of my newly realized 'availability', not really expecting I'd ever get a response from the busy President and CEO of the Zoo, or at best a glancing referral to the HR department. To my surprise (and great relief), he responded nearly immediately, tossing me the one-sentence life-preserver I most needed at the time: "Let's meet right away." These four words would set in to motion the next phase of my professional life, and the opportunity to get to know a man who has been such a powerful influence on myself and so many others.

His prompt response was only the first of many Terry Maple surprises. I had become so used to hearing why projects couldn't or shouldn't be done; where basic concepts of good science and conservation had to be meticulously justified and actively defended to gain the "boss's" conditional approval, that I was shocked to be in a room where just the opposite was the case. Every meeting was a constructive discussion of how the Palm Beach Zoo could contribute to wildlife research and conservation outside its walls, in my case through the study of hawksbill turtles in Palm Beach County waters. "Sure, let's find some support for it" seemed to be the norm. I was amazed...I actually looked forward to meetings with my boss. He recognized the connectivity sea turtles create among local residents, and offered to the Zoo's professional development team to help me identify funding sources. I sat there like a sponge, watching and listening to how he simultaneously managed non-profit Board members (never easy), budgets, short and long-term goals, a large, diverse, and often challenging staff, and everything else the Zoo had in store for him, all during economically terrible times, while still finding the time to support and encourage my sea turtle work. I remember him saying while discussing the Zoo's future, from the physical space limitations to the the dismal economic climate: "You don't have to *be* big; you have to *think* big." Terry Maple always thinks big, and taught me to do the same.

The next surprise he had for me was his desire to more closely link the Palm Beach Zoo with local institution(s) of higher learning; most notably Florida Atlantic University, located in Boca Raton, Florida. He had mentioned in passing how he had student support money at FAU that had followed him from his previous post, and wanted me to "get down there and sign up." Again, I was conditioned to be skeptical; and wasn't sure how serious this offer was, especially knowing the commitment both myself and he/the Zoo would have to make to get me through a Ph.D. program. To no one's surprise who is reading this, he was indeed quite serious after all, sternly reminding me that he only wanted Ph.D. biologists on his future research staff... so off I went, rather urgently, to get started. To my benefit, I had completed both my undergraduate and Master's degrees at FAU, so I arrived as a familiar face; but still to the bewilderment of a number of faculty members, who weren't yet familiar with Terry or his collaborative vision, as they tried to figure out who this "zoo guy" was and exactly how he and I would fit in with their program. It didn't take long to settle in to everyone's satisfaction, and though Terry's tenure at the Zoo ended before my completion of the Ph.D. program, his commitment to both me as my committee chair and FAU continues, and his 'thinking big' for me is about to culminate with my upcoming graduation.

From hatchlings to adults, day or night, sick or healthy, I've given a whole lot of sea turtles a second chance. As with many wildlife rehabilitators I'm sure, I can't help but lightheartedly wonder now and then if our subjects somehow know that, and occasionally get the chance to pay us back. That little green turtle flapping away in Terry Maple's hands unknowingly got that chance. Thank you, little green turtle, for capturing the fascination of the man who has since become a huge source of knowledge, guidance, and inspiration in my life. And, thank you, Terry, for your unwavering support of my work and career, with so much more to come!

FESTSCHRIFT FOR TERRY MAPLE

PART II: ZOO COLLEAGUES

16. MAPLE AND ME

Gail Eaton

By the time I met Terry Maple in 1990 I was already a grownup with over 20 years of professional experience in marketing and communications. In fact I was almost two full weeks older than Terry - a fact that he enjoyed pointing out to me. In all, we were colleagues for nearly 15 years.

Our professional relationship began over tacos in a little bar across the street from Zoo Atlanta. I was working for a start-up museum that was planning to open an IMAX theater with a wonderful film about the mountain gorillas of Rwanda. Since I have always been a firm believer in marketing collaborations, what could be better than a cross-promotional initiative with the zoo across town that housed one of the nation's largest collections of gorillas? They were lowland gorillas, but still - a brilliant idea. Terry was a thoroughly delightful guy. He listened attentively to my concept, and then embroidered on it with brilliant ideas of his own. By the last taco we had hammered together a plan that would drive attendance and membership for both institutions. I left feeling elated that I had done good work and found a fascinating new friend in my adopted city.

To my great surprise, the director of my little museum rejected the idea out of hand. She was not such a big fan of collaborations. As it turned out, she was also not such a big fan of me. We parted ways before the museum even opened its doors.

The next time I met with Terry was a job interview. I had made up my mind that I really wanted to work for this guy, but the complexity of the zoo structure made it impossible for us to work out a deal. Instead I went to work at the local children's hospital, managing communications and community relations. It wasn't long before another opportunity to collaborate with the zoo arose, and I was back at the taco joint with Maple. This time, the results were spectacular. The hospital wanted to build a state-of-the-art playground that engineered out all the dangerous features that caused so many children to end up in ERs across the country - hard surfaces under play structures, choking hazards, chains that trapped little fingers - the design was astounding. All we needed was a place to build it where healthy children and their families could enjoy it and learn from it. Voila! We could build it at the zoo where hundreds of thousands of people would see the hospital's brand and get inspired about playground safety. It was a win-win.

The next year, the hospital got involved in teaching hand-washing as a means of preventing the spread of disease. More tacos with Maple. More collaboration between the two institutions. Another big voila! Branded child-sized hand-washing stations at the zoo's contact yard. It was all fabulous. By this time I was determined to work for this guy. Fortunately he decided he was through kicking the tires. Our next lunch meeting was at a chic downtown restaurant. No tacos this time - just a very exciting job offer which I accepted on the spot: Senior VP for Marketing at Zoo Atlanta.

Maple had some very uncommon attitudes about how work gets done. He openly attributed much of his success to the fact that he kept himself surrounded by "smart women" - his wife, his three delightful daughters, and an impressive team of female executives at the zoo. As a seasoned veteran of the corporate and non-profit worlds, my opinions about the ways of the world were a bit jaded. Like most working women, I had a few war stories about gender equality and ethics in the workplace. Most men in positions of power claim to treat women fairly - even in the face of glaring injustices. But Terry Maple is the real deal. He actually trusts and respects women. He treats them fairly, promotes them when appropriate, and mentors them with enthusiasm. He gives them credit for their accomplishments and he gives them hell when they mess up.

And even though we have parted ways in recent years, I would still jump at an invitation to meet him for tacos.

17. TLM

Rita McManamon

Terry Maple changed my life. I know that sounds overly dramatic. But for anyone who knows our history, that statement rings true. Long ago, in June of 1984, my San Francisco State mentor Hal Markowitz invited me to meet the newly appointed director of the Atlanta Zoo at Hal's house in Pacifica. Hal introduced me, and Terry and I chatted while we watched a basketball game together. Terry was searching for a new zoo veterinarian, and I had been preparing for and dreaming of being a zoo vet. But I wasn't available in June, and the whole idea of being hired was so preposterous (to me) that I remember being quite calm. I was just grateful for the opportunity to talk about primate behavior, with the professor whose work I so admired. We chatted about zoo medicine, zoo politics, animal behavior and welfare, and formed a quick bond that has never broken (and never will). To my great surprise, I was later hired. I don't think either of us completely appreciated the challenges he had signed up for, in agreeing to lead the transformation of the Atlanta Zoo to the new Zoo Atlanta. For my part, every day was a new adventure - and Terry was the most supportive boss I could ever have imagined.

Terry has detailed some of the surprises and challenges of those early days (and some are best left unwritten, to avoid recriminations). But from the perspective of a new and idealistic veterinarian, I was most impressed by three major facets of Terry's personal approach to each challenge we faced together. The first is Terry's deep concern for animals, and his burning commitment - no matter what perspectives might be advanced - that animal welfare and animal health, trump all other considerations. He always set the bar high in that regard - thus ensuring that all zoo employees and supporters had a clear path for daily decision-making. Secondly, he has enormous, unflagging confidence in the intellectual capacity of others to re-think and re-imagine solutions, and he truly delights in helping to build the success of others. To me, this is the core principle that must drive all leaders and managers. To this day, I remember the plaque that sat on his zoo office desk "There is no limit to what a man can accomplish, if he doesn't mind who gets the credit." Terry has an uncanny ability to recognize talent - in keepers, researchers, zoo supporters, anyone - then motivate them and get out of their way, so they use their best abilities. This has been a brilliant and successful strategy, to build people, and thus to build the zoo. The third successful aspect of Terry's personality (but often frustrating to his pragmatic veterinarian) is his absolute, stubborn inability to accept that there are any obstacles to his dreams.

In fact, during my earliest days at Atlanta Zoo, my fellow zoo leaders Susan Hood (Assistant Director of Operations) and John Croxton (Assistant Curator of Mammals) and I had a little secret phrase for this annoyingly optimistic perspective. Although we grudgingly admired his positive outlook, most of our early days were spent slogging through unromantic and messy misery - broken hoses, busted water mains, sewage-obstructed pipes, rusty and dangerous cages whose doors or locks wouldn't work, limited veterinary equipment and staff, and a nonexistent clinic. Occasionally we would slog up the hill (a hot, empty, grassy field in the middle of the zoo) and we would trudge past Terry, leading a new group of potential donors. "Look over here", he would say. "This will be the site of our new gorilla habitats. Gorilla families will sit outside, foraging together, while their youngsters wrestle and play, rolling down these hillsides...And right there, we will build a huge outdoor aviary, with beautiful birds flying high in the trees above your heads...." Terry would sweep his big arm toward the sky, and all the donors would cast their eyes heavenward, and murmur appreciatively. So at the end of each tough day, we would whisper our new mantra to each other (with deep skepticism, mixed with fervent hope): "Ah yes, today was rough, but just remember: 'beautiful birds!'" and we'd live to fight another day.

So of course, it is now 2013. Everyone who has visited Zoo Atlanta knows that Terry's dream has come true. Four gorilla habitats replaced that hillside, and visitors can watch several gorilla groups at once. And on one of the proudest days of my life, I watched with Terry as the huge and gentle gorilla Willie B stretched up and reached for a leaf from a living tree, while his feet were buried in rain-soaked grass. Indeed, beautiful birds fly over the heads of zoo visitors every day. I am very proud and grateful, for all these life lessons - as well as happy professional experiences - that fateful basketball game brought to my life. Thanks, Terry, for leading us in this great adventure, and always believing that we are capable of doing our best, for all the wonderful creatures that are entrusted to us.

18. DR. MAPLE'S CONSERVATION EDUCATION LEGACY IN CHINA

Sarah M. Bexell

I'd had dreams of working for wild animals, animals that were still in their native habitats. Upon graduation with my master's degree studying physical anthropology, wanting to continue work with primates, I searched for jobs. I got an offer from Zoo Atlanta in the education department and needed to learn more about this institution. This is when I learned not only of Dr. Maple's wonderful work for primates, but also heroic work to transform Zoo Atlanta from one of the worst and most inhumane zoos in U.S. history, to one of the best. In fact a world class facility with animal health and welfare being the priority. I knew I could be proud to work for this man and learn from all the people who had helped him in this endeavor.

In 1999, Dr. Maple sent me to collect behavioral data on giant pandas for Zoo Atlanta's ongoing behavioral research program directed by Dr. Rebecca Snyder. While there, I was also asked to investigate the possibility of collaborating with Chinese colleagues on conservation education programming. Drs. Maple and Snyder had traveled to China many times and while there saw the lack of understanding of animals, and in many cases blatant abuse of animals. They had also become aware that China had not yet invested in creating conservation education departments, fostering and training education staff, and creating country and culturally appropriate conservation education programs in zoological institutions. Because of a combined background in animal behavior and informal and formal science education, both Maple and Snyder felt my background could prove beneficial in the establishment of conservation education programming in China. After spending five months in China, seeing the lack of understanding of animals, I wanted to find a way to connect people and animals so that these problems might be alleviated.

Luckily, in 2000, I was sent back to China to develop a memorandum of understanding to create the first functioning conservation education departments in zoological facilities in China at the Chengdu Research Base of Giant Panda Breeding and Chengdu Zoo.

Two amazing young women, Ms. Luo Lan (Research Base) and Ms. Hu Yan (Chengdu Zoo) were given the task of partnering with us and learning the skills and content knowledge for creating education departments and developing conservation education programs (Bexell, Luo, Hu, Maple, McManamon, Zhang, & Zhang, 2004). Over the years and with tremendous support from the Research Base and Chengdu Zoo leadership, we established successful programs (e.g., Bexell, Feng, Zhang, & Esson, 2008; Bexell, Jarrett, Xu, & Feng, 2009; Bexell, Jarrett, & Xu, 2013), conducted observations in schools in both the U.S. and China (Bexell, Jarrett, Yang, & Tan, 2005), conducted research into the power of giant pandas in conservation education (Bexell, Jarrett, Luo, Hu, Sandhaus, Zhang, & Maple, 2007) and brought Luo Lan and Hu Yan to the U.S. for intensive training at AZA's conservation education training and to visit 10 zoos, aquaria and conservation breeding facilities.

A most exciting and rewarding event occurred in 2004. Our colleague, Dr. Yu Jinping and I were asked if we would meet with Ms. Xie Zhong, assistant director of the Chinese Association of Zoological Gardens (CAZG). She told us she had been watching the success of our education departments in Chengdu with great interest. She felt they were important and critical for the future of wildlife conservation in China; would we be willing to help take this to zoos throughout China?

Luckily, with wonderful support from Zoo Atlanta, we were able to agree to this request and within a year had secured funding to hold trainings for appointed education staff from zoos throughout China, the first training being held at the Chengdu Zoo in 2006. For four years, with the tremendous effort and skillful coordination by Ms. Laurel Askue from Zoo Atlanta, this training program, named ACT (Academy for Conservation Training) was offered two times per year, bringing in leaders from the AZA education community, and building the conservation education capacity in China beyond our wildest dreams. With the end of the funding and tremendous success, CAZG took over the program in entirety and it continues to this day - not only training zoo and aquarium personnel throughout China but also many animal welfare and conservation NGOs send their education staff to learn and contribute.

Today, the two Chengdu facilities have the largest and most successful conservation education departments in all of China. Both facilities have been awarded as environmental education sites by Chengdu's city government and the Research Base is a nationally appointed environmental education site for the entire country of China.

This is only one of Dr. Maple's legacies in China. His panda program began another. Conservation education is beginning to be seen as our last hope of saving life on Earth as we know it. In no other country is the biodiversity crisis so severe and apparent than in China. This is indeed a legacy Dr. Maple can proudly beat his strong silverback chest about. I am indebted to him for his trust in me, and his trust that with hard work, we can make this a safer planet for other animals.

References

Bexell, S.M., Feng, R.X., Zhang, Z.H., & Esson, M. (2008). Conservation education and community pride as a tool f or protecting Mamize Nature Reserve, Sichuan Province, China. *Journal of the International Zoo Educators Association, 44*, 8-11.

Bexell, S.M., Jarrett, O.S., Luo, L., Hu, Y., Sandhaus, E., Zhang, Z., & Maple, T.L. (2007). Observing panda play: Implications for zoo programming and conservation efforts. *Curator, 50*, 287-297.

Bexell, S.M., Jarrett, O. S., & Xu, P. (2013). The effects of a summer camp program in China on children's knowledge, attitudes and behaviors toward animals: a model for conservation education. *Visitor Studies, 16,* 59-81.

Bexell, S.M., Jarrett, O.S., Xu, P., & Feng, R.X. (2009). Fostering humane attitudes toward animals: An educational camp experience in China. *Encounter: Education for Meaning and Social Justice, 22,* 25-27.

Bexell, S.M., Jarrett, O.S., Yang, J., & Tan, N.N. (2005, April). *Children and animals: Exploring empathic feelings with animals in four year olds in China and the United States.* Poster presentation at the biennial meeting of the Society for Research in Child Development, Atlanta, GA.

Bexell, S. M., Luo, L., Hu, Y., Maple, T.L., McManamon, R., Zhang, & Zhang, Z. H. (2004). Conservation education initiative in D. Lindburg, & K. Baragona (Eds.), *Biology and conservation of the giant panda* (pp. 264-267). Berkeley, CA: University of California Press.

19. INCOMPARABLE MEGAVERTEBRATE

Deb Forthman

Terry Maple is unforgettable. Once you have met him, you will never say, "Maple. *Terry* Maple, you say? Huh, the name rings a bell, but I can't seem to place him." That will not happen. Terry has an enormous presence, not just because of his physical size and hearty voice, but because of his personality. When he enters a room, he fills it. He is animated as he greets people; he smiles a lot; he is affable. Terry is also highly intelligent, as we all know - many have described him as a visionary. I had many occasions to witness that vision during the time I worked for Terry.

Let me back up. Although I said he is unforgettable, that does not mean that the exact time and place we met is indelibly imprinted in my mind. My chronological memory is not the best. Terry and I conferred on the subject. He thought probably Africa, but although some of the dates we were there overlapped, I had no entries in my journal mentioning a visit from him and his students. We may have met at a meeting of the Animal Behavior Society or American Society of Primatologists while I was at UCLA, but I tend to think I met him early on, while I was still an undergraduate and my advisor invited Terry to give a seminar at the University of California, Riverside. I was in the psychology department, specializing in primate behavior and was very familiar with Terry's impressive work well before we met - wherever and whenever that was. The book he edited with fellow student Joe Erwin and graduate advisor Gary Mitchell on the behavior of primates in captivity resonated deeply with me. Their observations and experiments addressed the effects of captivity and captive environments on the psychosocial behavior of primates. Having studied monkeys in captivity at Riverside, I agreed with their conclusions that the effects of inadequate captive environments were profoundly, and often permanently, damaging to the animals' psychological well-being. Shortly thereafter, I spent my first year in Africa studying wild baboons and that, combined with another two years in the field, informed all my subsequent work.

After finishing my dissertation at UCLA, I got a job in the research department at the Los Angeles Zoo. Immediately after I arrived, I attended my first American Association of Zoos and Aquariums conference (AZA) and it was there that Terry first had a direct influence on my career path. Pardon the alliteration, but sadly, many senior scientists are snobs. Perhaps they treat their own graduate and postgraduate students well - I hope so - but they are less than welcoming to other junior colleagues. At one of my first academic meetings, probably of the American Primatological Society, I introduced myself to a luminary I knew by reputation. His reply was, "I know who you are." I might have been flattered had it not been for his cold tone and swift departure. As a result of interactions like that, I became a bit gun-shy about approaching some scientists whose work interested me.

Therefore, I was both surprised and delighted when I ran into Terry at the AZA conference. He remembered me and, like the other scientist, was also familiar with my fledgling research. However, unlike the reception I received before, Terry took me under his capacious wing immediately and shepherded me around, introducing me to all of his friends and colleagues as "an up and coming zoo biologist." Because the words came from Terry, I found myself accepted readily and soon felt comfortable mingling with zoo professionals, especially his students, friends and close colleagues.

After a day of meetings, most conference participants repaired to the nearest bar to continue talking about the day's presentations or to relax and chat over many pitchers of beer. Terry definitely more than held his own in these beer-drinking blow-outs, and the parties often became quite boisterous, especially if Gary Mitchell and Joe Erwin were also there. Gary and Terry had, shall we say, an unusual relationship, rather like that of two silverback gorilla buddies. I well recall my astonishment at a conference in New Orleans when Terry ripped off Gary's shirt; buttons popped and flew in every direction. That was the first and only time I ever witnessed that particular interaction, but they were always an entertaining pair.

Terry became director of the shamefully inadequate Atlanta-Fulton County Zoo in mid-1984. He assembled a team to help him transform what later was known as Zoo Atlanta from one of the country's worst zoos into one of its best. Around 1986, he approached me to join his research team, which at that time was composed of several of his graduate students in the School of Psychology at Georgia Institute of Technology, where he was also a professor. I was thrilled by the invitation, but had to tell Terry that I was still involved in a USDA project and had other personal obligations at the time that prevented me from leaving Los Angeles. He told me to keep him in mind. I said I certainly would and had a hard time doing anything else.

Over the next year and a half, he asked me about my availability whenever we met at a conference and I continued to put him off. I was afraid that the invitation would be withdrawn if I did not act relatively quickly. When my USDA job was nearly finished and the personal obligations had been taken care of, I finally called Terry and told him I was ready to take him up on his offer to join the Zoo Atlanta team. I packed up, found a house outside Atlanta, moved everything in and went to the zoo, where Terry gave me the grand tour. I was as excited as he was about the naturalistic gorilla habitats that he had envisioned and built early in the zoo's renovation. Willie B., the sole gorilla when Terry became director, had already been introduced to a world of grass and trees such as he had never enjoyed. The gorilla habitats would remain the zoo's crown jewel, home to multiple family groups of the magnificent animals and the birthplace of many infants. After my visit, I turned around and moved to Galveston for three months to finish the USDA work. I started work at Zoo Atlanta as an Applied Behavior Analyst on January 1, 1989 - at least I can recall that detail.

Although I was thrilled to be at the zoo, particularly in those early years of change and growth, and liked my co-workers in research and the other departments, I was less than delighted with my own initial zoo habitat. The research department was housed in a small and windowless room in an old building at the very back of the zoo. The location did have some appealing features: the presence of an elderly lion and, on the other side of our room, the new gorilla indoor holding area. I arrived at work early in those days and Valentino, the lion, often roared in the morning. I liked to visit him and scratch his ribs while he chuffed in pleasure. Occasionally, the booms of gorillas displaying and banging on metal doors echoed through the building. We were allowed to visit them periodically, which was always an awe-inspiring experience. I had been that close to gorillas only once before, during a visit to the mountain gorillas in Rwanda. Unlike monkeys, for whom a direct gaze is a threat, gorillas often look deep into a person's eyes, their expressions enigmatic and solemn. Willie B., as it happened, was quite the lady's man and always came to the front of his enclosure to greet female visitors with friendly rumbles.

Terry's first assignment for me was to develop and study forms of behavioral enrichment for a solitary grizzly and Asiatic black bear and a pair of polar bears still housed in old-fashioned grottos. During that project, I encountered the same difficulties that I had at the Los Angeles zoo in working with keepers who had been at the zoo for many years and had ingrained notions of how animals should be managed. The study ended up having less than stellar results, but did give some idea of simple ways to offer the animals occupational activities.

I was given one of my first exciting assignments shortly after I started at the zoo. Terry asked me to come and see him. When I sat down, he told me that he had a volunteer who wanted to study the orphaned elephants of Akagera National Park in Rwanda. I was familiar with the horrific story of these elephants from a program I had seen on television. It aired periodically, but I was only able to watch it once. A group of elephants had become marooned in an agricultural area of the country and efforts to herd them elsewhere had failed. As a result, helicopters were called in and all of the adult elephants were shot, leaving only a small group of infants and juveniles, who were rounded up and put on trucks. During the capture operation, a photographer who happened to be the cousin of a friend of mine was killed by a little bull calf when the photographer became entangled in her camera cable. The elephants were translocated to the park and confined in a stockade before eventually being released. There they grew up without benefit of the tutelage of their female relatives. As adults, they were shy and secretive. I was immediately interested in studying them. Terry told me that the volunteer had no field experience, or experience as a behaviorist for that matter, and Terry wanted me to work with him on the project. So began my association with Wayne Esarove.

We worked in Rwanda, mostly trying unsuccessfully to find and observe the elephants, which were largely active at night. On one occasion, we prevailed on the Rwandan Army to take us up in a helicopter to see if we could find the elephants. We did locate them and finally saw them briefly the next day, venturing out of the vehicle to follow them as long as we could. That ended up being an eventful day, as the diesel Land Cruiser would not start when we were ready to head back to the little house where we stayed. After waiting in vain for rescue, during which we finished the water in my canteen - Wayne had forgotten his - we decided to set out and walk the thirteen miles to the nearest fisherman's hut.

It was brutally hot slogging along the road and was almost dusk as we neared our destination. A large pride of lions occupied the area and, equally worrisome to me, herds of hippos in the lake would soon be leaving the water to graze - with us between them and their destination. Wayne had terrible blisters by that time and just as I was putting on speed, he began to lag behind. I heard a piteous call, "Are you going to leave me?" I slowed and told him, "No, but you better get a move on before we run into these hippos." That news gave him enough incentive to pick up the pace. When we arrived at the fisherman's hut, they handed us a clean Prestone jug full of unclean lake water. We proceeded to guzzle it down, with the result that I contracted an unpleasant case of giardia. We continued to work on the elephant project, changing our focus from studying the elusive animals to pleading with the Rwandan Office of Research, Tourism and National Parks, as well as granting agencies, for protection for the elephants. Our efforts were halted by the outbreak of the civil war that led to the genocide of 700,000 Tutsi and moderate Hutu tribes - people in the space of one hundred days of slaughter.

About a year after I started work at the zoo, Terry promoted me to Coordinator of Scientific Programs. For several years, I had the pleasure of working daily with his many Georgia Institute of Technology graduate students. All of them were bright and enthusiastic and, in keeping with Terry's focus on the scientific study of animals in captivity, conducted their thesis and dissertation research on various species at the zoo. Quite a few studied the gorilla groups and addressed questions ranging from the behavior of the apes and staff in a post-occupancy evaluation of the exhibits to variables that influenced the behavior of regurgitation and reingestion shown by some of the older gorillas, as well as a thesis on the adaptation to the zoo of an adult male gorilla raised alone in a cage in a shopping mall.

During this period, two young drills arrived at the zoo. I was enthralled with the drills, so much like the baboons I had studied, and spent much time with them while they were in quarantine, making friends especially with the little male. Several studies were conducted on the drills after their move to the new Small African Primates exhibit, including research on mother-infant behavior, after the two youngsters grew up and began to produce what became a remarkable number of offspring. We had noticed as well that the drills and the mona monkeys with whom they shared the exhibit engaged in social interactions. An interesting study was subsequently conducted on instances of post-conflict reconciliation between members of the two species. A paper to which I contributed described another study conducted by one of Terry's students, Tina Chang. The research compared the behavior and activity budgets of a group of mandrills while in a barren, indoor exhibit and after their transfer to an "ecologically representative" outdoor exhibit. The paper became a lead article in the journal *Zoo Biology*, founded by Terry.

Most people do not like meetings. Usually they disrupt what might otherwise be a productive day. But there were two types of meetings at Zoo Atlanta that I really enjoyed: curators' and design meetings. In curators' meetings we discussed daily management issues and any problems the curators and keepers faced in providing safe and environmentally challenging exhibits for the animals. Environmental enrichment was one of my favorite subjects for study and discussion and was the area in which I felt I could contribute most. But as much as I liked curators' meetings, design meetings were my favorite, particularly during their first, "blue sky," phase. This was the most exciting period, when all of us could let our creativity have free rein as we brain-stormed about the ideal characteristics of new species - and environmentally-representative exhibits. It came before the many practical and economic constraints had to be considered. Often, research studies were a consideration from the beginning of exhibit design, so that no opportunities would be lost. Four major exhibits were designed and built while I was at the zoo: the small African primates exhibit, which housed the drills and mona monkeys, a habitat for Sumatran tigers, the giant panda exhibit complex after the arrival of a pair of pandas on loan from the Chinese, and the mandrill habitat. It was a challenging and educational experience to work on these design teams and I was also fortunate enough to participate, if only as a mentor sometimes, in research studies and papers on all but the tigers.

While I like to think, correctly or not, that Terry and I shared the trait of being "big picture" thinkers, he and I did not always see eye-to-eye. This was primarily because, aside from the "blue sky" phase of design projects, I tended to be a realist, while I considered Terry to be a sometimes overly-optimistic idealist, perhaps a trait associated with being a visionary. I recall vividly one meeting that Terry participated in, during which I made a dampening remark that caused him to say, "Your glass is always half-full." I responded with, "Yours is always overflowing onto the floor." That garnered laughs from the meeting participants. We once had a difference of opinion in which we swapped sides. I was opposed to acquiring white tiger cubs on loan, as it aroused my purist feelings about exhibiting animals with genetic anomalies just for the sake of visitors' reactions to their novelty. In that instance it was Terry who was the realist. He stated his opinion that whatever means brought increased numbers of visitors to the white tiger exhibit would also introduce them to the endangered Sumatran tigers. Usually, however, we were in agreement on matters related to design and management of the animals.

At that time, I also began a long-term collaboration with a visiting scientist and one of his graduate students. They studied thermal physiology and factors in captive environments that affected thermal stress and thus, the well-being of the animals. Their research at Zoo Atlanta focused on the elephants and I became fascinated by an area of study that was new to me, but most relevant to my interests. In some ways, this research, in which I ultimately became heavily involved, informed my later participation in a project that detailed "best practices" for the management and psychological well-being of elephants maintained in captivity. That project led to me acting as lead editor on a volume of collected essays that was distributed to every institution world-wide that manages elephants. Another significant study pertaining to the well-being of the elephants was conducted later by the below-mentioned Mollie Bloomsmith and the elephant keepers. That work compared the behavior of the elephants when they were chained during the night - standard zoo operating procedure to prevent aggression - to that when they were able to move freely. No aggression was observed.

There were many changes in the zoo management regime during the time I was Research Coordinator. First, department heads had moved to more pleasant quarters in the Administration building, where I even had a window. More importantly, though, Terry had envisioned a concept he referred to as the Conservation Action Resource Center (ARC), with a building to house it. The ARC would include a conference room, library, distance learning center and large auditorium for lectures. Terry promoted Beth Stevens, a hard-charging former member of the research department, to lead the ARC. She became the director of the research and education departments at that time. There followed a period of grant-writing in which I was much involved, as writing is one of my strengths. These included one for a National Science Foundation (NSF) Research Experiences for Undergraduates (REU), on which I collaborated with Duane Jackson, a professor at Morehouse College and the zoo's Curator of Insects. Morehouse was an undergraduate institution and Duane already had considerable experience in leading undergraduates in research projects. We had a difficult time obtaining the NSF grant, but finally did so after we were sent a copy of a successful application. I was primarily involved in the writing, while Duane executed the project and a group of undergraduates set up shop in the old research offices along with the graduate students. When Beth moved on to Disney, the zoo's long-time veterinarian, Rita McManamon, took leadership of the ARC. We continued to write grants for various programs. These entailed a great many meetings which, unfortunately, I did not enjoy as I had the curators' and design meetings.

Then, in 1997, my career at the zoo took a major turn. Terry called me into his office one day and, without much preamble, told me that he was hiring a former student of his, Mollie Bloomsmith, as

Research Director. My stomach dropped; I thought he was about to tell me that I was out of a job. A moment later, however, Terry made an extraordinary proposal. He said that he would like to create a Department of Field Conservation and thought I was the ideal person to lead that endeavor. I was as delighted as I had a moment before been in despair. I told him that I could not think of anything I would rather do. He outlined what he had in mind. The department would still be under the purview of the ARC, so I would continue to report to Rita. It would be small and would include projects conducted at the zoo, and small amounts of monetary support for conservation programs in various parts of the world. The main focus of the department would be field conservation in Africa. He planned to hire Tom Butynski, a well-respected zoologist who lived in Kenya, to run the program, loosely under my direction. This was more than I could have wished for and I left his office feeling like I had finally achieved the goal of a lifetime.

Ultimately, the department included three efforts besides the Africa program. I led a zoo-based project on golden lion tamarins (GLTs), a highly endangered species of Brazilian monkey, members of which were managed on a day-to-day basis by staff and volunteers in both the research and education departments. Zoo Atlanta was one of several zoos nation-wide that participated in the program. The immediate goal was to give zoo-born GLTs enrichment opportunities in a limited area on zoo grounds in which they could range freely and learn to move effectively in natural vegetation. They were also presented with complex foraging devices to teach them how to find food rather than eating out of bowls in an exhibit. Researchers and trained education volunteers conducted behavioral studies on the monkeys and interpreted the project to zoo visitors. Once the tamarins were deemed to be proficient in the skills needed to survive in the wild, they were translocated to Brazil for additional pre-release experiences. Finally they were released in areas where wild tamarins already lived. The goal was not so much that the tamarins born in zoos survive for long periods, but that they live long enough to breed and produce offspring competent to live successfully in the wild.

During the GLT project, I became the supervisor of a young woman in the education department, Sarah Bexell, who led the education branch of the GLT project. Sarah became involved in the giant panda program, led by Terry and Rita, while I became a member of Sarah's dissertation committee when she went to live in China. There she developed conservation education programs for youngsters. She became the first westerner to be hired by the Chinese to work on giant panda conservation. In addition to being a member of the giant panda facility design team, I also worked with then graduate student, Rebecca Snyder, who conducted her dissertation research on the Zoo Atlanta pair and wrote several papers on her research, to which I was fortunate to contribute. Rebecca later became Curator of Pandas.

The two small field research projects for which we provided some monetary support were a wildlife rehabilitation center in Belize conceived, built and run by a former Zoo Atlanta primate keeper, Robin Brockett. The project mostly dealt with Howler monkeys and parrots confiscated from private owners. Robin used methods similar to those of the GLT program to prepare the monkeys and birds for repatriation to the wild. After release, she conducted follow-up field observations on their progress. The third project was, again, a rehabilitation center, this one for Bornean orangutans, most of them orphaned as infants or juveniles. Several Zoo Atlanta great ape keepers volunteered at the project for short periods of time, lending their expertise on and assistance in raising infants in ways that would facilitate their eventual re-release in the wild. Some would become permanent residents of the center and the facility was always in need of funds.

During the years that I was Coordinator of Scientific Programs and Director of Field Conservation, my participation in the AZA conferences increased. Initially, that participation mostly took the form of presenting papers, but after I became the Field Conservation Director, I also sat on a number of important committees, including the Field Conservation and Behavioral Enrichment committees, where I met many interesting colleagues. I also became chair of the Animal Behavior Society's Animal Care Committee, during which time we revised the standards. That was a time during which I felt that I was really making a difference in a larger arena, not just at my own zoo. I much appreciated Terry's support of my participation on these committees. I also became the editor of *African Primates Newsletter*, which focused primarily on brief and up-to-date articles on primate field studies.

Around the mid-1990s, Terry began to offer a field research

course through Georgia Tech. It was a competition open to under-graduates nation-wide and about eight students participated each year. Terry asked me and one of his graduate students, Tara Stoinski, to lead the groups and teach the course. It was a great opportunity to spend time in Kenya each summer, although some of the female students - most were female - were definitely not field-worker material. One young woman had hysterics when a large grasshopper flew into the van. I usually added several weeks on at the end of the courses to conduct research on primates and lions that followed up on my dissertation research.

In the late 1990s there was considerable turnover in zoo staff, both at the managerial and keeper levels. Gradually, the tenor of the institution began to change from what it had been during the years that I think of as the salad days. I am not entirely sure when the zoo began to face financial difficulties, although I was aware of it on some level due to my participation in the budget process for my department. However, it really hit home when it affected me. In late 2000 or early 2001, Terry again called me into his office and told me first that my attendance at AZA conferences would be limited due to budget constraints. Then he floored me by going on to say that my position as Director of Field Conservation would be reduced to half-time. During the other half I would act as Associate Curator of Hoofstock. I was shocked. I had not worked my way up through the zoo ranks to attain my position; I had been hired for my field and research expertise and had never managed animals in captivity. As a result, I would be essentially at the mercy of the staff I supposedly supervised in order to receive the training I needed to manage the care of rhinoceros, giraffe, Thompson's gazelles, zebras, ostrich and a number of smaller birds.

I discovered immediately that I was indeed at their mercy and that mercy was in short supply. There were four keepers. One was kind, another relatively friendly, while two, including the lead keeper, were openly hostile. They did not receive me well because, in their minds, I was simply someone with book-learning and an academic title. I was forty-six years old and had a bad back. Although they did rotate me through the care of all the animals, their favorite thing was to tell me - remember I was the alleged supervisor - that I would be cleaning the rhino barn that day. It seemed that I heard that dread refrain every day. I had cleaned horse stalls for years, but this was

orders of magnitude more difficult, a truly Augean task. If you have
never seen a rhino stall after one night's occupation, you cannot
begin to appreciate what an appalling sight it is. There are probably
two hundred pounds of manure in piles or trodden into the floor, not
to mention what is smeared on the walls. And there is urine, of
course. Everything has to be shoveled into a wheelbarrow and
dumped on a truck, then the stall must be hosed, disinfected, brushed
thoroughly, rinsed and a squeegee used to remove excess water.
Now…multiply that by two. Of course we had two rhinos. I thought
I would die.

Then came the day I was informed that I had left the barn aisle
padlock unsecured. If the rhinos were let into the barn, they could
theoretically, although not likely, gain access to the keeper area. In
any case, it was an egregious oversight. It is possible that I did
commit the error; mistakes can be made. I was furious, however,
when they informed me that, prior to making their accusation to me,
they had gone directly to my dear friend Dietrich Schaaf, Director of
Collections, and ratted me out. They had even by-passed the Curator
of Hoofstock, my immediate supervisor. I told them in no uncertain
terms that their behavior was inappropriate. Needless to say, that did
nothing to endear me to them.

Not long after, Dietrich left the zoo for another position and, as
far as I was concerned, the atmosphere at the zoo took yet another
turn for the worse. At the end of 2001, I became ill and was obliged
to take a medical leave of absence. On the day I reported back for
work, the Human Resources Director called me in and told me that I
was being laid off. I was able to have my staff moved into lateral
positions, and Tom Butynski got a job with another conservation
organization, but I had to leave. It appeared that after 9-11, even
written commitments of support to the zoo evaporated like disap-
pearing ink. Other "non-essential" departments, including the
research department, were subsequently dissolved. When I went to
see Terry after being given the bad news, he told me that he would
hire me back, even if only in the capacity of a consultant, as soon as
he could. As it happened, however, Terry also departed the zoo soon
after.

Despite the sad ending, my career at Zoo Atlanta was the
happiest and most productive time of my life. And I owe it all to
Terry Maple, a person like none other I have met and one of the

most influential people in my life. Terry put together an outstanding team of professionals and trusted us to help him create what was one of the best zoos in the country. I am honored to know him and to have worked with someone whose primary goals were, like mine, to support conservation of wild animals, use information from the field to improve the lives of animals in captivity and to document the effects of those improvements scientifically in order to persuade others to do the same.

20. LIVING IN TWO WORLDS

Rachel MacNabb
Communications Manager
Zoo Atlanta

Dr. Maple and I have many memories in common, but the one that means the most to me is the one he never noticed. It was fall 2000, and I was the kid with the neatly-printed résumé sitting on pins and needles in the Administration Building at Zoo Atlanta, nervously anticipating my first job interview there. When you're a stranger waiting in what you hope will be your future workplace, anyone who walks past could be someone of great importance. That morning, it was.

A man came through the front door and hurriedly disappeared into the big office on the right. Having known him now for more than 12 years, I can hazard a guess that he was probably running late. But with no third eye for the future, I still thought instantly: *That's Terry Maple.*

It wasn't that I'd been up all night researching the faces of the zoo family. He was someone Atlantans recognized on sight, and to anyone who even remotely followed the news, his was a household name. I grew up not far from Atlanta, and even as a very small child awed by Willie B. and his fellow zoo residents during school field trips in the mid-1980s, I knew something wasn't right about this place. The animals were colorful, charismatic, magnificent wild emigrants from points around the globe, but something about their conditions occasioned shame and embarrassment, even in a first-grader.

I remember when the zoo was just one ugly newspaper headline away from being shut down forever, and I remember when Dr. Maple became the man tasked with turning things around. He was constantly in the news, on TV and in the paper. His quotes, interviews and photos were everywhere: I even remember a department store print ad featuring Dr. Maple sporting a Member's Only Jacket, which in my mind signified instant celebrity status.

This was the legend who hurried by that morning in 2000, but my interview wasn't with Dr. Maple that day. I wanted to work at Zoo Atlanta so badly I would have mounted any task, whether it be pouring coffee, making photocopies, or sweeping little pellets of goat poo in the petting zoo (all of which I did do). I was overjoyed to get a position as administrative assistant to one of the vice presidents.

In fall 2001, a staff restructuring suddenly required that I become Dr. Maple's Executive Assistant. I'd say I was honored, enthusiastic or over the moon, but I was scared out of my gourd. If I'd been offered a baby pacifier or permission to suck my thumb in public, I think I'd have availed myself of both opportunities. Maybe somewhere in a parallel universe, I listened to the naggings of what I believed to be my professional shortcomings and went and took a job somewhere else. Thank goodness there's no such thing as a parallel universe.

As it turned out, Dr. Maple wasn't so scary, and the office wasn't a lofty tower under siege by monsters from under the bed. On the contrary, I received what I still believe was the finest possible introduction to the work world for any new recruit learning the ropes of a demanding professional environment. I say "the work world" because I'm sure I was grossly immature; the "zoo world" was a beautiful added bonus, and I had the privilege of learning its inner workings from one of the most respected leaders in the field.

When Dr. Maple retired from Zoo Atlanta in 2003, I joined him at the Center for Conservation and Behavior at Georgia Tech. Dr. Maple knew that my background and interests were in writing; I think he saw that I was getting restless doing office jobs and wanted me to have the chance to take on something meatier. He gave me a shot at penning a zoo-centric article - a feature on Ivan the gorilla for the Center for Conservation and Behavior website. That story became the first of what are now more than 125 published articles I've written on Zoo Atlanta's animals and programs.

During my two years at Georgia Tech, I got to know many of the finer points of Dr. Maple's character - traits that never necessarily appeared in news headlines or press interviews. I learned that not only was he a strong executive, visionary leader and powerful public speaker, but he was also a wise mentor, a supportive friend, and an unfailingly generous person. I also learned that whenever I went on an errand around the corner to Junior's to pick up lunch, no matter how explicitly he requested a grilled cheese *without* fries, he was still going to "borrow" a few of mine.

I think both of us missed the zoo business, and it wasn't long before both of us jumped back into that rapid stream. In 2005, I got a new job back at Zoo Atlanta, and he accepted a position at the helm of Palm Beach Zoo around that same time. At the time, he told me I could choose any piece of zoo memorabilia I wanted from his office as a memento of the five years I worked for him. I don't think he expected me to point to his prized autographed photo of Clint Eastwood in "Every Which Way but Loose," but he gave it to me all the same.

That was where my professional relationship with Dr. Maple ended on paper, but I've had the honor of his influence and friendship for many years since. While I never took one of his classes or defended a dissertation in front of him, I still feel as if I were one of his students. There was much to be learned from him, and there still is.

He led Zoo Atlanta for more than 18 years, and I'm proud to have been part of just a fraction of that career. I still hear Atlantans and zoo visitors mention his accomplishments with reverence, and it's a reverence deeply earned.

A lady never reveals her age, but I do know that Dr. Maple wasn't much older than I am now when he took over at Zoo Atlanta. While I'm years removed from the inexperienced over-zealot who sat anxiously at the zoo waiting for an interview, I can't imagine shouldering such public responsibilities, against so many odds, and with so much success, as he did.

Thank you Dr. Maple! A legend is a legend and legends always endure.

21. THE EVOLUTION OF BWANA KUBWA

Tom LaRock
Managing Director & Founder, Safari Professionals
Managing Director & Founder, World Safaris

Dr. Terry L. Maple was initially a professional colleague and consultant, who, as my career in the zoo world moved forward, became a friend and mentor. I think the best way to illustrate the importance of Terry's influence is to relate stories of some of the times our paths crossed. His never-ending passion for and commitment to the quality of life of those animals placed in the care of zoological institutions is well known. These stories add to the documentation of his legacy.

I first met Dr. Terry Maple in 1983, when he served as a consultant to the Toledo Zoo. In 1978, the zoo had acquired the gorilla, Max, from the Frankfurt Zoo as its second silverback, with the expectation that he would become part of the zoo's gorilla breeding program. Unfortunately, Max had a behavioral issue - he was far more interested in self stimulation than in breeding with the zoo's female gorillas.

After the Toledo Zoo was privatized in 1982, Bill Dennler, the zoo's new director, sought Terry's advice. Public relations were part of my responsibilities and we wanted the community to begin to learn about the science behind the operation of the zoo. We advised the local media that we were inviting Dr. Maple to come to Toledo, as a consultant in the behavior of captive primates. The local press picked up the story, with one of the media outlets describing Terry as a "marriage counselor" for gorillas. While that wasn't exactly the message we were promoting, the light-heartedness it brought to the resulting stories helped the community begin to understand the challenges the zoo faced within its breeding efforts. Therefore, we considered the PR effort to be a success. Remember that this was in 1982 - long before most zoos publicly committed themselves to conservation and just a few months after the AAZPA began to create its Species Survival Plans (SSP).

A couple of weeks after Terry's visit, I found a copy of the Weekly World News on my desk, opened to a story that had a picture of a male gorilla (it wasn't Max) with this headline: "Max Won't Do It!" To put this in perspective, the World Weekly News was a supermarket tabloid that featured truly unbelievable stories. As I read the article, I found myself laughing at the sensationalized story until I read equally over-the top quotes from the zoo's general curator. I quickly checked and found out that no one from the World Weekly News had spoken with anyone at the zoo. The writer had simply made up a version of the story from the local news stories. While we all had a good laugh, Terry's visit provided me with a couple of my most important early lessons in public relations - you can never predict who will be interested in a story and what they will do with it. By the way, even with Terry's focus on behavioral enrichment, Max never did sire any gorillas and no one ever admitted to leaving the Weekly World News on my desk!

In 1986, I was serving as the executive director of the Alabama Zoological Society at the Birmingham Zoo. Bob Truett, the zoo's director, had invited me to participate in the planning of the next major exhibit. Bob's vision was to exhibit animals that shared behavioral adaptations. The first of these was "The Predators" and the second was to be called, "The Social Animals." The zoo had three of the great apes on exhibit - chimpanzees, gorillas and orangutans. But there was only room for two of the three in the plans and the chimps were chosen to be sent to another zoo within the SSP.

Unfortunately, there were members of the Society's board who wanted to champion keeping the chimps. As we moved forward with exhibit planning, they became quite vocal. Bob and I offered to bring in great ape experts to review the plans and comment on multiple issues, among them the decision not to include chimpanzees. We recruited three consultants, with Dr. Maple serving as the last one to meet with interested board members. After a tour of the zoo's primate exhibits and a review of the plans, Terry presented his reasons for his conclusion that removing chimpanzees from the zoo was the best decision, especially for the benefit of the chimpanzees. Terry explained the growing understanding that chimps required a larger social structure and more complex exhibits in order to encourage natural behaviors - rather than the stereotypical, and often, from a human perspective, negative actions captive chimps were famous for. The Birmingham Zoo simply did not have the resources to properly exhibit and care for a large troop of chimpanzees. I'll never forget his concluding statement: "If you exhibit chimpanzees, they will make you pay for every sin you've ever committed." The next day the board approved the plans for the Social Animals building, with just one dissenting vote. After the vote I learned that, while the other consultants were helpful, it was Terry's professional credentials and his passionate honesty that carried the day, allowing those two chimpanzees to move on to a zoo where they would be able to thrive.

In 1987, my next assignment took me to the Seneca Park Zoo - the zoo I had visited regularly as a child when I stayed with my cousins in Rochester, NY. During my interview as the potential executive director of the Seneca Zoo Society, Dan Michalowski, the zoo's director, was about to take me on a tour. Before we started, I told him what I remembered from my last visit, which would have been about 25 years earlier. I remember Dan telling me that much of what I remembered was still there and, to my disappointment, it was.

After moving to Rochester, we joined forces to create a new vision for the zoo. As with many zoos at the time, the zoos had some "star" animals. One of those at Seneca Park was Gambar - a male orangutan, who had become locally famous with stories that told of Gambar's apparent fascination with watching television. When behavioral enrichment was in its infancy, several zoos installed televisions in attempts to engage the attention of great apes (a result of the story about Willie B. and his television at Atlanta's Grant Park Zoo). Two of the zoo's most ardent donors donated the TV, becoming Gambar's adoptive "parents" in the process. It was said that Gambar was particularly interested when "I Dream of Jeannie" was on the air. While Gambar had old fire hoses to climb on, there was little else to encourage meaningful activity in his cage. As a result, Gambar was very overweight.

Realizing that the zoo did not have the resources to significantly improve Gambar's exhibit, Dan asked me for help in finding a new home for Gambar. I immediately suggested we enlist Dr. Maple, not only in his role as a great ape consultant but also as the chair of the orangutan SSP. Dan agreed and we arranged for Terry to come to Rochester to meet Gambar.

After setting up Dr. Maple's visit, I realized that I needed to involve the couple who were Gambar's "parents." We arranged to host a dinner, at which Terry explained the importance of Gambar as a potential father within the SSP and the necessity to provide Gambar with a larger, more stimulating environment. Once again, Dr. Maple's passion for the great apes and their well-being at the zoo came through. I'm not exaggerating when I tell you the couple was on the verge of tears when they told Terry that they wanted whatever was best for Gambar and they expected him to send Gambar to the best place he could find. In an interesting coincidence, Gambar was sent to the Toledo Zoo - my old stomping grounds - where he became a father.

Fast forwarding to 1994, I left the Seneca Zoo Society to start a travel company offering natural history travel throughout the world, with a heavy emphasis on African wildlife viewing safaris. When that business faced challenges in 1998, with shrinking markets due to the economy and the bombing of the U.S. embassies in Kenya and Tanzania, I began to look at returning to my zoo career. Zoo Atlanta had a position open for a deputy director and I called Terry to express my interest. He invited me to submit my CV for consideration. While it was initially disappointing when he called to tell me he'd selected another candidate, I was pleased that he had selected my friend, Steve Marshall, for the position. Terry encouraged me at the end of the conversation when he told me his goal was to find a place for me at Zoo Atlanta.

And the call came a few months later, in December 1998, when Dr. Maple opened the door for my return to the zoo world. The position of Corporate Vice President for Human Resources and Administration was open and Terry wanted to talk about my early business career, in what used to be called "Personnel Administration." Although I had not considered that experience, nor my degree in psychology, as important qualifications, Terry did. During a luncheon in Atlanta, Terry offered me the position, with an understanding that a part of my role would be as the "junior silverback." Understanding the trust implicit in that role, I gratefully accepted the opportunity to return to the unique world of zoos.

Without going into details, I look back at my five years at Zoo Atlanta as the most challenging and the most personally rewarding of my career. Dr. Maple always had high expectations of those of us who worked with him. In return, I received strong support and the freedom to do what I thought was the right thing. And, on those occasions when my decisions did not lead to the expected outcomes, Terry's support never faltered. I remain thankful for his trust and his friendship.

While I have many memories of my time at Zoo Atlanta, perhaps the most memorable for me took place on February 2, 2000. Dr. Maple was interviewing Dr. Dwight Lawson as a candidate for the general curator's position. I heard the "Code Green" announcement that there was a veterinary emergency at the Ford African Rainforest and saw Steve Marshall running toward the zoo entrance. A few minutes later, my phone rang and I saw that the call was coming from the gorilla building. I reluctantly answered the phone and heard Steve tell me that Willie B. – the Zoo Atlanta family's most famous and most inspiring resident – had died. It was Willie B.'s impoverished life at the Grant Park Zoo that led the Atlanta community to change the zoo. It was Willie B. who, when he first stepped out into the Ford African Rainforest, paused, looked out at the grass and trees that replaced his cage and quickly assumed the posture of a silverback. I think it's safe to say the Willie B. was the soul of the renewed zoo.

Because Willie B. had been ill, the news was not unexpected – but it was still a shock. And I was now the person who had to deliver the news to Terry. As I walked down the hall, the memory of the morning I had to go to the hospital to tell my dad that mom had died during the night came back to me. I knew how dedicated Terry was to Willie B. and how much he loved that big silverback. As I interrupted the interview and told Terry, he looked at me for a few seconds and then looked down. He took a deep breath, stood up and told Dwight they'd finish the interview at another time. Dr. Maple and I began walking from the Administration Building to the gorilla holding area. As we walked, he talked about the steps we needed to take now to help everyone involved with Willie B. and how to honor the role this magnificent gorilla had played in the life of Zoo Atlanta and the greater Atlanta community. Even during this – what I suspect was the lowest moment for Dr. Maple during his service to the Zoo – his commitment to the future remained his focus. The passion and commitment I had seen in my first encounter at the Toledo Zoo still burned within him. It's a part of his legacy that more people should know about. While Willie B. may have been the soul of the renewed Zoo Atlanta, I think Dr. Terry L. Maple was its heart.

22. GOING GREEN WITH TERRY

Kristen Cytacki
Director of Education & Sustainability
Palm Beach Zoo and Conservation Society

In the fall of 2005, Terry Maple became the President and CEO of the Palm Beach Zoo, where I had been employed as the Director of Education for eight years. Our little zoo had been without an executive leader for several years and I was looking forward to working with a legend from the zoo world. I had no idea at the time, but our zoo was about to be radically transformed, on every level, by the wealth of experience and extraordinary vision of Terry Maple aka Zoo Man.

When Terry arrived, he could have come in and cleaned the slate and handpicked his leadership team from a variety of accomplished zoo professionals he knew throughout the country. Fortunately for many of us he did not. He carefully studied and spent time with each of us and saw the talents each of us had and considered how we could be part of his bigger picture. Right from the beginning, I admired how driven but calm Terry was about everything that happened at our zoo. He had big plans for the organization but was patient with all of us in getting there. I learned quickly that he is clearly someone who plays chess - not checkers - and he certainly does not sweat the small stuff, which was so welcomed and refreshing!

Not long after he arrived he asked me to help with the zoo's quarterly membership publication. I needed to write an article about Terry, in which his new position at the zoo was announced. I entitled the piece, *From Pandas to Palm Beach,* highlighting Terry's impressive career. The research for this piece gave me the opportunity to get to know him better and understand what was important to him. The first thing that stood out very clearly is that family comes first. He spoke fondly of how he often had his children by his side throughout his career. He understood the importance of being there for your children and the commitment that parenting required. He wanted his team to embrace the role and enjoy parenthood while also doing important work. He personally understood the demands of working parents and was joyous, understanding, and very flexible with me when I wanted to start my own family. I have valued and admired these qualities of his more than words can say.

One of his key responsibilities at the zoo was fundraising. He hit the ground running and in 2006, just a few months after his arrival, our annual black-tie gala reached a one million dollar milestone! An amazing feat for a zoo our size which brought us from the minor leagues to the big leagues, joining the ranks of only three other zoos in the nation to reach this remarkable achievement; WCS-Bronx Zoo, Audubon Zoo, and Zoo Atlanta.

Terry also did an amazing job bringing zoo and wildlife conservation experts he knew to our facility for us to meet and learn from. In 2007, he established the zoo's annual Conservation Leadership Lecture. Our lead off presenter was Dr. Alan Rabinowitz, and each year brought more incredible speakers like the legendary Dr. George Schaller and Dr. Howard Quigley. A decade later, this popular program still continues.

Terry always dreamed big and thought carefully about how our zoo could be unique. Most importantly, he truly believed we could achieve great things and his confidence and drive encouraged and motivated all of us. In 2009, we opened the nation's first LEED certified zoo animal hospital, officially named the Melvin J. and Claire Levine Animal Care Complex. Although we had planned for a new animal hospital for many years, the fundraising was stagnant and the vision incomplete. Terry led us from a 1,000 square foot animal clinic to a 10,000 square foot state-of-the-art animal care complex - LEED certified at the gold level - complete with 2,000 square feet of solar panels on the roof.

My professional career grew immensely under Terry's leadership. He expanded my responsibilities to include the zoo's sustainability program and appointed me editor of the zoo's largest publication - the *Palm Beach Zoo Magazine*. I will always be grateful for the many ways he challenged and encouraged me to grow and expand. He always recognized and valued my work and inspired me to think big!

I sincerely admire Terry and will always be grateful to have had the opportunity to work for him and with him. Working for a true modern zoo pioneer has definitely been one of the highlights of my career. I will be forever thankful for all I learned from him.

23. A DOOR OPENED AND I WALKED IN

Holly Harris Reid

I first met Terry when I was the managing editor for a multi-authored book called *Wild Mammals in Captivity*. I especially loved his chapter(s) because of the enhancements that his expertise brought to the animals. In the mid to late 80's animals in zoos were often still living in unnatural environments and were largely intended to be for the public's entertainment. As I read his work, it was clear that he was dramatically changing the lives of animals in a very significant way. I pored over his work and I knew that he was helping to revolutionize a dated and often dismal industry, bringing education and conservation to the public's attention.

Terry's work with gorillas appealed to me since I'd always considered myself a frustrated armchair primatologist. One evening while watching National Geographic's *Urban Gorilla*, the narrator told of hopes that Ivan, a "strip mall gorilla," would one day be moved to Zoo Atlanta to live with other gorillas in a sprawling natural habitat. As I watched Ivan on the documentary peeling the unnaturally blue paint from the walls of his very tiny, isolated cement "yard," I was eager to reconnect with Terry and hear more about the possibilities of a better life for Ivan who was at the center of an endless bankruptcy case. Terry invited me for a visit to Zoo Atlanta, an invitation I eagerly accepted.

As so often happened with Terry, I went anticipating an interesting visit with a visionary leader to talk about gorillas, but

155

instead, walked out of his office with plans of dropping out of graduate school and accepting his offer to come and work for him as his executive assistant. I wasn't sure what an executive assistant was but hoped it wasn't a secretary! As it turned out, it was, however, I was thrilled to be working for a man who changed the lives of so many gorillas—with at least one more gorilla to come named Ivan. Graduate school would have to wait.

Working for Terry the following years was one of the most exciting and enlightening times of my life. Not only did I have the opportunity to be on the front lines observing Terry navigate the bankruptcy courts to have Ivan released and moved to Zoo Atlanta. I stood in awe as he so artfully played hardball to secure Ivan's future. And he succeeded in a way that will be etched in my memory forever as I watched Ivan step outside and onto grass for the first time since he had been captured as an infant over 30 years before.

Working with Terry also gave me the opportunity to experience the work that was being done by the Dian Fossey Gorilla Fund. It was 1994 and civil war had just broken out in Rwanda. I intensely manned my post by the phone to connect Terry to his contacts in Africa to learn the impact the war was having on the fragile gorilla population and the dedicated staff at the Karisoke Research Center. Terry brought calm to chaos and hope to the seemingly hopeless.

When I think of a visionary leader, I think of Terry Maple. He has a way of leading that engages even the most stubborn of personalities. His enthusiasm is contagious as he talks about the possibilities of a better future. Anyone walking out of his office wanted to be on his team and contribute to bringing his vision to reality.

I did eventually return to graduate school so that I could contribute in a more substantive way. Terry and I have stayed in touch through the years. I am honored to have spent such profound with him at Zoo Atlanta. I look forward to more opportunities to work together again.

24. TWENTY-EIGHT YEARS AND COUNTING...

Rich Block
Zoo Atlanta Alumni Association

It was 1986 and I was nearing the end of my first year as The Kansas City Zoo's curator of public relations. I had jumped right into my first zoo job after completing a five-year teaching appointment in the University of Michigan's School of Natural Resources. It was clear to me that the Kansas City Zoo was at an impasse with its nonprofit support society and I needed a zoo opportunity that would be more productive. The opening for an education curator at Zoo Atlanta caught my attention. I was ready to be inspired and their new director, a guy named Terry Maple, was preparing to take one of *Parade Magazine*'s "10 Worst Zoos" to world-class status. That's inspiring!

Terry Maple brought attention to this often over-looked, long-neglected community resource, putting it in the spotlight in Atlanta and nationally. His vision and passion were irresistible so I soon found myself bound for Atlanta. Though I had some teaching experience, Terry took a gamble and gave me the opportunity to begin shaping the education program under Zoo Atlanta's new management team. It was a great group of people, many of whom would move on to leadership positions in other accredited institutions. Though he might not have foreseen it at the time, Terry was actually building quite a distinguished "alumni association" for Zoo Atlanta and an even larger pool of Maple fans.

Terry gave me a wide playing field and always supported new

ideas for programs including Zoo Atlanta's first volunteer recognition program. When we were ready to redefine the zoo's relationship with Atlanta's public schools, he backed our ideas and the negotiations to take control of the "classroom" that was used as a laboratory for field trips. Terry never failed to work a message about education into all of his public appearances, making me feel that he always had my back. He consistently encouraged our networking and outreach efforts, including the Zoo's participation in World Wildlife Fund's *Future in the Wild* and the traveling exhibit *Cargo to Extinction*.

Shortly after Drs. Mark Plotkin's and Russ Mittermeier's Zoo Atlanta presentation of *Future in the Wild*, I received an offer to work at World Wildlife Fund (WWF) in Washington, DC, coordinating a new program to develop relationships with accredited zoos and aquariums. Though I had thoroughly enjoyed my work at Zoo Atlanta and had become a Maple fan, the offer to work on a national program in DC was too alluring. The deal-closer was the opportunity to work with Russell Train, WWF's president and a long-time conservation hero of mine.

Five years later, in 1995, Terry would again shape my professional development and experience. After launching several successful programs at WWF, I was open to a "next step," and there was Terry! This time Terry was suggesting a move to another organization, the Dian Fossey Gorilla Fund International. Terry was on their board of directors and the organization was looking for a new executive director. He told me, "Anyone that can bring direction and organization to the Gorilla Fund will be able to go anywhere after that!" We all know how difficult it is to say "no" to Terry, so I was off to Denver for my next professional adventure.

This new opportunity was fraught with challenges, but the greatest was a severe case of "founder's syndrome," a founding board member that could not distinguish between the responsibilities of a professional staff and those of a volunteer board member. As always, Terry was a good listener and a source of good advice, but the road to good management and implementing a broader vision for the organization was more challenging than either of us had anticipated. To further compound the issues, the Rwandan civil war was brewing and that winter the Rwandese Patriotic Front (RPF) invaded Rwanda from their refugee camps in Uganda.

Just as we had successfully pulled our field team at Karisoke from Rwanda and established an agreement with the RPF, World Wildlife Fund came back into the picture. I was asked to return as a Senior Fellow to work on a number of special projects with the likes of HBO, WQED, Microsoft, and Evian, among others. The timing was right for me. In the end, my departure from the Gorilla Fund created new opportunities to engage their board of directors and opened the door for Terry to move the organization to Zoo Atlanta's campus. Under new leadership and with Terry's support, the Gorilla Fund began to evolve into its current structure and scope of operation.

Meanwhile, my career path continued from WWF to the Indianapolis Zoo and ultimately on to my current CEO position at the Santa Barbara Zoo. During all of this time, it was always fun to keep in touch with Terry at conferences and to watch the evolving form of his leadership and vision in the zoo and aquarium community. In 2006, Terry helped shape the Santa Barbara Zoo's conservation program. Following a recommendation from Terry (and one knows you should follow those recommendations!), we interviewed one of his graduate students, a Ph.D. candidate, Estelle Sandhaus, to run our expanding field conservation program. We hired Estelle and never looked back! Our field programs have never stopped growing as the Zoo has become a significant contributor to the conservation of Channel Island foxes, California condors, amphibians of the Los Padres National Forest, and southern sea otters.

It is fair to say that Terry Maple has been an all too familiar figure in my professional development and experience since 1986!

25. A ZOO DIRECTOR'S JOURNEY: TEN QUESTIONS ANSWERED

Tony Vecchio
Director
Jacksonville Zoo & Gardens

1. What were you thinking when Dr. Maple recruited you to become Curator of Mammals at one of America's worst zoos?

   Surprisingly enough, I had no worries about it. Many of my friends and colleagues advised me not to take the job because it was one of America's worst zoos but I knew somebody who worked at the Zoo Atlanta and he had already told me about Terry, the team that Terry was putting together and how exciting it was. He described Terry's vision for the place and how everybody was starting to buy into that vision. He really saw that it was a zoo going in the right direction and I could just feel the energy and enthusiasm there. So I was excited about the opportunity.

2. What was your biggest challenge when you arrived in Atlanta?

   When I arrived it was still in the very early days, and Zoo Atlanta still deserved to be called one of the worst zoos in the country. It was in terrible shape. There were inadequate exhibits and inadequate management styles. There were a lot of processes and procedures that were still being done that were left over from the pre-Terry days. Terry had created a great vision but it was obvious there were going to be many, many, hurdles to overcome before we could fulfill that vision. It was difficult building the new zoo while we kept the old zoo running; there was a lot of drudgery, difficult personnel issues and a lot of challenges during that time.

3. What did you learn from your experience in Atlanta that prepared you to become a zoo director?

Zoo Atlanta was a really unique experience because it was, in fact, one of the worst zoos in the country. I can't image there are too many times where something like that comes up. But, when there is a clear vision of what we want the zoo to be, the experience was really educational because you could just see what it took to make a zoo great. We were starting from below ground level and to see all the steps involved and what it takes to make a zoo great is really an experience that probably couldn't be duplicated.

4. What was different about a zoo directed by a psychologist from Georgia Tech?

Zoo Atlanta was a whole different zoo because of Terry being there. The zoos of the past seemed to be almost run by tradition and gut feelings and Terry really brought the scientific method to zoo management. He asked really probing questions that people just hadn't asked before and demanded in the nicest way possible that your answers be based on evidence and the scientific method. He brought a nice blend of the science and academic communities into the zoo community and that was really new at that time.

5. Did you work with the elephants at Zoo Atlanta? What do you remember about that experience?

So much! I was intimately involved with the elephant program. I hired the staff and I was involved in picking the new elephants for the exhibit and training the elephants. Something that is clearly in my memory is that this was a time when elephants in most facilities were still being managed in the old fashion of the zoo keepers dominating the elephants to, "Show them who is boss!" Our team, Dr. Maple, Dr. Schaaf, and the elephant consultant we hired did not believe in that old method, but rather they believed in positive reinforcement. We were on the cutting edge of the work being done with elephants and that was a really exciting feeling. Training elephants using positive reinforcement was very different from what most other zoos and circuses were doing at the time and it was a very positive experience for me.

6. What are your memories of Dietrich Schaaf?

    Dietrich was a great guy, but sort of a fish out of water. Dietrich was a scientist and he was just a wonderful guy with a wonderful heart who I think loved being in the field. So, again… the good and the bad, the great thing was he was really a smart guy who brought the scientific method to everything we did, but every day you could see the frustration in him in trying to work in an organization that just had lots and lots of logistical challenges. Dietrich was a big picture thinker and didn't want to deal with all the day-to-day problems. We had lots of day-to-day problems, so I learned a lot from Dietrich, but I also felt for him. I felt like he wanted to be doing something else. He loved the animals, he loved research, he loved the science. He was not someone who liked being in a bureaucracy.

7. Were you surprised when Willie B. became a breeder?

    I was probably as surprised as anyone in the world, because again, I worked very closely with Willie B. and the whole gorilla team. I saw Willie B. when he was living in his horrible sterile cage. And I knew he had been in there for over 30 years. I could see the bond between him and his keeper. I really thought that Willie B. thought of himself as a person, not a gorilla. I didn't even know if he would ever be able to be housed with other gorillas, much less breed and be a father. When he turned out to be a great silverback leader of the group as well as being a great father to his offspring, it was amazing. It was just unimaginable when he was living in the old fashioned concrete and glass cage with a lack of social skills; it was amazing that he became a breeder and great father.

8. Any humorous incidents that you recall at Zoo Atlanta?
    Those times were so challenging it's hard to think. At the time nothing of it was funny. But now looking back some of the old fashion management things that I don't know if they were ever accepted anywhere in the zoo. One of the things the former staff used to do to keep the bears from breeding was to keep them overweight. They kept them so fat that they couldn't breed. We were moving animals to other zoos to get ready to build new exhibits and we had to ship out some of these grizzly bears that were so fat they looked like grizzly beach balls. They were just round. I remember we got one into the crate and we lifted the crate up and the bear fell through the bottom of the crate. He was so fat and overweight. That was a little scary at the time, but looking back on it just was really funny that the bear was so fat that the crate couldn't hold him. That's probably the best of it.

9. What was it like preparing for Zoo Atlanta's first accreditation in 1987?
    That was overwhelming, because I had come from a good zoo and I knew what it took to be accredited. We just had so many things to do. It was such a long laundry list that it was almost frustratingly overwhelming to try to knock all of these things off the list. But amazingly, we were able to do it because we had a lot of good people. As I said earlier, Terry put together a really good team and the list that looked overwhelming to me, wasn't so overwhelming when we had so many different people knocking things off the list every day. By the time that came around we were much ready for it than I expected we ever would be. We had to get a lot of really basic work done.

10. What is the most important attribute of a successful zoo director?

I think it's a mistake to think that there is any one attribute that can make the zoo director successful. I think it's a combination of things. I talked about what a great visionary Dr. Maple was. He was able to paint the picture of what the zoo should look like and what you're striving to get to; zoo directors need to have a vision. But you also have to be good at getting the day to day stuff done. I think the bottom line if you could pick out one thing that makes a zoo director good would be... it's all about attitude, about someone that cares. To be a good zoo director you have to care about the staff, because you are working with people who are always going to be underpaid. For that staff to be successful they've got to love their job and understand the importance of it. If you don't care about the staff enough to keep them interested in their jobs and motivated, they're not going to do the work. You also have to care about the community. The zoo is part of the community and has an obligation to the community and you have to care about the place where you live and the zoo is based. So many people are in the zoo business because they care about animals and the future of the animals. You've got to care about the individual animals that you're taking care of and their welfare and also care about the species, and working hard to save species.So, even though many people may not think that caring is the most important zoo directly quality, I give the zoo director caring about the staff, the animals, the zoo and the community as my number one vote.

FESTSCHRIFT FOR TERRY MAPLE

PART III: PROFESSIONAL COLLEAGUES

26. TERRY MAPLE: SCIENTIST, CONSERVATIONIST, ENTREPRENEUR, WRITER, CITIZEN, FRIEND

Newt Gingrich

When I think back about the many adventures I have had with Terry Maple it takes six different big words to capture the scope and the intensity of his life: scientist, conservationist, entrepreneur, writer, citizen, and friend.

In every area he brings the same energy, enthusiasm, good humor, and very powerful intelligence. He also manages to bring lessons and knowledge from one aspect of his life to another. He is interested in virtually everything and his good humor and sense of excitement gets others engaged in his dreams.

I first met Terry in the mid-1980s when he had undertaken a remarkable career change. At the time I think he imagined he was leaving his teaching and research post at Georgia Tech for a brief assignment to save the Atlanta Zoo. Little did he know this was the beginning of a lifetime of adventure.

By the mid-1980s the city of Atlanta had failed so decisively at managing the Atlanta Zoo that it was in grave danger of losing its accreditation. In a remarkable act of courage Mayor Andy Young concluded that the city bureaucracy could not run the zoo and turned it over to the Friends of the Zoo. They looked for an entrepreneurial leader and recruited Terry.

Terry was a remarkable zoo saver. He brought a vision of a strong research component, great animal exhibits, a showman's ability to attract news media, and an entrepreneur's ability to raise money (the Ford Rain Forest was one of his first big breakthroughs).

I think I first met Terry in the WSB TV Fourth of July Parade. I was there as a young member of Congress. He was there with a baby elephant drawing attention to the zoo. As an animal lover, zoo lover, and Republican, how could I resist? We found we had a lot in common. Many don't realize it but Terry's childhood was in the Republican neighborhoods of San Diego. He was very comfortable talking with an animal-loving Republican Congressman.

Over the years I was delighted to help Zoo Atlanta acquire some Rainbow Boas, 2 black Rhinoceroses, and 2 Komodo Dragons from the National Zoo. I was there with President Carter when the zoo opened the Giant Panda Exhibit (in some ways Terry's most famous achievement).

When I visited the zoo I would meet graduate students from a variety of universities monitoring the wildlife and, in particular, the gorillas who formed one of the best family exhibits in the world. With Terry's leadership a lot of research was being done at the zoo.

Terry and I worked to save the Endangered Species Act while I was Speaker and I suspect it would not have been saved without his leadership and involvement. He encouraged E.O. Wilson and other famous biologists and botanists to come to the Congress and help members understand the delicate web of life they were dealing with.

When I left the Congress Terry invited me to a meeting of the zoo directors from across the country. We were meeting at the then new Animal Kingdom at Disney World, and being allowed to visit with and learn from so many dedicated zoo leaders was one of the high points of my life.

Together we wrote a manifesto for an effective conservative environmentalism called *Contract with the Earth*. Johns Hopkins Press brought it out and it remains one of my favorite books. It really outlines an alternative to either big government bureaucracy or allowing the environment to be destroyed.

Terry followed up his great leadership at Zoo Atlanta with a dynamic tour of turning around the West Palm Beach Zoo. He seems to have an almost magical knack for arousing enthusiasm for a vision of a dynamic community-based zoo with a strong conservation component.

Terry has been one of the leaders in developing the public-private partnership model of zoo management which virtually every first rate zoo in America now uses.

Given the E.O. Wilson model of longer term leadership, Terry has another twenty or thirty years of contributing to science, to zoos, and to the community. I have no doubt he has big achievements ahead of him. I look forward to working with him on those achievements. I know it will be fun. With Terry it always is.

Hoff, Bloomsmith & Zucker, Eds.

172

27. A PHENOMENOLOGY OF ACADEMIC KINSHIP

Don Lindburg

Davis, California, was still a small university town when several graduate students from the departments of Psychology and Anthropology began meeting at a small bar near campus on Friday afternoons. All were relative newcomers to the emerging field of primatology. Terry Maple was a member of this group. The year was 1969. (This university would eventually develop schools in Engineering, Law, and Medicine.)

Psychology majors were enthusiastic about the "comparative" aspects of their discipline, a branch that was moving beyond the largely rat-oriented work of predecessors. Only a few years earlier, "primatologists" from zoology and biological anthropology had begun to publish results from studies of wild living primates. When research on captive colonies was included, that little bar in Davis would soon become an important extension of the more formal seminars, lectures, and classroom assignments directed by faculty.

I am honored to contribute to a festschrift in recognition of the scientific accomplishments of Dr. Terry Maple. I first met him when he began his above mentioned graduate work at UC-Davis. He had come there to study under the tutelage of Dr. Gary Mitchell, a recent graduate in Psychology from the University of Wisconsin. Gary had been recruited to a joint appointment at the Davis Primate Center and the Department of Psychology in 1967. Having just received a similar appointment in Anthropology, I was delighted to have a new colleague with broadly similar interests to mine, i.e., rhesus monkey development and behavior. On their own initiatives, graduate students in our respective programs began meeting at the afore-mentioned bar in order to discuss and sometimes argue vehemently about the issues emerging from intensified study of both captive and wild-living nonhuman primates.

UC Davis was one of seven campuses selected in 1962 by the National Institutes of Health for establishment of centers dedicated to the study of nonhuman primates. Two years later, while in graduate school at UC-Berkeley, I had been offered the opportunity to conduct a socio-ecological study of the rhesus monkey, stalwart of the research laboratory, in a stretch of its native habitat in north India.

Upon my return to Davis in 1964, the captive population of rhesus macaques at the Center was made available to me for follow-up studies. The Director, Dr. Leon Schmidt, whose primary efforts were aimed at finding a vaccine to immunize humans against malaria, was also interested in the deleterious effects of the drug thalidomide on human fetuses that were becoming known at that time. He began treating pregnant rhesus females at the Center with thalidomide in order to further elucidate its harmful effects. Infants were thus born with impaired forelimbs, and hopped around on their hind limbs like small kangaroos, but otherwise appeared to be normal. Dr. Schmidt asked me to record their behavior, in particular any adverse effects on maternal attachment and care.

At the University of Wisconsin, Gary Mitchell had studied under Harry Harlow, known for using extreme social deprivation to elucidate more clearly the course of rhesus neonatal development. Eventually, Gary would acquire for the Davis Primate Center a small number of Harlow's then fully grown males for further study of their impaired behavior.

Terry's mentor, Gary Mitchell, and I received joint appointments at the Primate Center and our respective Departments of Psychology and Biological Anthropology in 1967. Virtually all of the primates in residence at the Center were rhesus monkeys. Given their position as the stalwart of US research laboratories, this population offered an ideal opportunity to engage in newly developing initiatives. Terry would conduct studies on this population for his Ph.D. in

Psychobiology, awarded in 1974. His first academic appointment was at the highly esteemed Emory University in Atlanta, Georgia. In 1978, Terry ultimately began a 30-year appointment to the faculty of the Georgia Institute of Technology. Our paths were destined to cross many, many times in the near and distant future.

Two events that no one could have anticipated had a profound impact on Terry's early career. One of these was his learning of an aged gorilla at the Atlanta Zoo that had not been outdoors since his birth 27 years earlier. This unfortunate circumstance had a dramatic ending years later, after Terry had rebuilt the zoo, and when national television broadcast the gorilla's first tentative steps into a world of blue skies and grass. "Willie B.," as he was known, went on to produce offspring. But, more importantly, his emancipation from the world of indoor cages would lead to establishment in Atlanta of the nation's finest research program in gorilla psychobiology. Other species and other zoos would benefit from this more enlightened approach to captive living as well.

The second event was the nearly concurrent characterization of the Atlanta Zoo by *Parade Magazine* as one of the 10 worst zoos in the entire United States. The profound embarrassment suffered by the city fathers led to recruitment of Terry as CEO and Director of Zoo Atlanta, a position he would hold concurrently with his faculty appointment at the Georgia Institute of Technology. Despite limited familiarity with zoos at the time, Terry's excellent performance in revitalizing Zoo Atlanta led to an entirely new world of engagement in that zoos all over the country began to seek his advice. Ultimately, Terry would attain the highest possible accolade from the world of US zoos in becoming the executive director of the American Zoo and Aquarium Association. With his campus ties and an inviting arena in which to embrace the new field of zoo-based research, he immediately began to attract to his program a cadre of graduate students, many of whom have emerged as leaders in this field.

It is worth pointing out that zoos had engaged in very little research before the 1960s, a notable exception being Drs. Duane Rumbaugh and Chris Parker, who did their research at the San Diego Zoo as faculty at San Diego State University. Duane Rumbaugh later went to Yerkes and Georgia State University and Chris Parker died tragically in a motorcycle accident. Their publications would influence all future zoo-based research on the great apes.

The timing of Terry's appointment to leader of the AZA would prove fortuitous since, on July 1, 1975, the Convention on Trade in Endangered Species (CITES), sponsored by the IUCN, came into effect. This treaty closed the door to further wildlife imports from native habitats. Zoos would never be the same, since they would henceforward have to learn how to breed exotics in captivity if they wanted to continue to exist. Embracing captive breeding would now offer much more than entertainment to the American public. This new emphasis on breeding required the enlistment of geneticists to establish a viable founder population from the stock on hand, and to construct models in genetic management that would insure viability some 200 years into the future. Although continually refined, these models are still a fundamental component of the captive breeding of zoo-based animals. In concert with genetic management, research on behavior, endocrinology, veterinary medicine, pathology, exhibit design and, consequently, enrichment of the lives of zoo denizens, began to flourish.

As Terry's extensive Curriculum Vitae demonstrates, he is an internationally recognized scholar. This document reveals that he has been an entrepreneur, launching programs new to his academic discipline. A laudable example is seen in convincing the prestigious Wiley-Liss publishing firm in 1982 to inaugurate a new journal, *Zoo Biology*, which is now into its 33rd volume. Terry served as its Editor-in-Chief for its first seven years of publication.

It cannot be overemphasized that Terry has become a renowned consultant, not only to zoos, but to such esoteric programs as the launching of a chimpanzee into space. On six occasions, he has testified before the US Congress, including two opportunities to comment on the Endangered Species Act. In 2002, he was appointed by President George W. Bush to the Institute of Museum Science Board of Directors, an appointment that was subsequently approved by the US Senate.

Terry testified before the United States Congress on CITES in four successive years, 1995-1998. In 2007, he gave an invited address at the annual meeting of the "Republicans for Environmental Protection." The following year he became a member of the Environmental Advisory Committee of the McCain for President campaign.

With respect to his zoo associations, Terry became a

professional fellow of the American Zoo and Aquarium Association (AZA) in 1998, and served as co-chair of the Taxon Advisory Group for Great Apes from 1990 to 1997. He served as President of the AZA from 1998 to 1999. In 1990 he was elected to the International Union of Directors of Zoological Gardens, and received Life Membership from the World Association of Zoos and Aquariums in 2012. In 2005, he was elected as a Fellow of the Georgia Academy of Science. He has also become a Fellow of the Association for Psychological Science.

In providing this document, I have summarized some of Dr. Maple's the more obvious achievements. One can easily access his Curriculum Vitae via Google for more information. (Editors' note: See *"Publications from the Maple Lab, 1977-Present"* in this volume.)

28. ZOO MAN; TECH MAN

Anderson D. Smith
Georgia Institute of Psychology

The School of Psychology at Georgia Tech always had an emphasis on Animal Behavior. When I arrived on the campus in 1970, one of the senior faculty members was Richard Davenport, a well-known primatologist who was affiliated with the Yerkes Primate Center at Emory where he did his research. He worked with orangutans. When he died unexpectedly, there was no doubt among the faculty here that we should hire someone who could keep that connection between Yerkes and Georgia Tech. Terry Maple had recently been hired by the Department of Psychology at Emory and he was a perfect fit to continue Dick Davenport's role at Georgia Tech. After just three years at Emory he became a faculty member at Georgia Tech. Just six years after coming to Georgia Tech, the then mayor of Atlanta, Andrew Young, asked him to take over Atlanta's zoo, a zoo that everyone agreed was one of the worst in America. A friend of mine at the time, Carolyn Boyd Hatcher was Atlanta's Commissioner of Parks and was responsible for the zoo. I can remember her asking me about Terry. Of course, I gave her a strong recommendation, even though at the time, I thought it would be a big loss for Tech. He became CEO at Zoo Atlanta and for two decades transformed the zoo into one of the very best zoos in the country.

The amazing fact about Terry's career is that he never gave up his role at Georgia Tech as a professor, a teacher, and a research scholar. There was no loss for Georgia Tech, but instead a strengthening of Terry's career. The entire time he was directing the zoo, he remained an active faculty member and colleague. He always attracted the very best graduate students to the School of Psychology. When I became Chair of the School, I tried to facilitate Terry's different roles. He was just too much an asset to Georgia Tech to allow him to turn away from academia. My predecessor as Chair, Ed Loveland, and I both agreed that Terry was one of our strongest faculty members even with his dual roles as zoo CEO and college professor. I was excited when Terry resigned from the zoo and came back full-time to Tech with an endowed chair. I was equally dismayed when the call of the zoo world enticed him again. After just two years full-time at Tech, he accepted the position of CEO of the Palm Beach zoo. Terry is always looking for new adventures.

He actually encouraged me to be involved with the animal world. I even supervised the dissertation of one of the students Terry attracted to Georgia Tech. My research area is human aging and cognition, and Yerkes had the two oldest chimpanzees in the world. We were able to study cognition in these chimps. Along with Jack Marr, also on the faculty at Tech, we went on to study recall memory in rhesus monkeys at Yerkes. I have remained active at Yerkes for the remainder of my career and I attribute much of my career broadening to Terry's enthusiasm when we were both young Tech faculty members. I seemed to always have fun when Terry was around. He and I were in a private box in Sanford stadium when Georgia Tech beat the University (sic) of Georgia. The box was owned by Bulldog fans, and Terry and I were the only ones left in the box when the game ended. There were always those great Darwin birthday parties he had. We were not always successful in our attempts to swim for exercise, but the fellowship was great. I thank Terry for letting me be a part of his career. He certainly has been an important part of mine.

29. DR. MAPLE AND THE LASH'S

Nevin Lash

It was 1986, and I had just gotten a new job with CLRR, Inc. in Philadelphia, a zoo design firm recently expanding due to receiving a big commission - Zoo Atlanta's Redevelopment. Dr. Maple had just taken over as director and there was lots to be done; a new era was unfolding. I had come from 8 years of commercial landscape architecture, which meant designing parking lots and shopping malls. My heart had always tended towards environmental issues and this zoo design world was brand new and offered such promise to create 'places' of great educational and environmental value. In order to get my head around my new responsibilities, I started reading everything I could about great apes, including *Gorillas in the Mist*, Schaller's *The Year of the Gorilla*, and of course I found and read Maple and Hoff's *Gorilla Behavior* as well as two others. I was immediately drawn in by the novelty of this scientific pursuit. To me, this was all new and held infinite interest and awe. When I finally got to meet Dr. Maple, I was star-struck! He was a god walking amongst us and I was always tongue tied when he and I met. He was the first zoo director that I had known and was so much more respectable than my previous clients - land developers!

Luckily that phase of idol worship passed and I was able to see him as a man, and one who had his opinions that, because he was my client, I had to take seriously. There were many memories from those early days that I still remember clearly and I will try to convey some of the color of those events: I was the Project Manager for CLRR and we had a huge task of rebuilding the zoo. Central to that project was the designing of the state-of-the-art gorilla complex. There were holding buildings to design, utility systems to layout, mature trees to protect and a unique visitor viewing experience to create. We had completed several months of detailed planning work with three firms that had teams hard at work on a very specific set of drawings to initiate construction for this very important exhibit. Then we got a call from Terry. He found himself presenting our large-scale model of the exhibit to someone when he realized that we had designed a situation where at key overlooks we had placed small buildings. Instead of the standard "moated" separation between humans and gorillas, we decided to provide close-up, through-glass viewing. To us, we thought this would bring gorillas and humans together for a glare-free close-up experience. To Terry it was architecture and why would we have architecture in our newly created "tropical forest?" He wanted those buildings gone. Jon Coe and I jumped on an airplane and within 24 hours the buildings were gone and we were re-designing all the overlooks, re-grading, re-working and re-directing the design team according to our new plan.

Terry is a big picture guy and his influence over our work was always big. He didn't usually sweat the details, he would listen to the issues at hand and decide what needed to be done. I remember one construction meeting we were discussing some pipelines that needed to be run that would effect a major tree (and there were many "major trees") and we all took the position that it had to be done, and that tree would have to go - all of us except Terry. He said, "We need someone to be the Ombudsman for the trees! If it was up to you guys - all the trees would be gone." And thus a new position was created, and Don Jackson was hired as Zoo Horticulturalist, a position rare in the zoo community at the time. I'm sure that pipe was run, and that tree did eventually die, but the zoo's trees have had an advocate ever since.

I remember another time when Coe and I were presenting concepts for our interpretive signage package and we were all packed into Terry's tiny old Director's Office, and Jon was showing slides of signs in African parks that were all wobbly and hand carved, and out comes Terry's booming voice, "Coe - that looks like shit!" and he went on to say that he wanted a more finished look, not some cobbled together sign. From that point on our interpretive signs were made of the highest quality, beautifully painted, baked enamel panels that have lasted 30 years without a fuss. Those wobbly wooden signs would have been replaced 10 times in that same period. We did maintain some of that wobbly, hand-carved feel on many of the gateways and building signs, but they were always a notch above what was originally proposed and the zoo was better off with his insistence.

Terry brought a true family feeling to the zoo staff. Even though some of the facilities were not up to snuff in some cases, the morale and camaraderie was always high during his years as director (which I can't say was the case at other times). He made people see how important the work was and encouraged everyone to contribute and take on a role of responsibility.

The Zoo Atlanta project for me was all-consuming. I worked non-stop on all the facets of the project from 1986 through 1992 before I was free to get involved with other jobs at the office. I was traveling from Philadelphia to Atlanta almost monthly and at times, weekly. It's not surprising that I did not have much of a social life beyond work - but I did have a social life. It revolved around a young woman Terry hired to be his Zoo Biologist. Gail Bruner had been persistent in capturing Terry's attention at one particular zoo conference and she was encouraged to apply for the job of Primate Curator. While she didn't get that job, she did eventually get a job when Tony Vecchio and his wife Trish moved to Roger Williams Park Zoo and the Zoo Biologist position became open. Gail moved from the Los Angeles Zoo and took on the role as liaison between the architects and zoo staff. The project was well underway so she needed to get up to speed quickly, and I took on the responsibility of teaching her the ropes - how to read drawings, how to use the architectural scales, etc. Well, one thing lead to another and soon, Gail and I were dating. Our two roles often put us on opposite sides of the table at meetings and debate was often heated. We each took our jobs quite seriously; to others it might have seemed a bit too seriously. Of course we thought that we needed to keep our social lives discreet and we went to extremes to not be suspected of any inappropriate behavior. This went on for over a year until we decided, it would be best to let Dr. Maple know and relieve ourselves of the burden of secrecy. We scheduled a meeting, walked in and said, "Dr. Maple, we have something to tell you..." and he looked up and asked, "Are you pregnant?" Of course he knew all along, he was a master at primate behavior and we apparently exhibited all the signs of the displaying male and receptive female. Luckily we weren't pregnant, but we were quite in love and would soon be getting married, which he heartily approved.

The classic moment during those early years at Zoo Atlanta of course was the time Willie B. came out of holding into the natural world for the first time. The stage was set - hundreds of zoo supporters, media and dignitaries had turned out, the keeper staff had prepared for weeks, and animal trainer, Tim Desmond was hired to make sure there were no mistakes. Everything was riding on the success of this particular moment. Tim brought out the big gun - strawberries! All that needed to happen was for him to open the door and Willie B. would follow the breadcrumbs and Zoo Atlanta would step into the history books. It was noon on a hot, sunny day in May 1988. We all pointed our cameras at a slot in the rocks where Willie would emerge (or not). We held our breath and waited, and waited. I remember turning around to look back to where Terry was positioned and snapped a photo of him. I knew that no matter what Willie did that day - it was Terry who would either sink or swim and he was sweating a bit more than the rest of us, but he offered a confident gesture of "just wait" and the rest is history. Willie B stepped out onto the grass that day for the first time in 28 years like he was walking on egg-shells. He looked up to the sky, then tore off a low-hanging branch and stood defiant for all to see as he claimed our habitat to be his own. Then, the sky opened a bit and rain began to fall, and the pampered gorilla beat a hasty retreat. But that was enough for all who were present, Willie B. was on his way, and so was Dr. Maple and Zoo Atlanta. Zoo Atlanta had gone from being one of the worst zoos in the U.S., to a highly respected zoo, with the largest collection of gorillas and award-winning exhibits and programs.

Gail left the zoo in 1993 to go back to school full time for her masters and a Ph.D., that Terry had always encouraged her to do, and I moved down to Atlanta and set up a zoo design firm, Ursa International, just down the street from Zoo Atlanta. For the next 20 years we have provided exhibit design services on many occasions as the zoo's go-to designer. We have Terry to thank for so many positive and encouraging words to us and to others. He has been a steady supporter and continues to recommend us on projects in his role of "leader of the pack" to other zoo professionals. There were occasions where I would be touring someone around the zoo in hopes that they would select Ursa for their project. Terry would always go out of his way to sit down with them and make sure they knew he supported us as experts in the field.

Gail and I continue to cross paths with Terry and hope to continue to do so for many years to come, as projects come up for him and for us. One such project is in Miami at Monkey Jungle. This is one of those original Miami attractions that grew organically out of the DuMond family's scientific research center to a small visitor attraction. As a private facility, there were years that funding was limited and visitors slowed to a trickle. Then in 1992, Hurricane Andrew put the "coup de grâce" on the facility. After several years of rebuilding, the park was rebuilt and re-opened, but much of the jungle-feel had been lost. By 1998, they began planning a new gorilla habitat for a circus-owned silverback gorilla, named "King," to help the struggling facility get back on its feet. Terry, then AZA president, spoke up against "roadside zoos" as one of his major platforms and encouraged Sharon DuMond to place King at Zoo Atlanta and not Monkey Jungle, which didn't have AZA accreditation. The media frenzy came to a head with Jane Goodall and local leaders lining up on either side to make this a national humane/animal rights issue. The family and Terry were at odds and in the end the DuMonds built King a lush habitat where he could live out his days. Because of Terry's strong opposition, no other zoo would think of sending a female playmate for King to this day and he lives alone in his wooded kingdom.

I found myself working with the DuMond family recently and seeing the sad situation of the lone silverback and immediately "stuck my foot in it." Not remembering the fuss back in 1998, I said, "Let's see if my friend Dr. Maple could come here and work on King's behalf to get him a friend." The look on Sharon's face when I mentioned his name almost got me fired on the spot! Even though time had passed and the ability to make physical accommodations for a small group of gorillas was now possible, there was no way Dr. Maple was going to be invited to help!

Not everyone is a big Terry fan, but most are. He is a great scientist, academic, storyteller and family man. To me, he has always been someone I admire and respect. He modeled the role of zoo director that few can compare with and as a teacher, he has spawned a host of our leaders in the field today. Many have contributed to this volume, and I feel honored to be asked to stand with them to pay our respects and share our stories about Dr. Terry L. Maple - Zoo Man.

30. REMEMBRANCES OF MY ZOO COLLEAGUE

Dave Towne

It is difficult to highlight the highs and lows of my 25 year friendship with Terry since it encompasses both numerous profess-sional and personal experiences. And, other than working with some of his excellent post docs, I had limited connection with his academic accomplishments except being the recipient of his many interesting books! The vast majority of our experiences involved the zoo and aquarium world where we were consecutive Chairs of the American Zoo and Aquarium Association (AZA) as well as our joint efforts to help negotiate Giant Panda Conservation Loan Agreements with China and our U.S. partners.

During our AZA leadership period, we hoped to move the organization forward to a new era. First emphasis was the major upgrades to the accreditation standards for all members and the second was the push to attract and keep minorities in the profession, woefully lacking at the time. Terry turned out to be much more strident than I, and enlisted his friends like Newt Gingrich who, along with Terry, made stirring speeches to the Association which did help move the organization to fully recognize the issue and take affirmative steps to correct. It always amazed me that that two conservative figures such as Terry and Newt helped make this happen.

The giant panda efforts were probably the most involved and challenging for both of us; Terry, who was determined that Zoo

Atlanta would be the second zoo to obtain giant pandas in North America, and me who was assigned the responsibility of overseeing the controversial negotiation efforts between China and the competing interests of the many institutions who wanted to be involved. Terry's desire for the pandas, at times I thought overruled his good judgment, regarding the fiscal and operational impacts they would have on a relatively small zoo. But his optimism and personal force did make it happen, and very successfully, I might add, given their several births and general public acclaim they have provided.

The process of these never-ending negotiations with Chinese officials was marked by two scoldings we received when we showed up following the bombing of a Chinese Embassy in Eastern Europe and an invitation to the Taiwan President by our President to visit and speak in the U.S. After being lectured for the better part of the first day on those two actions, we reconvened the negotiations without further reference to our imperialistic behaviors. Terry was a real diplomat and soon the issues were forgotten, except in our memories.

Terry had a very winning way with the Secretary General, who was a strong woman with high-level Communist Party connections, and in time the Loan Agreement was approved, and the rest is history. In this process before cell phones, changing schedules, world travel and agenda negotiations were the numerous morning and night calls or e-mails. This allowed me to become well acquainted with Terry's long-suffering wife Addie, who deserves a gold medal for her patience, sense of humor as well as helping keep him out of more mischief to which he was always attracted. But he did make a difference and I love the "old man" and our long, memorable relationship!!!

31. TERRY MAPLE AND THE SIOP SPEECH

Larry James

Terry Maple and I have been close friends for over 30 years. We met when we were both new to the Georgia Tech psychology faculty in the early 1980s. Shared interests in sports, politics, San Diego (both of us had lived there), and psychology evolved into both personal and professional relationships. I would like to relate a professional experience when Terry's friendship saved my bacon.

Terry had become Director of the Zoo Atlanta, a story better told by others in this volume. In a weak, uncharacteristically prosocial moment, and comprising a single trial learning experience, I had agreed to be the local area coordinator for the annual convention of my APA division. It had just become the Society for Industrial and Organizational Psychology (SIOP), which is long for Division 14. The hardest part of my duties was to recruit a luncheon speaker for our primary convention meal. I was given $1,500, which in the mid-1980s was kind of a big deal, or so we thought.

Now, we need to set the context. It's the mid-1980s, and Terry was on leave from Tech to rebuild the Zoo Atlanta. As part of this effort, Terry is eating grits and red-eye gravy three to four mornings a week trying to raise money to rebuild the Atlanta Zoo into a respectable venue. He was well-suited for this task. He raised a serious amount or money, he made the zoo a showpiece and a well-known research base, and he became a charismatic, respected, and well-liked personality in Atlanta and beyond. But at the time of this story, while his work had started and was in progress, his reputation as a successful leader and executive was just approaching the Atlanta city limits.

We had a maturing experience of a different nature. I say "we" because two very able graduate students, Lois James and Sigrid Gustafson, accompanied me on this venture. Allow me to demonstrate what this entailed. We called the office of our US Senator from Georgia (Sam Nunn) to ask if he would address our luncheon. After being put off by aides for several calls, we reached the alpha aide who set Sam Nunn's schedule. We gave our pitch, starting with being from Georgia Tech, reaching our high point with this being for educators (well, mostly), and ending on a strong note of having a whole $1500 for an honorarium. The aide responded that Senator Nunn customarily gets $5,000 for luncheon speeches. We immediately played the education card again, hoping that a claim of poverty would cut us a break. The aide, and it was now becoming clear why she was the alpha aide, countered with "How many of these educators vote in Georgia?" I don't know, 12 maybe. And so went what became known as the "Nunn Experience," which did not have a positive connotation in our shop.

We went on to build some expertise at these experiences. I think that we were about 0 for 10 (it could have been 15 or 20, memory fades). Desperation set in; the convention was approaching and we had no luncheon speaker. It was time for a change in strategy. Our meeting went something like this: "OK, we have talked to most of the people in Atlanta who don't need $1,500. So, who does?"

Terry's name came up pretty quickly. He was giving speeches for free, so $1500 might look pretty good. He did not have to get up early for us. He was building a successful identity as an executive/academic. And, he was a psychologist who could give a psychologist's perspective on rebuilding an organization. Finally, Terry is great in front of an audience. He, Bob Liden, and I jointly taught a leadership class, and I had witnessed what Terry could do with an audience on the subject of leadership.

Maple was our candidate. He agreed to give the speech. He thought $1500 was too much, but I convinced him to take it, fearing what others that knew the going rates would think if we got someone for less than $1500. I then informed the elected officials of the Society of our choice and his acceptance. Their first response was

"Who the .... is Terry Maple?" My response, mostly true, was to describe his recent exploits in rebuilding the Atlanta Zoo. They went along with it, largely because they had no choice, on what they referred to as "James' Guy." Indeed, the Society President, in introducing Terry at the luncheon, made it clear who was responsible for selecting the speaker.

And Terry proceeded to blow them away. It was clearly the best luncheon speech in the history of the Society. (Of course, it was only the second, given the Society had formed the prior year). After the speech, Terry became "our speaker" to the executive committee. Most important, however, Terry was used as the standard for quality speakers at the Society for years to come. A consensus exists to this day among those who attended that Terry was rarely equaled and never exceeded. He became our "Gold Standard."

32. HUGE AND HAIRY-YET LEPRECHAUN-LIKE

Joseph M. Erwin
Research Professor of Anthropology,
George Washington University, Washington, D.C.

One afternoon in 1966, as I sat in the office of my first academic mentor, Martin Gipson, at University of the Pacific in Stockton, California, Marty read to me from the student newspaper an account of a UOP varsity baseball game. The piece described, as I remember it, a walk-off game-winning triple hit by Terry Maple. "He's a psych major, you know," said my grinning professor. Soon after that, I first met Terry. He expressed interest in the work we were doing with animal learning and behavior in the psychology lab.

At that point I was serving as the animal caretaker for the rats involved in a thesis project for one of Marty's grad students. This was one of my many part-time jobs as an undergraduate, but it was not my first rodeo. I had grown up on a remote ranch, caring for various domestic animals and livestock, as well as occasional rescued wildlife. Later, as a custodian for a biology building, care of research rodents was included in the scope of my duties. While in community college, a couple of other students and I initiated a project using Skinner boxes to train rats, and - of course - someone had to provide for the care and feeding of the rats. Guess who!

One day the Psychology Department Chair, W. Edgar Gregory,

came to me and asked if I would like to enter the M.A. program. He knew me pretty well because I had taken independent study courses from him and had served as his "reader." He said the department could offer me a paid teaching assistantship and graduate fellowship with full tuition remission if I would be able to start mid-year. A grad student was finishing and would be leaving. They needed to replace him as he was vacating one of the teaching assistant slots. Dr. Gregory said that if I was interested, I should discuss the matter with Martin Gipson, as I would be serving as his teaching assistant.

I was already quite well acquainted with Martin from taking his very challenging classes in experimental psychology and learning theory. I had really struggled with these classes. At the time I took these courses, Martin was finishing up his dissertation at Vanderbilt University under the supervision of Keith Clayton - who apparently was meticulous and demanding as a professor. In the learning theory course we were required to master Hullian learning theory and notation, in addition to having a thorough grasp of the work of Thorndike, Watson, Pavlov, Tolman, Terman, Lashley, Spence, Estes, and other central figures who dominated scientific psychology in that era. For the experimental psychology course, we were expected to internalize the exceptionally detailed and excellent *Experimental and Quasi-experimental Design* treatise by Donald Campbell (and Stanley). These two courses, probably more than any others, formed the foundation of my interest and orientation in psychology and science. So I visited Martin in his office in the old war surplus Quonset hut next to the rat lab.

Martin said he would be glad for me to serve as his teaching assistant, but, if I accepted the grad school offer, there would be a need for someone else to feed and weigh the rats and clean their cages. Did I know of anyone would do that? I thought of Dennis Farrell, but he had multiple sclerosis and multiple allergies - possibly including allergic reactions to animal dander - so he was out. Or maybe Dan Wakeman, but he already had a full-time job as an electrician at the county hospital. He did not really have time for another job. Both Dennis and Dan had already completed military service, as had I. Martin and I tried to think of some undergraduate who was a good student and also had an interest in animals. At pretty much the same time, we thought of an obvious choice: Terry Maple. Terry accepted the offer. At the same time, he unknowingly put himself in line for the graduate assistantship I would leave after a year-and-a-half - just in time for him to enter the masters program.

Terry and I both began doing research in Gipson's psychology laboratory at Pacific sometime late in 1967 or early 1968. The lab was adorned with psychedelic signs I had painted - one of a blue rat and the other painted on glass with a Calaveras jumping frog sticker in the center. The rat sign that hung outside Martin's office was stolen. I was quite flattered by that. Terry was studying learning and aggressive behavior in fish (Oscar ciclids and Siamese fighting fish), while I was working on learning, stimulus selection, and development with fruit flies (*Drosophila melanogaster*).

My collaboration on fly research with Professor Robert Murphey (another former Clayton student) at University of California, Davis, led me to enter the Ph.D. program in psychology there. The sub-program was "psychobiology," and it was broadly interdisciplinary, incorporating behavioral genetics, comparative psychology, neuroscience, ethology/animal behavior, and developmental and evolutionary psychology. Even though I had moved from Stockton to Davis, I kept in touch with my mentor, Marty Gipson, and others at UOP - including Terry Maple.

In September of 1969 I was offered a position as research assistant to the Director of Research at Stockton State Hospital, a notorious mental hospital. Dr. Robert Earl, the Director of Research, graciously offered me the position with the understanding that I would continue to be enrolled full time in the Ph.D. program at Davis. When I arrived I found that Terry Maple, now in the graduate program at UOP, was employed as a research assistant in the psychology division at the hospital. And so our association continued.

Time passed. I returned to Davis after about a year. By this time, after working with many different kinds of animals, including humans, on various studies of learning, I began to work with Professor Gary Mitchell at Davis on social development in nonhuman primates - rhesus monkeys. Mitchell, a very personable fellow, became a close friend, as well as an enthusiastic mentor. My first published research reports were with him. He encouraged teamwork among students, and one of the people who joined his team, also in the psychobiology Ph.D. program, was Terry Maple!

Terry and I formed a very productive collaborative team and

published a number of papers together as graduate students. We "egged each other on." Ours was a very compatible and constructive competition. We both finished our dissertations and were awarded our Ph.D. degrees in 1974. Terry stayed at Davis for a post-doc with Mitchell, while I moved to the University of Washington for a three-year research post-doc under the supervision of Professor Gene P. "Jim" Sackett (whose mentor at Claremont Graduate School was Robert Earl). Jim had also been a post-doc under Harry Harlow at Wisconsin at the same time as was Gary Mitchell.

Just as we were starting our post-doctoral careers, Terry and I met at Larry Blake's Restaurant in Davis to discuss our proposed participation in the Congress of the International Primatological Society in Japan. We had both submitted papers that had been accepted. Now we were discussing making the necessary travel arrangements. As we decried the expense of the trip, our friend Jim Welles joined us. Jim explained that he already had his tickets for travel to Japan. Terry and I, as if by instinct, proposed that Jim take our papers along and read them for us. We were very relieved at not having to spend thousands of dollars we did not have, and we ordered another round of drinks - including a large bottle of Pepsi Cola for Jim.

After another round or two, we grew bolder, and the thought that impoverished young scientists like us had to spend so much money to attend a primatology meeting grated on us. More than that, we were dissatisfied with the primatology journals that existed at the time. Their review processes were insufficiently rigorous and latency to publication was too long. We began to think that we knew how to do better. That night we conceived of the *American Journal of Primatology*, and that concept led to incorporation of the American Society of Primatologists two years later, in 1976. By 1980, we had a commitment from Alan R. Liss, Inc., to underwrite and publish the journal. I was the founding editor of *AJP*, but Terry played a pivotal role by arranging a meeting between Alan Liss and me. Not long after, Alan agreed to start another journal, *Zoo Biology*, with Terry as the Founding Editor. Here I should mention that *AJP* initially had a dark red cover - what could be called "wine" or "burgundy." Terry was the inspiration for this cover. Following a visit to Leningrad in the early 1970s, Terry came down with an affliction he fondly referred to as "Lenin's revenge." His physician prescribed drinking red wine to address his intestinal distress. The color of the journal cover was selected in honor of that prescription.

Terry had moved to Atlanta, working first at Emory and then at Georgia Tech. He had also become involved with the Atlanta Zoo. His immersion in the zoo world as a research resource for himself and his students led to increased involvement in initiatives for constructive change. His chapters in the book we edited together, *Captivity and Behavior: Primates in Breeding Colonies, Laboratories, and Zoos* (New York: Van Nostrand and Rheinhold, 1979) drew attention to the needs for improved facilities and care.

He ascended to the position of Director of Zoo Atlanta, while I became Curator of Primates for the Chicago Zoological Society's Brookfield Zoo. The interests we shared led us to travel abroad. Terry made many trips to Africa in search of wildlife and to assist students in developing research and conservation projects. I moved to work as a scientific editor for the National Geographic Society, and developed the Sulawesi Primate Project - a project that took me to Asia once or twice a year for about 15 years. We each spent a little time in each other's territory. I visited places so familiar to Terry in Kenya and Rwanda, where I sat with mountain gorillas and visited Dian Fossey. He visited Indonesia to float the Sungai Alas and look for orangutans.

Around the time Terry was elected President of the Association of Zoos and Aquariums, I was completing a term as President of the American Society of Primatologists. While Terry became President and CEO of Zoo Atlanta and simultaneously held an endowed chair at Georgia Tech, I became VP and division director of an NIH contract research organization and held several unpaid adjunct appointments. My old pal was always several steps ahead of me, and deservedly so. He's a born leader.

Across the years our paths have differed, but our interests have often brought us together. We currently work together from time-to-time on consulting projects - most often related to helping organizations intended to promote conservation and care of primates and other animals advance their missions more effectively. We both care about conservation of animal populations within their natural ranges, but we also appreciate individuality and systematic scientific research on behavior and health. We love to learn from animals, and I think we are both fully committed to learning more from each one.

It has been a great ride, old pal. We've been through a lot, together and apart. I look forward to many more good times with you. Warm wishes to you and your family, and to your distinguished academic progeny. I love it when they call me "Uncle Joe."

33. A FEW WORDS OF TRIBUTE TO TERRY

Rich Tenaza
University of the Pacific, SEAZA and Micke Grove Zoo

I've known Terry Maple for over 40 years, I'm proud to say. We both started graduate school at University of California at Davis in Fall of 1968, and we met shortly thereafter, brought together by our mutual interest in primate behavior. Terry was working towards his Ph.D. in Psychology and I was doing the same in Zoology, and so we both were primatologists in training. We started getting better acquainted in 1973, after Terry returned from a year studying sociology at University of Stockholm and I returned from two years in the field in Indonesia.

One of the places in Davis I'd run into Terry was a funky (and now defunct) pub called the Antique Bazaar. Terry often played football in the afternoon before heading to the Antique Bazaar and I can still picture him striding into the pub clad in sneakers, shorts, and football jersey, carrying a football, and attended by an entourage of smaller males. Sometimes Terry would make an even more dramatic entrance, appearing in a full head gorilla mask and accompanied by his old friend Joe Erwin dressed like a giant chicken. Quite a duo they were!

One day late in 1974 I was walking across the Davis campus when I ran into Terry near a campus coffee house. We both would be leaving UC Davis soon so we took advantage of this opportunity to sit and chat a bit. While we talked Terry doodled, sketching out a hollow, robotic female elephant powered by methane produced from elephant dung. As I recall, Terry's "Pachydermobile" was meant to be a self-propelled moving blind from which to observe wildlife on African savannas; I think it was also designed to be mounted by collect semen from male elephants. Even now, more than 40 years later, I chuckle when I contemplate Terry's Pachydermobile.

Terry and I both left Davis in 1975, he hired by Emory University and I by the University of the Pacific in Stockton, CA. I knew that Terry had been an undergraduate at UOP but I didn't know what a mark he'd left on the place. When his old professors learned I knew Terry they barraged me with accolades about him. I started at UOP nearly seven years after Terry had graduated, but the legendary stories about Terry maintained his presence there. Though we were on opposite sides of the continent there was no way to forget Terry in my new job at UOP.

Terry was a star athlete at UOP and in 2004 the university honored him with the Amos Alonzo Stagg Award, recognizing lifetime achievements of a former student-athlete. In 2008 - 40 years after he graduated - the university honored Terry again by inviting him to be keynote speaker at the commencement ceremony and bestowing an honorary Doctorate of Law degree on him.

In the 1980's and early 90's I was active in the American Association of Zoological Parks and Aquariums so I'd see Terry at AAZPA annual fall conferences and sometimes at their winter professional management school. That allowed me to observe Terry's rise to prominence in the zoo world as he turned Zoo Atlanta from a municipal embarrassment into one of world's finest zoos.

Recently our paths have been crossing again, as Terry consults with the Micke Grove Zoological Society to improve Micke Grove Zoo, located in Lodi, 12 miles from the UOP campus. This little zoo has a special meaning for Terry because it's where he and his wife Addie went on their first date.

I used to take groups of students and tourists to East Africa to study wildlife and so did Terry. On August 7th of 1982 I was scheduled to take a group to Kenya but on August 1st there was a coup attempt and all my people canceled out. Terry, on the other hand, was in Nairobi when the coup attempt occurred, and he and his students were holed up in a hotel while the city was being shot up. That added a bit of spice to the professor's life and was an experience none of his students will ever forget. (*The coup failed and by the time I reached Nairobi on August 8th the city was all cleaned up.*)

A toast to you Terry for a great career that contributed - and continues to contribute - so much to your students, your several universities, the zoo world, and conservation worldwide! And I'm but one of thousands who have benefited from knowing you.

34. SOME GREAT RIDES ON "AIR MAPLE"

Erika Archibald
Communications Director
Dian Fossey Gorilla Fund

Even though I'm a journalist by trade, Terry Maple opened the door to the animal kingdom for me like no else could have, and offered me the privilege of working in a world like no other.

It began with the late, great zoo gorilla Willie B., when I came to write about him for ATLANTA magazine in the late 1980s, as he got ready to make his outdoor debut. Just a few months later, I found myself on the zoo staff and soon became Willie B.'s chief publicist, as well as taking on the mission of showing how the Atlanta zoo was zooming from worst to first. I had the absolute assurance from Terry Maple that the zoo's ethics would be the highest in the land and that its operations would be transparent to all. That was enough for me and soon I invited a pool of top media to join me in seeing everything that transpired in this "new" Zoo Atlanta, something that could only be done because of the total trust one had in a zoo run by Terry Maple. To this day I still get thanks from media folks for providing that kind of inside access.

It was serious business but we also often had a LOT of fun doing the job of publicizing the zoo! Here's an example: Sometime around 1990 I convinced ATLANTA magazine to do a big feature on Terry Maple and the zoo's turnaround and they hired a top-notch

New York photographer to come down and shoot for the piece. Terry graciously agreed to whatever shots they might want. The first one wasn't too hard – they dressed him in a safari outfit and put him in a field tent we had erected near one of the gorilla habitats, where he could pretend to be like Dian Fossey in the wild.

But the final photo shoot was the kicker. They asked Terry, dressed in his safari suit, to get into the flamingo pool (lagoon) so his head could be at the same level as the flamingos, for a dramatic photographic effect. Terry gamely climbed over the concrete wall and lowered himself carefully into the gooey lagoon, with the water coming up to about chest height. The photographer then proceeded to take a series of photos with Terry in different spots in the pool and was done. They started packing up and told Terry he could get out of the lagoon. But after sloshing around for a few moments, it became clear that he couldn't.

"Get out the same way you came in," I said to him. "I can't find any foothold on this wall," he said, as he moved along feeling the inside of the concrete retaining wall, knowing that he couldn't get out by just being lifted from above and would need a leg up. Around that time John Fowler, the bird curator, came along, and proceeded to give various types of humorous advice, as did a few other zoo staff. Soon various curious visitors were watching too. Terry was a very recognizable zoo director and they couldn't figure out why the zoo director was in the flamingo lagoon. Had he fallen in, they asked?

So I got on the radio to the maintenance department to see if they could bring a ladder to the flamingo lagoon right away. They asked why it couldn't wait and when I explained they said they'd do their best to drop other work and get there as soon as they could. By now there was such a hub-bub going on around this exhibit that we all kind of stopped paying attention to Terry. By the time maintenance arrived with full gear, Terry had wandered through the water to the back of the lagoon and found some way out by crawling up a muddy slope. And he was still in good humor, although he asked if he could go home now...

On the academic side, Terry of course wanted everyone on his staff to go to graduate school. I already had a master's degree and had thought of a Ph.D. but hadn't done it. Still, with Terry's influence I decided I probably should before I got too old. So I got a teaching fellowship at the UGA journalism school and was surprised (or not) when Terry asked me if I wanted him to be on my committee! But the UGA dean said while they'd love to have him, it would be my problem if he didn't show up for my final defense. They seemed to know his propensity for being a little bit tardy. But I did manage to get the head of the UGA Ecology school instead, given my zoo background. And by then, I knew that any further work I did in journalism would be related to conservation and animals.

For many years now I have done communications for the Dian Fossey Gorilla Fund, also a "Terry Maple" organization, since he brought it to Zoo Atlanta in the mid-1990s to save it from a slow demise in a non-professional setting elsewhere. Today it's a smashing success story at saving gorillas in the wild. I've also since studied veterinary technology (nursing) and wildlife rehabilitation, helped found a large nature preserve in Atlanta, become a master naturalist, and am creating an urban naturalist program. I can catch a wild hawk in flight and have rescued everything from beavers to opossums to vultures. And each time, I think of all the things we "made" Terry Maple do for various TV shows and publicity purposes, the animals we put in his hands and the places we had him go...

At the zoo, we used to say that a staff meeting with Terry was a "ride on 'Air Maple'" – a presentation of wild ideas that we never knew if we could pull off. Well, now I operate my own rides, with what I hope is at least a little bit of the vision, courage, determination, ethics, spirit and good nature of the original, the one and only Dr. Terry L. Maple - the highest-level, alpha, uber-charismatic megavertebrate that I've ever had the pleasure of knowing.

FESTSCHRIFT FOR TERRY MAPLE

PART IV: FAMILY AND FRIENDS

Hoff, Bloomsmith & Zucker, Eds.

35. DADDY MAPLE FESTSCHRIFT

Molly Maple

I still have the photograph. I dug it out recently, as I have done so many times, during the most recent of countless moves. It is still in the frame, signed, though not dated. It reads: "To Molly. With love - your daddy."

I don't know where he had been during that trip, though I can guess it was Africa. I don't remember receiving the picture and I had not truly pondered it until now, but as far as I am concerned, I could have had it my entire life. It has moved with me across the country and back.

In the picture he stands in the foreground of a landscape that seemingly reaches for miles. In it squints that familiar face - the eyes gleaming with excitement - for this place, its creatures, for what his experience can, *will* teach the world. This photo is the one that I will always imagine - have always imagined - when thinking of my father.

He is an agent of change. As the eldest of the Maple girls, I have both observed this for the longest time and am the greatest beneficiary of this characteristic. The man lives to dream, to improve, and to aspire.

He has given his energy, and devoted his life to the betterment of the world's creatures. In doing so, he has brought on levels of change in the world's zoos that can only be measured in the millions: the millions of children and parents, students and researchers —

beasts of the upright, two-legged variety – who have discovered the love and wonder of God's beautiful creatures.

However, he is nothing if not restless. More can always be done, and more *will* be done, whether it is under his direction or through his influence over the countless number of zoo and research professionals who consider him among the greats.

I know that he will never stop achieving – at least not willingly. His retirements – yes, two of them – have each resulted in new career doors opening. The only thing that I wonder is – will I be able to keep up?

36. MY DADDY THE ZOO MAN

Emily Maple

I had a magical childhood. One full of creatures kids only dream about seeing, much less touching or being encouraged to study, adore and work with. We were brought up in a way that we always felt connected with nature. Dad would love seeing our "catches" from the creeks in our backyards each time we went exploring, from salamanders to moths, praying mantis, crayfish, or lizards. He would then ensure our critters would end up safely back in their homes where we found them.

We also had many pets in our home, as both my mother and father loved animals. We had cats, dogs, bunnies, and later my parents let my sisters and I keep reptiles in our home. My mother, although deathly afraid of snakes, did not try to extinguish my love for all things that creep and crawl, possibly at the prodding of my father, who just wished us all to love creatures as much as they both did, despite if they had scales or feet or not. Once I found an injured garter snake that had been lacerated by a neighborhood cat, and I coddled it for a time to try to help it heal. Although shooed out of the house, I was never told to fear or hurt them, but instead, to love and protect somewhere far away from where my mom could watch. There was this one memory that is still very vivid. I was sitting in the living room, still young enough to drink out of a bottle, and Dad was picking up a pile of poop from our family dog. What he said to me that day would then define much of my adult life as a pet owner, the gecko breeder and of course, zookeeper; "Emily, poop is science." Truer words were never spoken.

At the age of 8, I was allowed to get my very first reptile pet. I don't remember much about the big day of picking out Gizard, the Green Anole, but I remember going to the pet shop every week to get crickets for my dear pet. Gizard lived a long life in our family, and he and my father helped to ignite my passion for reptiles. I recognized early on how intelligent and misunderstood these creatures were, and it soon became my goal to learn as much about reptiles, amphibians and insects as I could, and then teach all of my classmates or anyone who would listen, how important they were. My father is also a visionary for the future of reptile keeping. He has been inspired by the reptiles that I have introduced him to, and has come up with new ways to better the lives of captive reptiles by enriching their lives and igniting more natural behaviors for them through wellness and enrichment programs.

I will always love my Dad and everything he has done for me. Perhaps the best thing of all was loving me for who I was, and helping to mold me into a better, stronger person with a good sense of humor for life's unpredictable moments. Daddy, I love you!

37. A MAN AMONG BEASTS

Sally Maple

I've been described as wild a time or two. It's really no surprise, my life began in a very wild household. I mean it in the very literal sense, the wild that conjures images of the African Serengeti, tropical rainforests, and the splashing of a New Zealand shoreline. You could go on a tour of the world just walking our hallways. My father's epic travels, safaris, and research adventures meant a gathering of incredible items from all over the globe (many of which I've been thankful to inherit). Each time he ventured off, we got to look forward to the next unique item to return home with him, as well as the stories that accompanied it.

I was the youngest child, and always drawn to things my sisters weren't (like writing, music and sports). Still, I was never the black sheep. We were a family of black sheep. We were about as different as a baboon and a wildebeest. Yet there were two similarities we all shared: a ridiculous, off-the-wall sense of humor, and a fondness for nature and animals.

The beasts that filled the zoo and our home helped inspire many of the stories I've written, and also led me to keep my own pets, and protect animals whenever I can. Both of my cats are rescues; runts that may not have had much chance on their own. They are a little ragged, but aren't we all? Fishkeeping is also passion of mine. Though work and life prevents me from really diving in (pun intended), I love the saltwater and freshwater ecosystems I've built, and I look forward to continuing to cultivate that hobby.

The work my father has done has touched the lives of many (both human and otherwise). I'm proud to say that beyond his work in conservation, animal welfare, and research, he's made another great stride that others may not know about: he took a zany, misfit family and held it together like a pride on the grassland. No matter where his travels took him, he was always looking forward to seeing his family back home - perhaps more wild than any creature he went off to study.

There are plenty of brilliant, hard-working people at the top of their field. But I would venture to say that few are as good, generous, and dedicated to their family as my father is and always was. I'm glad he is able to retire and spend even more time with us. And if he needs any reminder of the incredible places he's been, all he has to do is walk from one room to the other!

38. THE OTHER MAPLE

Kathryn T. Hoff
Dalton State College

This series of writings honors Dr. Terry Maple, a good friend and colleague. But, there is another Maple who has helped make Terry what he is, and that is his wife, and my good friend, Addie. I first met Addie when I was in graduate school and she was a young, re-settled Californian, the first "faculty wife" I had the pleasure of meeting. Little did I know that our friendship would last decades, outlasting career changes, long-distance moves, and family troubles and joys. Addie has the ability to find humor in most situations, and she laughs like her late, lovely mother, Jean. She definitely has her own opinions, but she doesn't steal Terry's limelight. I remember when Terry first became the director of Zoo Atlanta. It was Addie who quietly pushed for the restrooms to be checked and cleaned on a standard schedule. The mother of three daughters, she had spent a lot of time in restrooms and knew exactly how they should be equipped and cleaned. To this day, I think of her every time I walk into a restroom at the zoo!

Did I mention she and Terry have three daughters? Three beautiful, talented daughters who have made their parents proud. I distinctly remember the birth of the first daughter, Molly. When I had my first peek at Molly, she was the most pink thing I had ever seen; pink skin, pink clothes, pink socks, pink blankets. Emily, the second, was born on the fourth of July. Starlet, the famous zoo elephant, would unfurl a banner wishing her a Happy Birthday as it passed by in the parade, so of course Emily thought the July fourth parade was for her! Then there is Sally who, taught by her older sisters, would scream "Daddy!" at every man Addie would pass with the stroller. The girls grew, learned, achieved, and became amazing young women because they had parents who loved and supported them in whatever they tried. I remember looking at the calendar in the Maple household when the girls were in elementary, middle and high school. It looked like every hour of every day was filled in with an activity, an appointment, or a meeting. To me it looked like a time management nightmare, but Addie knew where Terry and the girls were supposed to be at any given moment.

Terry lives large and somehow Addie manages it quietly, often behind the scenes. She keeps him organized and grounded. She tolerates moving, which she and Terry have often done as his career expanded. She somehow figures out where to put all the artwork Terry brings home from his world jaunts. She has a penchant for animal prints, maybe because she's had to deal with so many animals in her life; dogs, cats, birds, turtles, lizards, and more lizards. She also loves family history and has great stories about both her and Terry's relatives. Through Addie, I have come to know a different Terry Maple than I otherwise would have known. I know Terry not just as the celebrated educator, scientist and zoo director he has become, but as a deeply dedicated family man who made the incredibly intelligent decision to marry and spend his life with Addie.

FESTSCHRIFT FOR TERRY MAPLE

PART V: RETIREMENT CELEBRATION

(Editors' comment: The works in Part V: Retirement Celebration are written pieces and comments from various people at the **Celebrate the Zoo Man**, honoring Dr. Terry Maple, Director Emeritus, Zoo Atlanta, on September 4, 2003, following his retirement from Zoo Atlanta. They were provided by Bob Petty.)

39. CELEBRATE THE ZOO MAN

Anonymous

Tonight we pay tribute to Dr. Terry L. Maple for his extraordinary and dedicated leadership of Zoo Atlanta. His invaluable contributions to conservation, education, and the City of Atlanta are a tremendous source of community pride. The impact of his work extends well beyond our community to the whole State of Georgia, global conservation efforts, and the entire zoo and aquarium field.

In December 2002, after 17 ½ years at the helm of Zoo Atlanta, Dr. Maple announced his retirement as President & CEO to accept an appointment as Founding Director of the Center for Conservation & Behavior at Georgia Tech. He is continuing his relationship with the Zoo as Director Emeritus, but his day-to-day guidance and inspiration will be missed. While many people have played a part in the Zoo Atlanta story throughout its 114 years, Dr. Maple has undeniably had the biggest influence on shaping the beloved zoological park we enjoy today.

What started as a temporary Interim Director appointment in 1984 evolved over nearly two decades into a phenomenal success story known throughout the zoo world. That year, Atlanta Mayor Andrew Young appointed Dr. Maple, a Georgia Tech psychology professor and former member of the Atlanta Zoological Society, to the post of Interim Zoo Director in hopes he would lead an ailing institution. Three months later, Maple, an expert on great ape behavior and former Deputy Director of the Audubon Zoo, was appointed permanent Zoo Director. Following the privatization of the Zoo in 1985, Dr. Maple was elected as the first President & CEO of the newly established nonprofit organization.

Within three years under Dr. Maple's direction, Zoo Atlanta was accredited by the American Zoo and Aquarium (AZA) and named "Atlanta's Best-Managed Nonprofit Corporation" by the Community Foundation for Greater Atlanta, an honor is achieved again in 2000. Zoo Atlanta has been named one of the nation's worst zoos in 1984 by Parade Magazine; in 1994, it was named one of the ten best and was chosen to host the National Conference of the AZA. The renowned Ford African Rain Forest, in which Zoo Atlanta's venerable icon Willie B. took his first steps outdoors in 27 years, opened in 1988. This remarkably naturalistic exhibit quickly became a model for gorilla habitats. The first gorilla birth for Zoo Atlanta followed in 1989, with the 13th gorilla birth celebrated 13 years later in spring 2002. The culmination of Zoo Atlanta's progress and Dr. Maple's drive came in November 1999 with the arrival of Zoo Atlanta's giant panda pair. Dr. Maple had devoted more than a decade to his dream of exhibiting and studying this critically endangered species. Having giant pandas cemented Zoo Atlanta's place as a star in the zoo industry, and attracted a record breaking one million visitors in 2000. During his tenure, Dr. Maple not only redeemed Zoo Atlanta - he took it to a new level of excellence not previously imagined.

As Zoo Atlanta's reputation was gaining international significance under Dr. Maple's guidance, so was that of its leader. In 1995, Dr. Maple testified before Congress on behalf of the Endangered Species Act, and the Smithsonian Press published *Ethics in the Ark*, a groundbreaking work on the future of zoos and animal welfare on which Dr. Maple was an editor. 1998 marked milestones for Dr. Maple in both his zoo and academic endeavors. He was elected president of the AZA, and he became the first occupant of the Elizabeth Smithgall Watts Chair in Conservation and Behavior at Georgia Tech. That same year, the Atlanta Chapter of the Stanford Business School Alumni voted Dr. Maple "Entrepreneur of the Year." In 1999, as he realized his dream of giant pandas at Zoo Atlanta, he was honored with the Atlanta Convention and Visitors Bureau President's Award. The story of bringing giant pandas to Zoo

Atlanta was proudly told in Dr. Maple's 2000 book, *Saving the Giant Panda*. President George W. Bush named Dr. Maple to the prestigious national board of the Institute of Museum Services in 2002. As he entered his 25th year on the faculty of Georgia Tech, the unique opportunity to found the university's Center for Conservation & Behavior and return full-time to his passion for research prompted Dr. Maple's decision to retire from a distinguished career at Zoo Atlanta.

A lion's share of credit is owed to Dr. Maple for making Zoo Atlanta what it is today - a thriving wildlife park for families and an invaluable resource for recreation, education, and conservation. His name will forever be synonymous with Zoo Atlanta's amazing transformation and success. It took a man of Dr. Maple's unyielding vision to see what Zoo Atlanta could become, and to work tirelessly to achieve a world-class status that many would not have thought possible. His legacy of growth and excellence will continue to guide the future of Zoo Atlanta.

40. COMMENTS BY THE CHAIR

Bob Petty
Former board member and chair of Zoo Atlanta and of
Friends of Zoo Atlanta.

"Terry Maple is a wonderful friend, a big, larger-than-life, lovable, compassionate, loyal, dedicated and determined man who has made, and continues to make, this world a much better place. He selected, mentored, and developed a cadre of people who have made and still make very meaningful contributions. Terry's vision, effectiveness, team building, tenacity, and dedication in involving politicians, donors, board members, volunteers, and staff in creating a wonderful zoo will pay dividends for many years to come. He is truly a man who saw what needed to be done, did it, and left his indelible mark on zoos and animal welfare everywhere. We are grateful to him for all he has done and proud to count him as a friend.

There is a virtually unlimited supply of people here tonight who could pay proper tribute to Terry Maple. You will be relieved to know that only three have been chosen to speak. I am pleased to introduce these three great personal friends of Terry Maple and Zoo Atlanta who are here to help you honor this unique man we love and respect so much.

Jeff Swanagan, head of the Georgia Aquarium is a former member of the Zoo Atlanta staff. Terry attracted many stellar people to make up the team that now supports Dennis Kelly. Others, like

Jeff, have acceded to important positions elsewhere in the zoo world.

Jeff, originally a science teacher, got his start at the Columbus Zoo. He worked with Terry at Zoo Atlanta for 11 years until the Florida Aquarium offered him the directorship and tremendous challenge of rescuing that institution. Earning a reputation as a strong administrator and creative marketer, Jeff has returned to Atlanta to build and lead the Georgia Aquarium.

Syd Butler is Executive Director of the American Zoo and Aquarium Association - the AZA. Prior to Syd's tenure, Zoo Atlanta was so bad that the AZA expelled Zoo Atlanta from its membership rather than merely refusing to accredit Zoo Atlanta.

At the time, little did we know how big a favor they did us. Since then Terry achieved accreditation and national recognition for turning Zoo Atlanta around to the extent that Terry was elected President of the national zoo organization. During the time of Terry's presidency, Syd and he worked closely together to create new and significant initiatives for diversity and for assessing the state of science in zoos. Syd has served as Executive Director of the AZA since 1992. Prior to that he was vice president for Conservation at the Wilderness Society. Syd has practiced environmental law and holds a University of Virginia law degree.

We are honored to have as our third speaker The Honorable Andrew Young. Ambassador Young is Chairman of GoodWorks International, a specialty consulting group providing strategic services to corporations and governments operating in the global economy. He also serves as public affairs professor of policy studies at Georgia State University's Andrew Young School of Policy Studies. An ordained minister, a top aide to Martin Luther King, Jr., and former vice president of the Southern Christian Leadership Conference, he was elected to three terms in the U.S. House of Representatives. In 1977, he was named Ambassador to the United Nations. He served two terms as Mayor of Atlanta, and was Co-Chairman of the Centennial Olympic Games in 1996. Zoo Atlanta and Terry are beholden to our friend Andy Young for his administration's bold move to privatize Zoo Atlanta. Ambassador Young's moving tribute to Willie B included the statement that ' ... thanks to Terry Maple ... this was the first and still the most successful privatization by Atlanta city government.'"

41. READING OF RESOLUTION BY BOARD OF DIRECTORS, ZOO ATLANTA

Bob Petty

"How fitting each of your remarks were! What an act to follow. Our thanks to Jeff, Syd, and Andy, and kudos to those who brought us the video tribute.

We also thank Terry's spouse, Addie Maple and their daughters Emily, Molly, and Sally for the support they have given Terry and, thereby, to Zoo Atlanta. Terry, you're the recipient of resolutions by the city council, and the state House and Senate, offered in your honor and displayed here tonight. Printed in the program are a lovely letter from Mayor Franklin and playful insights from Lessie Smithgall. In addition I want to read the resolution offered by the Board of Directors of Zoo Atlanta:

RESOLUTION OF APPRECIATION

WHEREAS: Dr. Terry Maple contributed immeasurably to the success of Zoo Atlanta; and,

WHEREAS: On August 31, 2003, Dr. Maple officially retired as President and CEO of Zoo Atlanta; and,

WHEREAS: His efforts in leading Zoo Atlanta brought pride and national acclaim to Zoo Atlanta, to the Atlanta community, to the City of Atlanta, to Fulton County, and to all the people and staff associated with Zoo Atlanta; and,

WHEREAS: Under the direction of Dr. Maple, Zoo Atlanta

pioneered efforts in animal conservation, science, and research for which the Zoo has been recognized throughout the world; and,

WHEREAS: Out of ashes he brought a Phoenix of bold and grand vision for animal exhibition, treatment, and conservation, while enhancing the visitor experience and education at Zoo Atlanta; and,

WHEREAS: Dr. Maple opened the eyes of Atlanta to its inadequate treatment of Willie B. and all the animals of Zoo Atlanta and showed the world that zoo animals possess near-human traits; and,

WHEREAS: Dr. Maple set new goals and standards for significant fund raising and capital improvements for Atlanta and its zoo; and,

WHEREAS: Dr. Maple attracted, retained, and developed a staff of highly professional individuals who afford quality and stability to Zoo Atlanta: and,

WHEREAS: Dr. Maple was a loving parent to Zoo Atlanta, remaining true to himself while resolving conflict and crisis, providing stability and strength, and came to be loved by all of us in his extended family; and,

WHEREAS: Zoo Atlanta has, through the efforts, leadership, and inspiration of Terry Maple, become one of America's premier zoos; and,

WHEREAS: Terry Maple has been duly recognized by Zoo Atlanta as a stellar recipient of its Silver Backer Award; and,

NOW, THEREFORE, BE IT RESOLVED: That the Board of Directors of Zoo Atlanta extends to Dr. Terry Maple their most sincere appreciation for exceptional service and significant accomplishments; and,

BE IT FURTHER RESOLVED: That the Board of Directors of Zoo Atlanta has bestowed upon Dr. Terry Maple the honorary title Director Emeritus, and that he shall hold this title in perpetuity."

42. STEPHANIE POWERS LETTER

Read by Bob Petty

"One response to tonight's invitation is very unique and special. Only a man of Terry's talents and charisma would receive a retirement letter like the one I am about to read. It is from Stephanie Powers - the Hollywood actress who notably founded the William Holden Wildlife Foundation to carry on Holden's conservation efforts in Kenya.

Dear Terry,

You are far too young to retire! But since you have decided to do so, you have to be prepared to suffer hearing all the things people will be saying to extol your virtues and herald your accomplishments.

Most of all, I have my fondest memories of you at the beginning of your challenges with the zoo. I too became excited by your vision and belief that you could create a magical place for animals and people, and you did it.

I also remember the intrepid explorer, as we tramped through jungles and ran the river rapids in Sumatra. Your tent making techniques were ... how shall I say ... exemplary ... of what? I cannot say.

You are a special person, Terry, and your presence will be greatly missed. You do take up a big space - not only with your size - but most of all with your HEART - be well always.

I love you too!
(signed) Stefanie Powers"

43. PRESENTATION OF THE PORTRAIT

Bob Petty

"Terry, will you come forward? And I'd like to ask Carl Strobe, Zoo Atlanta's Artist-in Residence, to join us. Terry, we have framed this letter for you. Addie, will it frame him? Terry, I know that you and Carl became friends over his panda paintings, and that you are the owner of an original Panda painting and a Willie B. drawing of his. For this gift, Carl very wisely chose as his subject our male lion Farasi, and painted him especially for you, our "Lion King" for so many years.

In May at the Beastly Feast, Terry was honored with Zoo Atlanta's highest honor - the Silver Backer award. Tonight I am pleased to announce that Zoo Atlanta has commissioned an oil portrait similar to those surrounding you in this room. The portraits of Bob Holder, Carolyn Hatcher, Bob Strickland and soon that of Terry will occupy a spaces of honor as Terry joins to this esteemed group of influential and effective friends of his and of Zoo Atlanta. The artist who is painting Terry's oil portrait and who also painted the Holder and Hatcher portraits is here tonight. Ellen, would you please stand and be recognized? Also in this room there is a terra cotta drawing of Terry. This is an early step in the process of capturing Terry in oil and will be given, courtesy of an anonymous donor, upon completion of the portrait. One of your colleagues was heard to remark upon seeing that drawing, 'Why I once knew that man.' The fountain of youth lies in the hands of an artist."

229

44. "OWED" TO TERRY
(from the Program)

Lessie Smithgall

Why do I admire thee?
Let me count the ways.

You and Carolyn Hatcher developed the beloved zoo of my childhood from one of the ten worst in the country to one of the best.

You negotiated the loan of a pair of giant pandas form China for a stay at Zoo Atlanta…

You took me on two safaris to Africa, where you were a knowledgeable and delightful companion.

You nurtured Atlanta's icon, Willie B., to become the most famous gorilla father in captivity.

You have done Georgia Tech proud for many years as a distinguished professor of psychology, and now as director of the new Center for Conservation and Behavior.

You love animals, wild or tame (except possibly poisonous snakes) as much as I do.

You are a caring husband, and a father to three accomplished daughters.

You were a great friend of my daughter, Bay.

Let other tell funny stories about you (and I could do the same)...I have to be serious about why you mean a lot to me.

With admiration and affection.

Lessie Smithgall

45. FROM THE OFFICE OF THE MAYOR
(from the Program)

The Honorable Shirley Franklin
Mayor

Dear Terry:

On behalf of the City of Atlanta, I would like to express our sincere gratitude to you for nearly two decades of service to one of the city's most beloved attractions, Zoo Atlanta. Under your charismatic guidance the zoo has emerged a tremendous cultural resource for Atlanta, and we are proud to claim you as our own!

As a member of Mayor Andy Young's administration, I witnessed firsthand your remarkable leadership in action. You had the vision necessary to make Zoo Atlanta great, and the ability to gather a team of high level staff and concerned volunteers to help translate that vision and make your dreams for Atlanta's zoo a reality. In the years since, I have continued to be amazed by your accomplishments. Zoo Atlanta will forever represent one of our city's greatest success stories.

Atlanta is fortunate and honored to have had such an extraordinary mind establish the mission of animal welfare,

conservation and scientific progress at Zoo Atlanta. I have no doubt
that your work at the Center for Conservation & Behavior at Georgia
Tech will continue to bring acclaim to our city and state. I wish you
the best in your future endeavors.

Sincerely,
Shirley Franklin
Mayor

46. REMARKS AT WILLIE B.'S MEMORIAL SERVICE FEBRUARY 5, 2000

Ambassador Andrew Young

Two of the things for which this city is most famous were named for our beloved mayor, William B. Hartsfield. We named the airport for him because he conceived the importance of aviation when very few cities did. On my first trip to the Atlanta airport in the 50's, it was just a single runway with a temporary Army Quonset hut, but even then Mayor Hartsfield saw to it that the runway was long enough to land jet aircraft. So when a little baby gorilla was found in Africa, people loved him and named him for the mayor that they loved, and he had the same kind of impact on our city that the mayor did. We looked at him in his cage, and we knew that he didn't belong there. He was brought here in captivity but he found a way to appeal to our hearts so that we were moved to find ways to set him free. And in setting him free, perhaps we set ourselves free to help us learn that we can live together in peace with all of the animals that God has created. We were able to do that, and thanks to Terry Maple and Zoo Atlanta this was the first and still the most successful privatization by Atlanta city government. And you make the case very well. Certainly a group of private citizens with a cause, who love the zoo, can do better with their own funds, with their own love, and with their own dedication to the animals of the Earth than we ever could have done simply with tax payers' money. We celebrated Willie B.'s freedom and we laughed with him when he got his first girlfriend. But, you know, he was always a flirt. He was always very, very fresh, and the last memory that I have of Willie B. was at the Beastly Feast last year when he came down right to the glass and looked at my wife and started making eyes at her. And I was so glad there was a partition there, because I didn't want to have to slug him. But in loving Willie B. and having Willie B. love us, I think we've begun to get a clue of the relationships that are possible between God's children who are human and God's children of other species. And how we relate together in a peaceful, loving environment. We've demonstrated that some few animals can be set free, but I go to Africa all the time and there are wonderful, beautiful game parks there where animals and people live side by side and where they help each other to prosper in areas that were formerly impoverished until the animals and the people got together. And I hope that we can find ways through this zoo, through this community to extend the communication. We don't know what the animals think of us, but we sure know we love them. And I think that love can be multiplied and can bear fruits that are yet unimagined by any of us at present. But when we do see wonderful things happening between men and women and animals, let's remember this giant, lovable gorilla who was almost human. Or maybe we were almost really and truly God's animals when we related to him.

Thank you, and thank God for Willie B.

FESTSCHRIFT FOR TERRY MAPLE

PART VI: COMMENTARY AND ADDENDA

47. VOYAGE OF THE ETHICAL ARK

Terry L. Maple

Other than Heini Hediger, I know of no other tenured university professor who has had the experience of leading a zoo. Of course Professor Hediger was the best role model I could hope to emulate as he managed to carry out his administrative duties at the zoo while serving on the faculty of the University of Zurich as a mentor, lecturer, and highly productive disseminator of scholarly papers and books. I don't know how Hediger did it, but whatever success I enjoyed was a function of teamwork. I recruited talented, hard-working students and colleagues who helped to expand the footprint of our collective endeavors. Acknowledging our debt to the academy, the title for this volume was influenced by a textbook on animal psychology (*Tierpsychologie*) that shaped Hediger's ideas, written coincidentally by his German mentor, Robert Sommer (1925).

The Robert Sommer who mentored me is now Distinguished Professor Emeritus at UC Davis. As a member of my graduate advisory committee in 1970, he suggested I take the time to study Hediger, but he did not foresee that I would learn as much from Hediger's leadership as I would learn from his publications. Like Hediger my career is a unique blend of scholarship and leadership. When I was summoned by Mayor Andrew Young to take the reins of Atlanta's struggling municipal zoo, I was delivered the perfect storm to manage. The zoo crisis had bottomed out, although I didn't recognize it at the time. As a theoretician, I dared to put my ideas and core values to the test, and subject all of it to scientific scrutiny. My team understood we were conspiring to create a truly empirical zoo, but we also understood that our efforts to put the animals first was also a highly ethical commitment. My students were the real beneficiaries of this institutional *tabula rasa* as they immediately went to work examining all aspects of zoo planning, husbandry, education, science, and management. Together we restructured Atlanta's zoo, from top to bottom. Our work prospered from the awesome power of a community mandate for change. Zoo Atlanta, depicted by its very name as a 180-degree turn-around, was an unprecedented organizational experiment and a model for all zoos on the verge of serious, sudden and dynamic change.

Origins of the Empirical Zoo

On my first day on the job I was visited by veterinarians from the United States Department of Agriculture (USDA). There wasn't much time for small talk as they wanted to examine the zoo's animal records. As the reform director I wanted to cooperate, but there was no sign of any animal records. When some paperwork eventually turned up in the trunk of the consulting veterinarian's automobile, they were quickly subpoenaed, never to be returned. Eager to save face, I assigned my newest and most quantitative graduate student, Lorraine Perkins to invent and install a new state-of-the-art records system that could not be corrupted or ignored. Within one year, Lori had succeeded in elevating our records to a user-friendly version compatible with the newest hardware and software invented for systematic records management in a zoo. She also assisted our new veterinarian, Dr. Rita McManamon, in putting together an advanced medical records system, vaulting our zoo out of the dark ages and into the modern world of the International Species Inventory System (ISIS). These were huge leaps forward for us and our official entry into the fraternity of reputable zoos.

To show our new face, and to advance our standing among peers, I sent Lori all around the world to learn and to share her ideas with other young colleagues. Years later, she has become the top animal manager at Zoo Atlanta and one of the most astute general curators in the Association of Zoos and Aquariums (AZA). Our IT/IS unit eventually became a cornerstone of Zoo Atlanta's empirical approach to problem-solving. One day when our IT manager reported that technology geeks at the San Diego Zoo proclaimed that Zoo Atlanta was the only zoo in America that could match their expertise I knew we had achieved a benchmark.

The quantitative resources at Georgia Tech became a major advantage in preparing students for careers in academia and in the zoo world. Several of my students touted their quantitative preparation as a means to win jobs in universities. Dr. Lawrence James was particularly helpful to our students and he appeared as a co-author on several publications. Georgia Tech's ability to teach statistics and methodology enabled several graduates of our program to win jobs and opportunities to grow their academic credentials. Another student who benefitted from quantitative courses at Tech, Chris Kuhar, has published important methodology papers in the scientific journal *Zoo Biology* and these contributions have helped to advance research metrics utilized by zoo biologists (Kuhar, 2006) throughout the world. The faculty at Georgia Tech provided access to useful specialized knowledge in ethics (Bryan Norton), environmental design (Jean Wineman), behavior analysis (Jack Marr), and cognitive science (Anderson Smith). Our collaboration with architects and engineers at Tech resulted in a number of innovative products including "Virtual Gorilla," the first use of virtual reality in a zoo environment. Additional intellectual talent assembled at the zoo (Debra Forthman, Duane Jackson, Dietrich Schaaf, Beth Stevens) provided breadth in all aspects of animal behavior and biodiversity. When Mollie Bloomsmith arrived at the zoo to direct our research program, she took all of the students under her wing and turned the Georgia Tech Laboratory for Animal Behavior (TECHlab) into a disciplined behavior research unit. I don't think any zoo has ever assembled so many scientific colleagues who worked so well together.

Following this chapter, the list of publications from the Maple lab illustrates the breadth and depth of the research we conducted together. We published 39 papers, chapters, and books on gorillas, 19 on pandas, 13 on orangutans, 9 on chimpanzees and 17 on great apes. There were 7 publications on elephants, 5 on giraffe, 4 on tigers, and 2 on lions. 33 publications concerned zoos and zoo research, 7 discussed animal welfare and wellness, and 6 articles were focused on leadership. We also wrote about teaching, behavior analysis, enrichment, education, and conservation. Flamingos, macaques, mandrills, okapi, otters, prosimians, and tamarins were also subjects of our research publications.

The Ethical Ark Evolving

The challenge of building an ethical ark was greatly facilitated by my business mentors who supported my priorities and guided my business decisions. Carolyn Boyd Hatcher and Robert C. Petty kept me focused on the tough day-to-day problem-solving that raised the bar on our aspirations. We were the first AZA zoo to privatize in 1985. Our first chairman, Robert M. Holder, Jr., was an inspiring and uncompromising leader in the City of Atlanta who rallied the business community to take responsibility for the zoo's *renaissance*. Over the years, we continued to attract talented board members who linked us up with financial and human resources necessary to achieving our full potential as a non-profit and a leadership position among world zoos. During the early stages of privatization, the planning and implementation of a new operating system was nurtured by Susan Hood. Without her creativity and skill and her commitment to excellence, the new zoo would not have been possible. Whenever I had a problem that could not be solved by the city bureaucracy she found a way to get it done. I am also grateful for the stewardship of Lynn Flanders who successfully managed our accounting division and served as our first CFO.

Along the way to the zoo's recovery and restoration, we built iconic exhibits such as the Ford African Rain Forest, arguably the finest gorilla exhibit in the world at the time of its opening in 1988, and the innovative giant panda exhibit opened in 1999 as the second pair of pandas entered the United States under the new, stringent requirements of the U.S. Fish & Wildlife Service (San Diego was the first). All of these exhibits were designed by CLR, the Philadelphia design firm started by Gary Lee and Jon Coe, now recognized as the best zoo designers in the world. (Gary was kind enough to serve as the principal sponsor of my *festschrift* party in Atlanta.) Everyone who served in my administration or afterwards beat their collective chests when Zoo Atlanta in 2011 was honored with the prestigious Bean Award for fifty years of success with lowland gorillas, and shared the Conservation Award for its work benefitting giant pandas in China. These honors were the culmination of a community's commitment to save its zoo and nurture it to prosperity and achievement.

The crisis in Atlanta was as much a medical as a management emergency. For that reason one of my first steps forward was the recruitment of Dr. Rita McManamon to serve as the organization's first fulltime veterinarian. She was an immediate success, a testimony to her calm demeanor, decisive leadership, medical expertise, and unwavering ethical principles. Humane animal management was firmly enforced with Dr. Rita at the helm of our medical program. In the early days we also benefited from two talented curators of mammals, John Croxton and Tony Vecchio. They joined Dr. Dietrich Schaff to reinforce a system of best practices and superior standards. Soon thereafter we hired the zoo's first bird curator, Guy Farnell, and he was a steady hand as we fledged our bird program. Sadly, Guy died early in his tenure at the zoo, but his imprint on our programs and our wildlife vision will live forever.

Launching Leaders

My colleagues have observed that no zoo director in my peer group has produced more successor directors. While most of these emerging zoo and aquarium leaders worked as members of my staff, many of my graduate students have been recently recruited to lead organizations. Former senior staff who became directors throughout the nation include Jeff Swanagan (Florida Aquarium, Georgia Aquarium, Columbus Zoo), Bert Castro (Oklahoma City Zoo, Phoenix Zoo), Tony Vecchio (Roger Williams Zoo, Oregon Zoo, Jacksonville Zoo), Rich Block (Santa Barbara Zoo), Craig Piper (Denver Zoo and WCS-affiliated city zoos), Steve Marshall (El Paso Zoo), Dwight Lawson (Oklahoma City Zoo), Bert Davis (Milwaukee County Zoological Society), Tom LaRock (Friends of the National Zoo), and Clare Richardson (Dian Fossey Gorilla Fund International).

Former graduate students who have become directors include Chris Kuhar (Cleveland Metroparks Zoo), Tara Stoinski (Dian Fossey Gorilla Fund International, succeeding Clare Richardson), and Jackie Ogden (Disney's Animal Kingdom). Jackie enjoys the singular achievement as the only one of my academic offspring who succeeded me as Chair of the Board of Directors of AZA. I was Chair in 1999; Jackie is the current Chair fifteen years later. I'm sure this unique succession is unprecedented in the long history of AZA. Waiting in the wings are Kyle Burks, former Deputy Director of

Denver Zoo and a metrician at DAK, and Megan Reinertsen-Ross, General Curator of the Lincoln Park Zoo, sure bets to become the next zoo directors with earned doctorates from Georgia Tech. From my perspective, the Zoo Atlanta-Georgia Tech partnership was an incubator for both scholarship and leadership. This generation of new leaders is already making a difference in the realm of animal welfare, conservation, and public education, and they are building better zoos with creative architecture and better standards and practices. One of my students exercised her leadership in academia when Gwen Murdock became Chairman of the Psychology Department at Southwest Missouri State University, while Mike Hoff recently ascended to the Chair of Social Sciences at Dalton State College. There had to be something in the Atlanta water to produce so many leaders, or was it the ominous challenge we faced together, in a situation that required heavy lifting by each and every one of us? Beyond the truths expressed in their essays herein, I hope to learn more about the wellspring of their aspirations as their careers unfold and evolve.

Inspiration and Aspirations

This *festschrift* volume spans a long period of time, from graduate school in Davis when I was just beginning to mine zoos as a research resource to the days when the entire team was immersed in studying and managing Atlanta's zoo in some way or another. Although Professor Sommer directed me to Hediger's work during graduate school, I was inspired by the wildlife exhibited at my hometown zoo at an early age. Growing up in San Diego, important family outings and holidays were almost always spent at the San Diego Zoo in Balboa Park. In those days, you could picnic in the zoo and we carried Grandma Maple's home-cooked chicken and famous mustard-based potato salad packed into our very own picnic basket. Fueling my devotion to nostalgia, I recently acquired Grandma's yellow Pyrex potato salad bowl, now a Maple family icon in our pantry. Those were the days!

As a kid I was fascinated by giant snakes and I would always race to the reptile building after entering the zoo, beckoning my family to follow me. This was, even then, the world-famous San Diego Zoo and we were lucky to be able to visit the zoo so often. As much as I enjoyed it, I never knew you could make a living working in such a place. Zoo directors, curators, and veterinarians didn't have the high public profile they enjoy in the 21st century. Many of the animals were iconic but they weren't marketed to the extent they are today. Given my personal history, it is not surprising that my daughter Emily became a herpetologist/zoo keeper. Her fearlessness in the garden is evoked in her childhood nickname; "the bug-master." Like her dad, she is drawn to big critters; she cares for alligators and Komodo dragons among the other reptiles at the Palm Beach Zoo.

I may have been the first San Diego county kid to become a zoo director, in my case at the ripe age of 38, but I wasn't the only one. In another weird coincidence, Jackie Ogden was also raised in San Diego and she too considers it to be her home town zoo. As Jackie became CEO of Disney's Animal Kingdom (equivalent to a zoo director) this is a distinction we both share now. During my formative professorial years in Atlanta, I used to dream of how I might help the City of Atlanta to upgrade the zoo so the kids in Atlanta could experience the joy of exploring a truly great zoo, as I did in San Diego. It was a dream of course not based in reality as professors don't normally morph into zoo directors. How it happened in my case is a long story more appropriate for another book. With some help from Tony Vecchio and Jackie Ogden, I plan to write my next book, *Professor in the Zoo*, with input from staff at Jacksonville and Disney's Animal Kingdom, and conversations and questions from eager undergraduates at Florida Atlantic's Honors College. Like everything I've accomplished in my career, this book will be a team effort.

Zoo research, in my case, evolved out of monkey watching at the California Primate Research Center. I supervised a large cadre of undergraduate students during a post-doctoral year when I was employed in the Behavioral Biology unit of the UCD Medical School. My best observer was Mike Hoff and he took an interest in studies I was doing at the nearby Sacramento Zoo. My girlfriend at the time (now my wife, Addie) helped me discover two oddities at this zoo. The first was a two-species social system comprised of South American spider and capuchin (Cebus spp.) monkeys. We were surprised when the spiders presented their backs to the smaller capuchins and took them around the monkey island as if they were a taxi service. As I later learned, this unusual behavior had not been previously documented. With the approval of Sacramento Zoo director Bill Meeker, I visited the zoo often to gather data with my students and we published a paper on this two-species phenomenon in the journal *Applied Animal Ethology* (Maple & Westlund, 1975). Addie also helped me generate a hypothesis about fear of reptile houses, when she refused to enter the reptile building at the Sacramento Zoo. Mike Hoff subsequently conducted observations summarized in another publication based on Sacramento and Atlanta Zoo data, confirming our discovery of a distinct gender difference in refusals to enter reptile buildings (Hoff & Maple, 1982). This was the first time that I clearly understood the full research potential of zoos. I was fascinated by the biodiversity in zoos and aquariums and encouraged by the many species that had not yet been studied by psychologists. My career was beginning to take shape.

Opportunity Knocks

When I was offered my first academic appointment at Emory University I was very excited at the prospect of being able to study the largest collection of great apes in the world at the affiliated Yerkes Primate Research Center in Atlanta. As a native Californian, moving to the south was daunting, but my advisors kept me from chickening out. The Emory opportunity was the best job in my field in 1975. After a week of contemplation at Larry Blake's Rathskeller bar in Davis, I was sufficiently fortified to accept the challenge. Once Addie and I had settled in Atlanta, we began our adjustment to a new way of life, a completely different world than Davis. The best aspect about the move was the quality of the students. At the graduate and undergraduate level they were bright and curious, hand-working and ambitious, easily the equal of UC students I had mentored, although Hoff and Bloomsmith, whom I knew as undergraduates at Davis, were as good as it gets. The research at Yerkes was slow to develop, but I quickly gained access to the Yerkes apes living at the zoo and I made the most of this opportunity. My strategy from the beginning was to open doors and create opportunities for bright young minds to do their best work on behalf of the wildlife we were privileged to observe. Early in my career, my research mentors, Martin Gipson and Gary Mitchell, taught me to eagerly share scarce resources.

My very first graduate student at Emory was Evan Zucker and he immediately impressed me with his positive attitude, great sense of humor, and his patience. You have to have an abundance of patience to watch orangutans watching you. On the first day that we visited the Atlanta Zoo together we observed intense play between a fully adult male and his four-year old male offspring. This had never been described in the literature for this species. We also witnessed rough and tumble copulations and left the zoo convinced that the Atlanta Zoo would become our laboratory. And so it did.

One of the best undergraduate students who worked in our group was a straight-A student who was pre-med at Emory. Mary Beth Dennon was looking for an Honor's Thesis when she discovered our lab. As a psychology major she liked what we were doing at the zoo and started to observe orangutans under Evan's tutelage. The three of us suspected something was up when an adult female began to vigorously pursue her male consort. We had been led to believe that orangutans were the only apes that did not exhibit "proceptive" courtship behavior, that is, the aggressive pursuit of a male to initiate sexual contact. Beth's project was a game-changer as she documented three successive months of thirty-day peaks in proceptive female behavior. We had the data and a convincing super-8 mm film to document our discovery. She published these data in her 1976 Honor's Thesis and we later published the findings in the journal *Behavioural Processes* (Maple et al, 1979). My largely under-ground film became famously known as "Deep Throat Sac" amusing a succession of undergraduates in my animal behavior classes. I doubt that I could show this film today. Beth's passion for orangutans led her to change her focus to veterinary medicine. She received a degree from Georgia and took up private practice in the Atlanta area. Our highly successful ape research lab influenced a number of other undergraduates who went on to graduate studies in animal behavior, veterinary medicine, and other fields.

In 1976 Mike Hoff drove from California to Atlanta to become my first recruited graduate student. He fortuitously arrived at a time when Ron Nadler needed a research assistant so we formed a collaboration to take advantage of the birth of three gorillas at the Lawrenceville Field Station. They lived in a family unit equivalent to free-ranging lowland gorillas, comprised of one silverback male, three adult females and their offspring in a large compound suitable for daily observations. Many publications resulted from this collaboration and set up Mike to become the greatest gorilla watcher of all time, now 38 years and counting. When I left Emory after three years to take a superior position at Georgia Tech, I kept my ties to Evan and Mike who managed to jump through all the hoops without me as their official faculty supervisor. This may have been my first experience with "stealth" leadership as I continued to guide them unseen by my former Emory colleagues. Evan and Mike were my first academic offspring who knew me when I was a much younger and more playful professor. I am especially gratified that Evan and Mike both became highly successful college professors committed to undergraduate instruction but still engaged in research.

Conservation Priorities

Mike's gorilla expertise enabled us to write an important book on the biology and behavior of gorillas designed to improve captive management (Maple & Hoff, 1982). As he writes in his essay, Mike also accompanied me on my first forays into Africa with my "Fieldwork in Animal Behavior" travel program targeted to under-graduates. Beth Stevens, then an undergraduate at Duke, was one of the students who travelled with me. Africa changed my life, just as my former student Bruce Westlund promised it would. Once I had observed wild baboons in East Africa, in Bruce's company, I no longer thought of primates from the perspective of their confinement. To me, all monkeys and apes reflected their natural propensities shaped by their evolution in the wild. Experience in the bush, with twenty-five excursions to Africa recorded to date, has greatly influenced my thinking about zoo design, and this has been revealed in my publications (e.g. Maple & Perdue, 2013). I met many field scientists in Africa and hired two of them, Debra Forthman and Tom Butynski. They both contributed immensely to Zoo Atlanta's conservation mission. In Debra's essay she discusses the ignominious end of this unit due to financial problems in the late nineties. In my seventeen years at the helm we confronted and overcame every impediment, but our aspirations were frequently challenged by a highly variable economic climate. Some things I could not change, although as CEO I had to confront every issue, no matter how unpleasant. My business mentors, Bob Holder, Bob Petty, Llew Haden, Terry Gordon, Terry Harps, and many others, taught me that business was cyclic even though my aspirations were linear. Unlike academia, I learned, the highs of business were very high indeed, and the lows were abysmally, painfully low. The demise of our highly regarded field unit was a bitter disappointment.

During my career as a zoo executive, conservation became the highest priority of zoos and aquariums. In recent years I've suggested that animal welfare should be regarded as an equally high priority as it is synergistic with conservation (Maple & Perdue, 2013). In addition to supporting the field work of Dr. Butynski in East Africa for nine years, Zoo Atlanta also became the home for the Dian Fossey Gorilla Fund International. While serving as its President I authorized the organization's move from Denver to Atlanta in 1995. Under the direction of Clare Richardson DFGF International has become one of the most important conservation organizations operating in Africa today. The unique partnership of DFGFI and Zoo Atlanta complements the zoo's commitment to lowland gorilla conservation and science, and provides a framework for understanding all species of gorillas. Our collaborations with field scientists and conservation biologists always informed and improved our work with captive animals.

All in the Family

One of the key factors in the success of our research group was the idea that we were ourselves a primate troop, essentially a family concept. This was first revealed to me when I worked with Gary Mitchell, a student of Harry F. Harlow. Harlow produced a large number of developmental psychologists who studied monkeys. Gary landed at the California Primate Center in its formative years and took a position in the Psychology Department at Davis. His office mate at the primate center was a young anthropologist, Don Lindburg, a student of the esteemed Sherwood Washburn. Offspring of Harlow and Washburn were among the leaders who formulated American primatology, and this support system greatly influenced my thinking about how psychology labs should work.

During my graduate student days and early in my academic career I collaborated with my good friend Joe Erwin who thought big about primatology, founding with other young Turks and a few silverbacks, the American Society of Primatologists and then putting together a deal to publish the *American Journal of Primatology*, now in its thirty-fifth year of continuous publication. Joe's success in the founding of *AJP* encouraged me to start the journal *Zoo Biology* in 1982 utilizing the same publisher, Alan R. Liss. Both journals were purchased by John Wiley years later but we will always be grateful to Mr. Liss for his confidence in our vision for these two journals.

The family model illustrated by Harlow's group, required trust and opportunity so each member of the team was inspired to gather information, organize it, publish it and talk about it. The Harlow system was revealed in full bloom at the Tucson *festschrift* celebration for Harlow in 1976. Each of his represented students brought one of their own to provide a good look at the impact of the extended family. Mitchell invited me to represent his line. This was my first academic reunion and it was extraordinary. The Harlow family has always been characterized by hard work, an active network, high productivity, and loads of fun (especially at conventions). I continue to advise my students to never forget their academic brothers and sisters, stay connected, and expect to be helped by their academic aunts and uncles. After forty-seven years of friendship, Joe Erwin and I continue to collaborate in the Harlow tradition and I still write papers and books with many of my students long after they graduated. Looking back, now in semi-retirement, my students are continuing the line, from Harlow to Mitchell, to Maple, to each of them, and to their academic offspring. In recent years, I have had the privilege of meeting several of my academic grand-offspring. What a pant-hoot!

Beginning in 1975 and continuing when my last Georgia Tech student, Allison Martin, obtains her Ph.D., nearly forty years as I write this in 2014, it has been a great run. Like the speed of parenting itself, academic mentoring goes by at a fast pace but I still enjoy the memories, basking in the glory of our achievements, and I continue to write about our work as I am doing now with the ending chapter of this *festschrift* volume edited by Mike, Evan and Mollie. I hope my students have learned a thing or two from me over the years, and I have certainly learned from each and every one of them. In a recent workplace discussion with Kristen Lukas I enjoyed a debate in which she gave as good as she got. I am now regularly lectured and often corrected by my former students. It is humbling but in a joyful, paternal way that I fully accept as a blessing of their continuing colleagueship.

The Voyage Continues

I feel great loyalty to Georgia Tech where I spent thirty years on the faculty, but my retirement in 2008 didn't stop me from teaching and mentoring. I am now affiliated with Florida Atlantic University as a Research Professor with an office on the Honors College campus not far from my home. I supervise the fieldwork of two graduate students in the FAU Integrative Biology program and collaborate with several students in California where I have been active as a consultant. One of these distant students is my co-author on an important paper we've written, recently published in *The Behavior Analyst* (Maple & Segura, 2014). The work we are doing in the west is based on the "wellness initiative" I introduced at the San Francisco Zoo in 2010 (Maple & Bocian, 2013; Maple & Perdue, 2013). Happily, there is still work to be done to benefit zoo and aquarium animals and the people who care for them. This work was inspired and shaped by my long collaborative partnership with Professor Jack Marr.

Fifty-six of my current and former students, collaborators, colleagues and my three children have contributed to this volume with insight, emotion, and humor. They have contributed essays, poems, and art, much appreciated to be sure. I want to thank them all for taking the time to offer their kind words and share their memories of working in Atlanta (and elsewhere) with me. In some cases, essays have reflected more worldly venues in Africa, China, and beyond. I regret that some of my former associates and students could not participate in this volume, but those who missed this chance can always utter a few words at my wake. They'll have plenty of time to compose the words as I intend to keep going for a long, long time. Years ago I contributed *festschrift* papers to honor the long and distinguished careers of Harry F. Harlow and Heini Hediger. The current volume was a different kind of *festschrift*, planned as a joyous celebration of an organized group of scientists and managers who built an institution together, and celebrated while the retiring scientist-practitioner was still young enough to enjoy it. We announced the *festschrift* on the occasion of my sixty-fifth birthday. On that day I was already thinking of myself as younger and certainly looking leaner with each passing day that I hit the pool and pushed away from the dinner table. It was the Willie B. diet that inspired me, more roots and tubers, less pasta and bread, lots of water, and a daily banana or two. Time spent in the company of monkeys and apes has truly shaped my life (and my body).

Looking back on the life of TECHlab and the Center for Conservation & Behavior, I am especially grateful to Lessie and Charles Smithgall who provided funding for the endowed chair at Tech named for their daughter, Dr. Elizabeth Smithgall Watts. Bay, as she was known, was a physical anthropologist and primate behavior expert at Tulane University and a dear friend of mine. Prior to her untimely death, Bay was working with me to set up a fund at the zoo to encourage student research in primatology and zoo biology. She wanted this fund to honor her grandfather, Charles Bailey, a former City of Atlanta alderman, who first introduced little Bay to nonhuman primates exhibited in the collection of Atlanta's zoological park. After she passed, her mother confirmed Bay's intentions with a $1M gift to establish the Bailey Fund at Zoo Atlanta. A second gift of $2.5M to Georgia Tech established the endowed chair that I occupied for a decade. It was a great honor to work in this capacity to recognize Bay's contributions to primate science and conservation, and to support the many talented graduate students who worked in our program. As the father of three daughters, I am especially happy that so many of these fellowship recipients were young women.

To Mike Hoff, Evan Zucker and Mollie Bloomsmith, I can never thank them enough for organizing this personal history told in the creative devices of our colleagues and friends. The words are inspiring and uplifting to me as I approach my seventh decade of life. Addie and I also appreciate and fondly remember the opportunity we've had to spend quality time with my students and their loved ones, including offspring, outside the academic setting, and for the inside look at the impacting lives they lead. We joyfully share their many achievements and special events including unique ceremonies such as the annual Charles Darwin Birthday Party. May we enjoy copious quantities of Survival-of-the-Fittest punch each and every year until the end of time. On this occasion Addie and I offer our special congratulations on the publication of this wonderful book.

Terry L. Maple
Tequesta, Florida
August 15, 2014

References

Hoff, M.P., & Maple, T.L. (1982). Sex and age differences in the avoidance of reptile exhibits by zoo visitors. *Zoo Biology*, 1, 263-269.

Kuhar, C. (2006). In the deep end: Pooling data and other statistical challenges of zoo and aquarium research. *Zoo Biology* 25, 339-352.

Maple, T.L. (1988, November). The contributions of Heini Hediger to the founding of *Zoo Biology*. Festcolloquium for Professor Dr. Heini Hediger. Switzerland: University of Zurich.

Maple, T.L., & Bocian, D. (2013). Commentary: Wellness as welfare. *Zoo Biology* 32, 363-365.

Maple, T.L., & Hoff, M.P. (1982). *Gorilla behavior*. New York: Van Nostrand Reinhold.

Maple, T.L., & Perdue, B.M. (2013). *Zoo animal welfare*. Heidelberg: Springer-Verlag.

Maple, T.L., & Segura. V. (2014). Advancing behavior analysis in zoos and aquariums. *The Behavior Analyst*. Advance online publication. doi: 10.1007/s40614-014-0018-x

Maple, T., & Westlund, B. (1975). The integration of social interactions between cebus and spider monkeys in captivity. *Applied Animal Ethology*, *1*, 305-308.

Maple, T.L., Zucker, E.L., & Dennon, M.B. (1979). Cyclic proceptivity in an adult female orangutan. *Behavioural Processes*, 4, 53-59.

Sommer, R. (1925). *Tierpsychologie*. Leipzig: Verlag Quelle & Meyer.

48. PUBLICATIONS FROM THE MAPLE LAB, 1977-PRESENT

1977
1.   Maple, T., Zucker, E. L., Hoff, M. P., & Wilson, M. E. (1977). Behavioral aspects of great ape reproduction. *Proceedings of the Annual Meeting of the American Association of Zoological Parks and Aquariums* (pp. 194-200). Topeka: Hills Riviana.

1978
2.   Maple, T.L., & Zucker, E.L. (1978). Ethological studies of play behavior in captive great apes. In E. O. Smith (Ed.), *Social play in primates* (pp. 113-142). New York: Academic Press.

3.   Zucker, E.L., Mitchell, G., & Maple, T.L. (1978). Adult male-offspring play interactions in a captive group of orang-utans. *Primates, 19,* 379-384.

4.   Maple, T.L., Wilson, M.E., Zucker, E.L., & Wilson, S.F. (1978). Notes on the development of a mother-reared orang-utan: The first six months. *Primates, 19,* 595-602.

5.   Maple, T., & Southworth, K. (1978). Breeding the pygmy chimapanzee. *Yerkes Newsletter, 15(1),* 23-25.

1979

6.   Erwin, J., Maple, T.L., & Mitchell, G. (Eds.) (1979). *Captivity and behavior: Primates in breeding colonies, laboratories and zoos.* New York: Van Nostrand Reinhold Co.

7.   Mitchell, G., Maple, T.L., & Erwin, J. (1979). Development of social attachment potential in captive rhesus monkeys. In J. Erwin, T. L. Maple, & G. Mitchell (Eds.), *Captivity and behavior* (pp. 59-111). New York: Van Nostrand Reinhold Co.

8.   Maple, T.L. (1979). Primate psychology in historical perspective. In J. Erwin, T. L. Maple, & G. Mitchell (Eds.), *Captivity and behavior* (pp. 29-58). New York: Van Nostrand Reinhold Co.

9.   Maple, T.L. (1979). Great apes in captivity: the good, the bad, and the ugly. In J. Erwin, T. L. Maple, & G. Mitchell (Eds.), *Captivity and behavior* (pp. 239-272). New York: Van Nostrand Reinhold Co.

10.   Maple, T.L., Zucker, E.L., & Dennon, M.B. (1979). Cyclic proceptivity in a captive female orang-utan. *Behavioural Processes, 4,* 53-59.

1980

11.   Maple, T.L. (1980). *Orang-utan behavior.* New York: Von Nostrand Reinhold Co.

12.   Maple, T.L. (1980). Breaking the hand-rearing syndrome in infant great apes. *AAZPA Regional Proceedings,* 199-201.

13.   Maple, T.L. (1980). *Chimpanzee reproduction, rearing, and rehabilitation in captivity: Report presented to the Ad*

Hoc Task Force, National Chimpanzee Breeding Program, Tanglewood, NC. Atlantal: Georgia Institute of Technology.

14. Maple, T.L. (1980). *Report of the subcommittee on behavioral aspects of reproduction: Report of the Ad Hoc Task Force to develop a national chimpanzee breeding program, interagency primate steering committee.* Washington, DC: U.S. Department of Health and Human Services.

1981

15. Hoff, M.P., Nadler, R.D., & Maple, T. (1981). Development of infant independence in a captive group of lowland gorillas. *Developmental Psychobiology, 14,* 251-265.

16. Hoff, M.P., Nadler, R.D., & Maple, T. (1981). The development of infant play in a captive group of lowland gorillas (*Gorilla gorilla gorilla*). *American Journal of Primatology, 1,* 65-72.

17. Maple, T.L. (1981, August/September). A zoo story: Confessions of a zoo psychologist. *APA Monitor, 12(8),* 20-21.

18. Maple, T.L. (1981). Comparative psychology as an East African field course. *Teaching of Psychology, 8,* 237-241.

19. Maple, T.L. (1981, November/December). Wounded impala in possession of the herd. *East African Natural History Society Bulletin,* 97.

20. Maple, T.L. (1981). Audubon's apes move uptown. *At the Zoo, 2(4),* 4-7.

21.   Maple. T.L. (1981). No tool like an old tool. [Review of the book *Animal tool behavior,* B. B. Beck]. *Zoo Biology, 1,* 103-110.

22.   Maple, T., & Cone, S. (1981). Aged chimpanzees at the Yerkes Primate Research Center. *Laboratory Primate Newsletter, 20(2),* 10-12.

23.   Maple, T.L., Murdock, G.K., & Lukas, J. (1981). Birth weights of African antelopes on St. Catherine's Island. *Der Zoologisches Garten, 5/6,* 388-390.

1982
24.   Brown, S.G., Dunlap, W., & Maple, T.L. (1982). Notes on the water-contact behavior of captive lowland gorillas. *Zoo Biology, 1,* 243-249.

25.   Clarke, A.S., Juno, C.J., & Maple, T.L. (1982). Behavioral effects of a change in the physical environment: A pilot study of captive chimpanzees. *Zoo Biology, 1,* 371-380.

26.   Gerth, J.M., Lewis, C.M., Stine, W.W., & Maple, T.L. (1982). Evaluation of two computerized data collection devices for research in zoos. *Zoo Biology, 1,* 65-70.

27.   Hoff, M.P., Nadler, R.D., & Maple, T.L. (1982). Control role of an adult male in a captive group of lowland gorillas. *Folia Primatologica, 38,* 72-85.

28.   Hoff, M.P., & Maple, T.L. (1982), Sex and age differences in the avoidance of reptile exhibits by zoo visitors. *Zoo Biology, 1,* 263-269.

29.   Maple, T.L. (1982). Toward a unified Zoo Biology. *Zoo Biology, 1,* 1-3.

30. Maple, T.L. (1982). Inside *Zoo Biology. Zoo Biology, 1,* 173-177.

31. Maple, T.L. (1982). *Report of the subcommittee on behavioral aspects of reproduction: Report of the Ad hoc Task Force, National Chimpanzee Breeding Program.* Washington, DC: National Institutes of Health, Interagency Primate Steering Committee.

32. Maple, T.L. (1982). [Review of *The natural history of the gorilla,* by A.F. Dixson] *Quarterly Review of Biology, 57,* 480.

33. Maple, T.L. (1982). Orang-utan behavior and its management in captivity. In L. E. M. de Boer (Ed.), *Biology and conservation of the orang-utan* (pp. 257-270). The Hague, Netherlands: W. Junk BV.

34. Maple, T.L., & Hoff, M.P. (1982). *Gorilla behavior.* New York, Von Nostrand Reinhold Co.

35. Maple, T.L., Lukas, J., Murdock, G.K., Bunkfeldt, L., Bigg, K., Conradsen, L., Ellington, S., & Christensen, T.L. (1982). Notes on the birth of two sable antelopes (*Hippotragus niger*). *International Zoo Yearbook, 22,* 218-221.

36. Maple, T.L., & Stine, W.W. (1982). Environmental variables and great ape husbandry. *American Journal of Primatology, 3(S1),* 67-76.

37. Stine, W.W., Howell, L., Murdock, G.K., Newland M.C., Conradsen, L., & Maple, T.L. (1982). Progression order in the captive sable antelope of St. Catherine's Island. *Zoo Biology, 1,* 89-110.

1983
38. Hoff, M.P., Nadler, R.D., & Maple, T.L. (1983). Maternal transport and infant motor development in

a captive group of lowland gorillas. *Primates, 24,* 77-85.

39.   Maple, T.L., & Warren-Leubecker, A. (1983). Variability in the parental conduct of captive great apes. In M. D. Reite, & N. G. Caine (Eds.) *Child abuse: The nonhuman primate data* (pp. 119-137). New York: Alan R. Liss, Inc.

40.   Maple, T.L. (1983). [Review of *Reproductive biology of the great apes,* by C.E. Graham]. *American Journal of Physical Anthropology, 60,* 129-130.

41.   Maple, T.L. (1983). Something special for comparative psychology. *Contemporary Psychology, 28,* 680-681.

42.   Maple, T.L. (1983). Environmental psychology and great ape reproduction. *International Journal for the Study of Animal Problems, 4,* 295-299.

43.   Murdock, G.K., Stine, W.W., & Maple, T.L. (1983). Observations of maternal-infant interaction in a captive herd of sable antelope (*Hippotragus niger*). *Zoo Biology, 2,* 215-224.

44.   Puleo, S.G., Zucker, E.L., & Maple, T.L. (1983). Social rehabilitation and foster mothering in captive orang-utans. *Zoologisches Garten, 53,* 196-202.

1984-85
45.   Mitchell, G., & Maple, T.L. (1985). Dominance in non-human primates. In J. Dovidio, & S. Ellyson (Eds.) *Power, dominance and nonverbal behavior* (pp. 49-66). New York: Springer-Verlag.

1986
46.   Bloomstrand, M.A., Riddle, K., Alford, P., & Maple, T.L. (1986). An objective evaluation of a behavioral

enrichment device for captive chimpanzees. *Zoo Biology, 5,* 293-300.

47.   Finlay, T.W., & Maple, T.L. (1986). A survey of research in American zoos and aquariums. *Zoo Biology, 5,* 261-268.

48.   Maple, T.L., & Finlay, T.W. (1986). Evaluating the environments of captive nonhuman primates. In K. Benirschke (Ed.), *Primates: The road to self-sustaining populations* (pp. 480-488). New York: Springer-Verlag.

49.   Zucker, E.L., Dennon, M.B. Puleo, S.G., & Maple, T.L. (1986). Play profiles of captive adult orang-utans. *Developmental Psychobiology, 19,* 315-326.

1987

50.   Bloomstrand, M., & Maple, T.L. (1987). Management and husbandry of African monkeys in captivity. In E. L. Zucker (Ed.), *Comparative behavior of African monkeys* (pp. 197-234). New York: Alan R. Liss, Inc.

51.   Maple, T.L., & Finlay, T.W. (1987). Postoccupancy evaluation in the zoo. *Applied Animal Behavior Science, 18,* 5-18.

1988

52.   Bloomsmith, M.A., Alford, P.L., & Maple, T.L. (1988). Successful feeding enrichment for captive chimpanzees. *American Journal of Primatology, 16,* 155-164.

53.   Finlay, T.W., James, L.R., & Maple, T.L. (1988). Zoo environments influence people's perceptions of animals. *Environment and Behavior, 20,* 508-528.

54. Maple, T.L., & Bloomstrand, M. (1988). Feeding, foraging and mental health. In T. P. Meehan, & M. E. Allen (Eds.), *Proceedings of the third annual Dr. Scholl Conference on the nutrition of wild animals* (pp. 1-8). Chicago: Lincoln Park Zoo Publications.

55. Maple, T.L. (1988). *The contributions of Heini Hediger to the founding of Zoo Biology: Festcolloquium for Professor Dr. Heini Hediger, University of Zurich, Zurich, Switzerland, November 1988.* Atlanta: TECHlab.

1989

56. Jackson, D.M., Ogden, J.J. and Maple, T.L. (1989). Making visual contact at the gorilla interpretive center: A study of visitor traffic flow. *Visitor Studies, 2*, 225-237.

57. Maple, T.L., & Finlay, T.W. (1989). Applied primatology in the modern zoo. *Zoo Biology, 8(S1),* 101-116.

1990

58. Bloomsmith, M.A., Finlay, T.W., Merhalski, J.J., & Maple, T.L. (1990). Rigid, plastic balls as enrichment devices for captive chimpanzees. *Laboratory Animal Science, 40,* 319-322.

59. Ogden, J.J., Finlay, T.W., & Maple, T.L. (1990). Gorilla adaptations to naturalistic environments. *Zoo Biology, 9,* 107-121.

60. Perkins, L.A., & Maple, T.L. (1990). The North American orang-utan SSP: Current status and progress in the 1980's. *Zoo Biology, 9,* 135-139.

1991-92

61. Maple, T.L. (1992). In Memoriam: Professor Dr. Heini Hediger. *Zoo Biology, 11,* 369-372.

62.   Maple, T.L., & Ogden, J.J. (1992). Designing for apes: The comparative psychology of gorillas and orangutans. *Zoo Design 4: Proceedings of the International Symposium on Zoo Design and Construction* (pp. 186-194). Paignton, UK: Whitley Wildlife Preservation Trust.

63.   Winslow, S., Ogden, J.J., & Maple, T.L. (1992). Socialization of an adult male lowland gorilla. *International Zoo Yearbook, 31*, 221-225.

64.   Ogden, J.J., Bruner, G., & Maple, T.L. (1992). A survey of the use of electric fencing with captive great apes. *International Zoo Yearbook, 31*, 229-236.

1993

65.   Hoff, M.P., Nadler, R.D., & Maple, T.L. (1993). Control role of an adult male in a captive group of lowland gorillas. *Zoo and Aquarium Topics from Abroad, 3,* 35-44 (published in Japanese).

66.   Maple, T.L., & Archibald, E. (1993). *Zoo man: Inside the zoo revolution.* Atlanta, GA: Longstreet Press.

67.   Ogden, J.J., Lindburg, D.G., & Maple, T.L. (1993). Preferences for structural environmental features in captive lowland gorillas. *Zoo Biology, 12,* 381-396.

68.   Ogden, J.J., Lindburg, D.G., & Maple, T.L. (1993). The effects of ecologically-relevant sounds on the cognitive and affective behavior of zoo visitors. *Curator, 36,* 147-156.

1994

69.   Gold, K.C., & Maple, T.L. (1994). Personality assessment in the gorilla and its utility as a management tool. *Zoo Biology, 13,* 509-522.

70.   Hoff, M.P., Forthman, D., & Maple, T.L. (1994). Dyadic interactions of infant lowland gorillas in an

outdoor exhibit compared to an indoor holding area. *Zoo Biology, 13,* 245-256.

71.   Hoff, M.P., Nadler, R.D., Hoff, K.T., & Maple, T.L. (1994). Separation and depression in infant gorillas. *Developmental Psychobiology, 27,* 439-452.

72.   Maple, T.L. (1994). Afterword. L. Koebner, *Zoo book: The evolution of wildlife conservation centers* (pp. 174-175). New York, NY: Tom Doherty.

73.   Ogden, J.J., Lindburg, D.G., & Maple, T.L. (1994). A preliminary study of the effects of ecologically-relevant sounds on the behaviour of captive lowland gorillas. *Applied Animal Behaviour Science, 39,* 163-176.

74.   Ogden, J.J., Carpanzano, C., & Maple, T.L. (1994). Immersion exhibits: How are they proving as educational exhibits? *AZA Annual Conference Proceedings,* 224-228.

1995

75.   Hoff, M.P., & Maple, T.L. (1995). Post-occupancy modification of a lowland gorilla enclosure at Zoo Atlanta. *International Zoo Yearbook, 34,* 153-160.

76.   Maple, T.L. (1995). Psychology is alive and well in the zoo. *Psychological Science Agenda, 8(3),* 8-9.

77.   Maple, T.L. (1995). The case for saving species. *Defenders, 70(3),* 41.

78.   Maple, T.L., & Perkins, L.A. (1995). Cage furnishings and environmental enrichment. In D.G. Kleiman, M.E. Allen, K.V. Thompson, & S. Lumpkin (Eds.), *Wild mammals in captivity: Principles and techniques.* (pp. 212-222). Chicago: University of Chicago Press.

79. Maple, T.L. (1995). Toward a responsible zoo agenda. In B. G. Norton, M. Hutchins, T. L. Maple, & E. F. Stevens (Eds.), *Ethics on the ark* (pp. 20-30). Washington, DC: Smithsonian Books.

80. Maple, T.L., Stevens, E., & McManamon, R. (1995). Defining the "good zoo": animal care, maintenance, and welfare. In B. G. Norton, M. Hutchins, T. L. Maple, & E. F. Stevens (Eds.), *Ethics on the ark* (pp. 219-234). Washington, DC: Smithsonian Books.

81. Norton, B.G., Hutchins, M., Stevens, E., and Maple, T.L. (Eds.) (1995). *Ethics on the ark: Zoos, animal welfare and wildlife conservation.* Washington, DC: Smithsonian Books.

1996

82. Hoff, M.P., Hoff, K.T., Horton, L.C., & Maple, T.L. (1996). Behavioral effects of changing group membership among captive lowland gorillas. *Zoo Biology, 15,* 383-393.

83. Maple, T.L. (1996). Epilogue. M. A. Rock, *Kishina: A true story of gorilla survival.* Atlanta: Peachtree Publishers, Ltd.

84. Maple, T.L. (1966). The art and science of enrichment. In G.M. Burghardt, J.T. Bielitzki, J.R. Boyce, & D.D. Schaeffer (Eds.), *The well-being of animals in zoo and aquarium sponsored research* (pp. 79-84). Greenbelt, MD: Scientists Center for Animal Welfare.

85. Stevens, B., Hutchins, M.P, & Maple, T.L. (1996). Zoos, aquariums, and endangered species conservation. *Endangered Species Update, 1996, 13 (1-2),* 7-9

86. Wineman, J., Piper, C., & Maple, T.L. (1996). Zoos in transition: Enriching conservation education for a new generation. *Curator, 39,* 94-107.

1997

87. Hoff, M.P., Burks, K., & Maple, T.L. (1997). Abnormal behavior in captive gorillas. In J. Ogden & D. Warton (Eds), *The management of gorillas in captivity* (pp. 21-28). Atlanta, GA: Zoo Atlanta/AZA.

88. Hoff, M.P., Powell, D., Lukas, K.E., & Maple, T.L. (1997). Social and individual behaviour of adult gorillas in indoor conditions compared to outdoor conditions. *Journal of Applied Animal Behaviour Science, 54,* 359-370.

89. Maple, T.L., Perkins, L.A., & Snyder, R. (1997). The role of environmental and social variables in the management of apes and pandas. In A. Zhang & G. He (Eds.), *Proceedings of the International Symposium on the Protection of the Giant Panda* (pp. 23-28). Chengdu, China: Chengdu Foundation for Giant Panda Breeding.

90. Maple, T.L. (1997, August). Research in AZA, 1972-1997. *Communique*, Silver Spring, MD: AZA.

91. Snyder, R., Maple, T.L, Zhong, W., & Huang, X. (1997). Breeding season behavior of female and male giant pandas at the Chengdu Zoo and the Chengdu Research Base of Giant Panda Breeding. In A. Zhang & G. He (Eds.). *Proceedings of the international symposium on the protection of the giant panda* (pp. 72-77). Chengdu, China: Chengdu Foundation for Giant Panda Breeding.

92. Chang, T.R., Bloomsmith, M.A., Forthman, D.L., Kneidinger, L., Feldman, J.M., & Maple, T.L. (1997). Development and scientific evaluation of a behavioral husbandry program at Zoo Atlanta. *Proceedings of the third*

international conference on environmental enrichment (pp. 248-250). San Diego, CA: The Shape of Enrichment, Inc.

1998

93.   Hoff, M.P., Hoff, K.T., & Maple, T.L. (1998). Behavioural response of a Western lowland gorilla group to the loss of the silverback male at Zoo Atlanta. *International Zoo Yearbook, 36,* 90-96.

94.   Lukas, K.E., Marr, M. J., & Maple, T.L. (1998). Teaching operant conditioning at the zoo. *Teaching of Psychology, 25,* 112-116.

95.   Maple, T.L. (1998). Foreword. In D.L. Shepherdson, J. Mellen, & M. Hutchins (Eds), *Second nature: Environmental enrichment for captive animals* (pp. xii-xiii). Washington, D.C.: Smithsonian Books.

96.   Stoinski, T., Lukas, K.E., & Maple, T.L. (1998). A survey of research in American zoos and aquariums. *Zoo Biology, 17,* 167-180.

1999

97.   Brockett, R., Stoinski, T., Black, J., Markowitz, T., & Maple, T.L. (1999). Nocturnal behavior in a group of unchained African elephants. *Zoo Biology, 18,* 101-109.

98.   Chang, T.R., Forthman, D.L., & Maple, T.L. (1999). Comparison of captive mandrills in traditional and ecologically representative exhibits. *Zoo Biology, 18,* 163-176.

99.   Maple, T.L. (1999). Zoo Atlanta's scientific vision. *Georgia Journal of Science, 101,* 159-179.

100.   Maple, T.L. (1999). Donald G. Lindburg: A decade of leadership and scholarship. *Zoo Biology,18,* 3-4.

101. Lukas, K.E., Hamor, G., Bloomsmith, M.A., Horton, C.L. & Maple, T.L. (1999). Removing milk from captive gorilla diets: The impact on regurgitation and reingestion (R&R) and other behavior. *Zoo Biology, 18,* 515-528.

2000

102. Maple, T.L. (2000). *Saving the giant panda.* Atlanta, Longstreet Press.

103. Stoinski T.S., Daniel, E., Liu, S., & Maple, T.L. (2000). Behavioral effects of feeding enrichment on African elephants. *Zoo Biology, 19,* 485-494.

104. Tarou, L.R., Bashaw, M.J., & Maple, T.L. (2000). Social attachment in giraffe: Response to social separation. *Zoo Biology, 19*, 41–51.

105. Tarou, L.R., Bashaw, M.J., & Maple, T.L. (2000). The empty nest: A case study of maternal response to separation in orangutans. *Journal of Applied Animal Welfare Science, 3,* 203-213.

2001

106. Bashaw, M.J., & Maple, T.L. (2001). Signs fail to increase zoo visitors' ability to see tigers. *Curator, 44,* 297-304.

107. Beck, B.B., Stoinski, T.S., Hutchins, M., Maple, T.L., Norton, B, Rowan, A., Stevens, E. F., & Arluk, A. (Eds.) (2001). *Great apes and humans: The ethics of coexistence.* Washington, D.C.: Smithsonian Institution Press.

108. Burks, K., Bloomsmith, M.A., Forthman, D.L., & Maple, T.L. (2001). Managing the socialization of an adult male gorilla (*Gorilla gorilla gorilla*) with a history of social deprivation. *Zoo Biology, 20,* 347-358.

109. Kneidinger, L.M., Maple, T. L., & Tross, S.A. (2001). Touching behavior in sport: functional components, analysis of sex differences and ethological considerations. *Journal of Nonverbal Behavior, 25,* 43-62.

110. Stoinski, T.S., Ogden, J., Gold, K., & Maple, T.L. (2001). Captive apes and zoo education. In B.B. Beck, T. Stoinski, M. Hutchins, T. L. Maple, B. Norton, A. Rowan, B. F. Stevens, & A. Arluk (Eds), *Great apes and humans: The ethics of coexistence* (pp. 112-132). Washington, D.C.: Smithsonian Institution Press.

111. Stoinski, T.S., Hoff, M.P., & Maple, T.L. (2001). Habitat use and structural preferences of captive lowland gorillas: The effect of environmental and social variables. *International Journal of Primatology, 22,* 431-447.

112. Stoinski, T.S., Hoff, M.P., Lukas, K.E., & Maple, T.L. (2001). A behavioral comparison of two captive all-male gorilla groups. *Zoo Biology, 20,* 27-40.

113. Bashaw, M.J., Tarou, L.R., Maki, T.S., & Maple, T.L. (2001). A survey assessment of variables related to stereotypy in captive giraffe and okapi. *Applied Animal Behaviour Science, 73,* 235-247.

114. Maple, T.L. (2001). The power of one. In G. Rabb (Ed.), *The apes: Challenges for the 21ˢᵗ century: Conference proceedings* (pp. 208-209). Chicago: Chicago Zoological Society.

115. Stoinski, T.S., Ogden, J.J., Gold, K., & Maple, T.L. (2001). The role of great apes in the educational efficacy of modern zoos. In G. Rabb (Ed.), *The apes: Challenges for the 21st century: Conference proceedings* (pp. 210-211). Chicago: Chicago Zoological Society.

116.   Erwin, J.M., Bloomsmith, M., Boysen, S.T., Perl, D., Zihlman, A., Maple, T.L., a& Hof, P.R. (2001). The great ape aging project: Caring for and learning from apes. In G. Rabb (Ed.), *The apes: Challenges for the 21st century: Conference proceedings* (pp. 344-346). Chicago: Chicago Zoological Society.

117.   Bashaw, M.J., Bloomsmith, M.A., Marr, M.J., & Maple, T.L. (2001). Effects of a live prey equivalent on the behavior of large cats. *Shape of Enrichment, 10(3),* 6-9.

2002

118.   Anderson, U.S., Benne, M., Bloomsmith, M.A., & Maple, T.L. (2002). Retreat space and human visitor density moderate undesirable behavior in petting zoo animals. *Journal of Applied Animal Welfare Science, 5,* 125-137.

119.   Stoinski, T.S., Hoff, M.P., & Maple, T.L. (2002). The effect of structural preferences, temperature, and social factors on visibility in western lowland gorillas. *Environment and Behavior, 34,* 493-507.

120.   Stoinski, T.S., Czekala, N., Lukas, K.E., & Maple, T.L. (2002). Urinary androgen and corticoid levels in captive, Western male lowland gorillas: Age-and-social group related differences. *American Journal of Primatology, 56,* 73-87.

121.   Tarou, L.R., Bloomsmith, M.A., Hoff, M. P., Erwin, J.M., &Maple, T. L. (2002). The behavior of aged great apes. In J. Erwin, & P. Hoff (Eds.), *Aging in nonhuman primates* (pp. 209-231). Basel: Karger.

122.   Stoinski, T.S., Allen, M.T., Bloomsmith, M.A., Forthman, D.L., & Maple, T.L. (2002). Educating

zoo visitors about complex environmental issues: Should we do it and how? *Curator, 45,* 129-143.

2003

123. Lukas, K.E., Hoff, M.P., & Maple, T.L. (2003). Gorilla behavior in response to systematic alternation between zoo enclosures. *Applied Animal Behaviour Science, 81,* 367-386.

124. Lukas, K.E, Stoinski, T.S., Burks, K., Snyder, R., Bexell, S., & Maple, T.L. (2003). Nest building in captive *Gorilla gorilla gorilla. International Journal of Primatology, 24,* 103-124.

125. Snyder, R.J., Zhang, A., Zhang, Z., Li, G., Tian, Y.., Huang, X., Luo, L., Bloomsmith, M.A., Forthman, D.L., & Maple, T.L. (2003). Behavioral and developmental consequences of early rearing experience for captive giant pandas (*Ailuropoda melanoleuca*). *Journal of Comparative Psychology, 117,* 235-245.

126. Stoinski, T.S., Beck, B.B., Bloomsmith, M.A., & Maple, T.L. (2003). A behavioral comparison of captive-born golden lion tamarins and their wild-born offspring. *Behaviour, 140,* 137-160.

127. Maple, T.L. (2003). Strategic collection planning and individual animal welfare. *Journal of the American Veterinary Medical Association, 223,* 966-969.

128. Anderson, U.S., Kelling, A.S., Pressley-Keough, R., Bloomsmith, M.A., & Maple, T.L. (2003). Enhancing the zoo visitor's experience by public animal training and oral interpretation at an otter exhibit. *Environment and Behavior, 35,* 826-841.

129. Bashaw, M.J., Bloomsmith, M.A., Marr, M. J., & Maple, T. L. (2003). To hunt or not to hunt? A

feeding enrichment experiment with captive large felids. *Zoo Biology, 22,* 189-198.

130. Maple, T.L., Bloomsmith, M.A., & Snyder, R.J. (Eds.) Special Issue on Management of Captive Giant Pandas. *Zoo Biology, 22,* 311-416.

131. Maple, T.L., Bloomsmith, M.A., & Snyder, R.J. (2003). Panda 2000: Conservation priorities for the new millennium. *Zoo Biology, 22,* 311-312.

132. Wilson, M., Kelling, A., Poline, L., Bloomsmith, M.A., & Maple, T.L. (2003). Post occupancy evaluation of Zoo Atlanta's giant panda conservation center: Staff and visitor reactions. *Zoo Biology, 22,* 365-382.

133. Bloomsmith, M.A., Jones, M.L., Snyder, R.J., Singer, R.A., Gardner, W.A., Liu, S.C., & Maple, T.L. (2003). Positive reinforcement training to elicit voluntary movement of two giant pandas throughout their enclosure. *Zoo Biology, 22,* 323-334.

134. Stoinski, T.S., Hoff, M.P., & Maple, T.L. (2003). Proximity patterns of female western lowland gorillas in the next six months after parturition. *American Journal of Primatology, 61,* 61-72.

135. Tarou, L.R., Bashaw, M., & Maple, T.L. (2003). The failure of a chemical spray to significantly reduce stereotypic licking in a captive giraffe. *Zoo Biology, 22,* 601-607.

2004

136. Anderson, U.S., Maple, T.L., & Bloomsmith, M.A. (2004). A close keeper-nonhuman animal distance does not reduce undesirable behavior in contact yard goats and sheep. *Journal of Applied Animal Welfare Science, 7,* 59-69.

137. Tarou, L.R., Snyder, R.J., & Maple, T.L. (2004). Spatial memory in the giant panda. In D.G. Lindburg, & K. Baragona (Eds.), *Giant pandas: Biology and conservation* (pp. 101-108). Berkeley, CA: University of California Press.

138. Snyder, R.J., Lawson, D.P., Anju, Z., Zhihe, Z., Lan, L., Zhong, W., Huang, X., Czekala, N.M., Bloomsmith, M.A., Forthman, D.L., & Maple, T.L. (2004). Reproduction in giant pandas: Hormones and behavior. In D. G. Lindburg, & K. Baragona (Eds.), *Giant pandas: Biology and conservation* (pp. 125-132). Berkeley, CA: University of California Press.

139. Wilson, M.L, Bloomsmith, M.A., & Maple, T.L. (2004). Stereotypic swaying and serum cortisol concentrations in three captive African elephants (*Loxodonta africana*). *Animal Welfare, 13,* 39-43.

140. Stoinski, T.S., Lukas, K.E., Kuhar, C.W., & Maple, T.L. (2004). Factors influencing the formation and maintenance of all-male gorilla groups in captivity. *Zoo Biology, 23,* 189-203.

141. Stoinski, T.S., Kuhar, C.W., Lukas, K.E., & Maple, T.L. (2004). Social dynamics of captive western lowland gorillas living in all-male groups. *Behaviour, 141,* 169-195.

142. Bexell, S.M., Lan, L., Yan, H., Maple, T.L., McManamon, R., Anju, Z., Zhihe, Z., Fei, L., & Yuzhong, T. (2004). Conservation education initiatives in China: A collaborative project among Zoo Atlanta, Chengdu Zoo, and Chengdu Research Base of Giant Panda Breeding. In D.G. Lindburg, & K. Baragona, K. (Eds.) *Giant pandas: Biology and conservation* (pp. 264-267). Berkeley, CA: University of California Press.

143. Burks, K., Mellen, J.D., Miller, G.W., Lenhardt, J.,
      Weiss, A., Figueredo, A.J., & Maple, T.L. (2004).
      Comparison of two introduction methods with
      African elephants (*Loxodonta africana*). *Zoo Biology, 23,*
      109-126.

144. Tarou, L.R., Kuhar, C.W., Adcock, D., Bloomsmith,
      M.A., & Maple, T.L. (2004). Computer-assisted
      enrichment for zoo-housed orangutans (*Pongo
      pygmaeus*). *Animal Welfare, 13,* 445-453.

145. Maple, T.L., & Sun, P. (2004). Zoological parks as
      naturalizing venues for people and their
      communities. *Proceedings of the 6th International
      Symposium for Environment-Behavior Studies* (pp. 394-
      396). Tianjin, China: Environment-Behavior
      Research Association/School of Architecture,
      Tianjin University.

2005
146. Tarou, L.R., Bloomsmith, M.A., & Maple, T.L.
      (2005). A survey of stereotypic behavior in
      prosimians. *American Journal of Primatology, 65,* 181-
      196.

147. Maple, T.L. (2005). Post-occupancy evaluation in the
      zoo: Toward a science of appropriate, functional,
      and superior exhibitry for animals and people. In A.
      B. Plowman, & S. J Tonge (Eds.), *Innovation or
      replication: Proceedings of the Sixth International Symposium
      on Zoo Design* (pp. 111-117). Paignton, Devon:
      Whitley Wildlife Preservation Trust.

148. Hoff, M.P, Tarou, L.R., Horton, L., Mayo, L., &
      Maple, T.L. (2005). Notes on the introduction of an
      11-week old infant gorilla to a non-lactating
      surrogate mother. *International Zoo Yearbook, 39,* 191-
      198.

149. Anderson, U.S., Stoinski, T.S., Bloomsmith, M.A., Marr, M.J., Smith, A.D., & Maple, T.L. (2005). Relative numerousness judgment and summation in young and old Western lowland gorillas. *Journal of Comparative Psychology, 119,* 285-295.

2006

150. Wilson, M.L., Bashaw, M.J., Fountain, K., Kieschnick, S., & Maple, T.L. (2006). Nocturnal behavior in a group of female African elephants. *Zoo Biology, 25,* 173-186.

151. Snyder, R.J., Bloomsmith, M.A., Zhang, A.J., Zhang, Z.H., & Maple, T.L. (2006). Consequences of early rearing on socialization and social competence of giant pandas. In D.E. Wildt, A.J. Zhang, Z.H. Zhang, D. Janssen, & S. Ellis (Eds.), *Giant pandas: Biology, veterinary medicine and management* (pp. 334-352). Cambridge: Cambridge University Press.

152. Maple, T.L., & Kuhar, C.W. (2006). The comparative psychology of Duane Rumbaugh and his impact on zoo biology. In D.A. Washburn (Ed.). *Primate perspectives on behavior and cognition* (pp. 7-16). Washington, DC: American Psychological Association.

153. Maple, T.L., & Mallavarapu, S. (2006). Values, advocacy, and leadership: an empirical philosophy for 21st century zoos and aquariums. In H.H. Genoways (Ed.). *Museum philosophy for the 21st century* (pp. 177-200). Lanham, MD: Alta Mira Press.

154. Zhang, Z. H., Zhang, A.J., Li, G., Fei, L., Wang, Q., Loeffler, K., Wildt, D.E., Maple, T.L., Mcmanamon, R., & Ellis, S. (2006). An historical perspective of breeding giant pandas *ex situ* in China. In D.E. Wildt, A.J. Zhang, Z.H. Zhang, D. Jannsen, & S.

Ellis (Eds.), *Giant pandas: Biology, veterinary medicine and management* (pp. 455-468). Cambridge: Cambridge University Press.

155. Maple, T. L. (2006). Tales of an entrepreneurial animal psychologist. *APS Observer 19(11),* 11-13.

156. Maple, T.L. (2006). Foreword to special issue on scientific elephant management. *Zoo Biology, 25,* 1-3.

157. Kelling, A.S., Snyder, R.J., Gardner, W., Marr, M.J., Bloomsmith, M.A., & Maple, T.L. (2006). Color vision in the giant panda, *Ailuripoda melanoleuca. Learning and Behavior, 2,* 154-161.

158. Mallavarapu, S., Stoinski, T.S., Bloomsmith, M.A., & Maple, T.L. (2006). Post-conflict behavior in a captive group of Western lowland gorillas. *American Journal of Primatology, 68,* 789-801.

159. Kuhar, C.W., Stoinski, T.S., Lukas, K.E., & Maple, T.L. (2006). Gorilla behavior index revisited: Age, housing, and behavior. *Applied Animal Behaviour Science, 96,* 315-326.

2007

160. Maple, T.L. (2007). Toward a science of welfare for animals in the zoo. *Journal of Applied Animal Welfare Science, 10,* 63-70.

161. Anderson, U.S., Stoinski, T.S., Bloomsmith, M.A., & Maple, T.L. (2007). Relative numerousness judgment and summation in young, middle-aged, and older orangutans. *Journal of Comparative Psychology, 121,* 1-11.

162. Bashaw, M. J., Bloomsmith, M.A., Maple, T.L., & Bercovitch, F.B. (2007). The structure of social relationships among captive female giraffe (*Giraffa*

camelopardalis). *Journal of Comparative Psychology, 121,* 46-53.

163. Bashaw, M.J., Kelling, A.S., Bloomsmith, M.A., & Maple, T.L. (2007). Environmental effects on the behavior of zoo-housed lions and tigers with a case study of the effects of a visual barrier on pacing. *Journal of Applied Animal Welfare Science, 10,* 95-109.

164. Bloomsmith, M.A., Marr. M.J., & Maple, T.L. (2007). Addressing nonhuman primate behavioral problems through the use of operant conditioning: Is the human treatment approach a useful model? *Journal of Applied Animal Behaviour Science, 102,* 205-222.

165. Gingrich, N., & Maple, T.L. (2007). *A contract with the earth.* Baltimore, MD: Johns Hopkins University Press.

166. Bexell, S.M., Jarrett, O.S., Lan, L, Yan, H., Sandaus, E., & Maple, T.L. (2007). Observing panda play: Interpretation for zoo programming and conservation efforts. *Curator, 5,* 287-297.

2008

167. Maple, T.L., Bloomsmith, M.A., & Martin, A. (2008). Primates and pachyderms: A primate model of zoo elephant welfare. In D. Forthman (Ed), *An elephant in the room: The science and well-being of elephants in captivity* (pp. 129-153). North Grafton, MA: Tufts University Cummings School of Veterinary Medicine, Center for Animals and Public Policy.

168. Gingrich, N., & Maple, T.L. (2008). Forging a new, bipartisan environmental movement. *Issues in Science and Technology, XXIV(2),* 24-26.

169.   Gingrich, N., & Maple, T.L. (2008, February). Decisive, effective incentives are prescriptions for breakthroughs on climate change. *The New Republic,*

170.   Maple, T.L., & Lindburg, D.G. (Eds.) (2008). Empirical zoo: Opportunities and challenges to research in zoos and aquariums. *Zoo Biology, 27,* 431-504.

171.   Maple, T.L. (2008). Editorial. Special Issue of *Zoo Biology. Zoo Biology, 27*, i-v.

172.   Anderson, U.S., Kelling, A.S., & Maple, T.L. (2008). Twenty-five years of zoo biology: A publication analysis. *Zoo Biology*, 27, 1-14.

173.   Gingrich, N., & Maple, T.L. (2008). Green conservatism. N. Gingrich & T. L. Maple, *A contract with the earth.* New York, NY: Plume.

2009

174.   Clay, A.W., Bloomsmith, M.A., Marr, M.J., & Maple, T.L. (2009). Habituation and desensitization as methods for reducing fearful behavior in singly housed rhesus macaques. *American Journal of Primatology, 71,* 30-39.

175.   Clay, A.W., Bloomsmith, M.A., Marr, M.J., & Maple, T.L. (2009). Systematic investigation of the stability of food preferences: implications for positive reinforcement training. *Journal of Applied Animal Welfare Science, 12,* 306-313.

176.   Wilson, M.L., Snyder, R.J., Zhang, Z.H., Luo, L., Li, C.L., & Maple, T.L. (2009). Effects of partner on play behavior in giant panda cubs. In C. D. Clark (Ed.), *Transactions at play: Play and culture studies* (Volume 9) (pp. 104-123). Lanham, MD: University Press of America.

177. Perdue, B.M., Snyder, R.J., Pratte, J., Marr, M.J., & Maple, T.L. (2009). Spatial memory recall in the giant panda. *Journal of Comparative Psychology, 123,* 275-279.

2010

178. Anderson, U.S., Maple, T.L., & Bloomsmith, M.A. (2010). Factors facilitating research: A survey of zoo professionals. *Zoo Biology, 29,* 663-675.

179. Perdue. B.M., Gaalema, D.E., Martin, A.L., Dampier, S.M., & Maple, T.L. (2010). Factors affecting aggression in a flock of Chilean flamingos (*Phoenicopterus chilensis*). *Zoo Biology, 29,* 1-6.

180. Maple, T.L., & Bashaw, M.J. (2010). Trends in zoo research. In D.G. Kleiman, K. V. Thompson, & C. Kirk Baer (Eds.), *Wild mammals in captivity: Principles and techniques for zoo management* (2nd ed.) (pp. 288-298). Chicago, IL: University of Chicago Press.

2011

181. Martin, A.L., Bloomsmith, M.A., Kelley, M.E., Marr, M., & Maple, T.L. (2011). Functional analysis and treatment of human-directed undesirable behaviors in a captive chimpanzee. *Journal of Applied Behavior Analysis, 44,* 139- 143.

182. Perdue, B.M., Snyder, R.J., Zhihe, Z., Marr, M.J., & Maple, T.L. (2011). Sex differences in spatial ability: A test of the range size hypothesis in the order *Carnivora. Biology Letters, 7,* 380-383.

183. Perdue, B.M., Gaalema, D.,Stoinski, T.S., & Maple, T.L. (2011). Technology at the zoo: The influence of a touchscreen computer on orangutans and zoo visitors. *Zoo Biology, 30,* 1-12.

2012

184. Perdue, B.M., Stoinski, T.S., & Maple, T.L. (2012). Using technology to educate zoo visitors about conservation. *Visitor Studies, 15(1)*, 1-12.

185. Maple, T.L. (2012). A zoo where the animals come first. *APS Observer, 25(4)*, 39-41.

186. Snyder, R.J., Perdue, B., Powell, D., Forthman, D.L., Bloomsmith, M.A., & Maple, T.L. (2012). Behavioral and hormonal consequences of transporting giant pandas from China to the United States. *Journal of Applied Animal Welfare Science, 15*, 1-20.

187. Kelling, A.S., Dampier, S.M.A., Kelling, N.J., Sandhaus, E.A., & Maple, T.L. (2012). Lion, ungulate, and visitor reactions to playbacks of lion roars at Zoo Atlanta. *Journal of Applied Animal Welfare Science, 15*, 313-328.

2013

188. Kelling, A.S., Bashaw, M.J., Bloomsmith, M.A., & Maple, T.L. (2013). Socialization of a single, hand-reared tiger cub. *Journal of Applied Animal Welfare Science, 16*, 47-63.

189. Ross, M.R., Gillespie, K.L., Hopper, L. M, Bloomsmith, M.A., & Maple, T.L. (2013). Preference for ultraviolet light among captive birds from three ecological habitats. *Applied Animal Behaviour Science, 147*, 278-285.

190. Perdue, B.M., Snyder, R.L., & Maple, T.L. (2013). Cognitive research in Asian small-clawed otters. *International Journal of Comparative Psychology, 26*, 105-113.

191. Maple, T.L., & Perdue, B.M. (2013). *Zoo animal welfare*. Berlin/Heidelberg: Springer-Verlag.

192. Mallavarapu, S. Stoinski, T.S., Perdue, B.M., & Maple, T.L. (2013). Can black and white ruffed lemurs (*Varecia variegata*) solve object permanence tasks? *American Journal of Primatology, 75*, 376-386.

193. Maple, T.L. (2013). Remembering Hal Markowitz. *Zoo Biology, 32*, 243-245.

194. Mallavarapu, S., Bloomsmith, M.A. Kuhar, C.W., & Maple, T.L. (2013). Using multiple joystick systems in computerized enrichment for captive orangutans. *Animal Welfare, 22*, 401-409.

195. Maple, T.L., & Bocian, D. (2013). Commentary: Wellness as welfare. *Zoo Biology, 32,* 363-365.

196. Maple, T.L. (2013). The empirical zoo director – Building a foundation of evidence-based welfare and wellness: Keynote. *Journal of Applied Animal Welfare Science, 16,* 382.

197. Perdue, B. M, Snyder, R. J., Wilson, M. L., & Maple, T. L. (2013). Giant panda welfare in captivity. *Journal of Applied Animal Welfare Science, 16,* 394-395.

2014

198. Hutchins, M., & Maple, T.L. (2014). Zoos and zoological parks. In B. Jennings (Ed.), *Encyclopedia of Bioethics* (4th ed.). Independence, KY: Cengage/MacMillian Reference.

199. Maple, T.L. (2014). Elevating the priority of zoo animal welfare – the chief executive as an agent of reform. *Zoo Biology, 33*, 1-7.

200. Mallavarapu, S., Stoinski, T. S., Perdue, B. T., & Maple, T. L. (2014, July 31). Double invisible

displacement understanding in orangutans: Testing in locomotor and non-locomotor space. *Primates*. Advance online publication. doi: 10.1007/s10329-014-0439-x

201. Maple, T.L. and Segura. V. 2014. Advancing behavior analysis in zoos and aquariums. *The Behavior Analyst*. Advance online publication. doi: 10.1007/s40614-014-0018-x

Made in the USA
Lexington, KY
17 October 2015